Shakespeare's I ry

The Marlowe Codes i nets

Peter Bull

Shake-scene Books

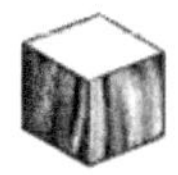

ISBN: 978-1-9193674-1-5

Front Cover: Vanitas by Harmen Steenwijck, c. 1640 - Public Domain.

Acknowledgements

A small but illustrious group of people have given me support and assistance over the years I have worked on this project. It was my enormous privilege to correspond with A.D. (Dolly) Wraight and to share ideas with her before her untimely death. Dolly's sparring partner in the Marlovian world, Peter Farey, was a hard man to please when trying out my early research findings, but his high standards of logic and evidence were exactly what I needed to raise my game. The mercurial John Baker was a gold-mine of bright ideas and his zany humour made for entertaining correspondence. Readers of the earlier version of this book who gave valuable feedback include Mike Frohnsdorf, Frieda Barker, Donna Murphy and Professor Robert Ayres. Of the non-Marlovians who have helped me Professor Alastair Fowler tops the list. His kindly interest, when my work was at an early stage, was hugely encouraging, and his books on literary numerology in the late Renaissance are a gold-mine. Arthur Neuendorfer, veteran of the 'humanities.lit.authors.shakespeare' newsgroup, made a couple of small but invaluable comments on my earlier ideas. Recently, I have had the pleasure of corresponding with Alan Green, whose profound knowledge of esoteric philosophy lies behind the discoveries he has made in the original Shakespeare publications, and elsewhere.

Finally, all credit goes to my wife Reyhan, who has supported me in a thousand ways through all the twists and turns of this long journey.

CONTENTS

Foreword

It was some time in the mid-1980s I first came across the idea William Shakespeare might not have been the man the history books claim he was. The source of this insight was a biography of Sigmund Freud, in which I discovered Freud firmly believed the historical record to be mistaken. Although made aware of this idea early in his career, Freud only took it seriously in his sixties following exposure to the work of John Thomas Looney. The unfortunately named Looney was an advocate of the theory that Shakespeare's works were written by Edward de Vere, the seventeenth Earl of Oxford.

I was initially sceptical of this challenge to the Shakespeare legend I had grown up with, but it didn't take long for the concept of a 'Shakespeare problem' to ignite my interest, and I began to investigate for myself. The deeper I dug into the evidence, the more I, too, became convinced there was something not at all right about the legend of England's most famous son.

Unlike Freud, Looney and the majority of doubters through to the present day, I was not attracted to the case for the Earl of Oxford. In essence, my objection was that Edward de Vere died long before Shakespeare stopped producing new work, and there is scant evidence in his surviving literary output that he attained a level of skill commensurate with the poetry and drama of Shakespeare. It seemed obvious for any alternative candidate to fill Shakespeare's shoes, he or she must have been a writer of superlative talent. In addition, his or her personal circumstances must also have somehow dovetailed with the life of William Shakspere from Stratford-upon-Avon. [*The spelling 'Shakspere' I shall use to distinguish the man from Stratford from that other person I believe to be author 'Shakespeare'*.]

It wasn't long before I found myself drawn to the argument for Christopher Marlowe. There is no doubt that Marlowe was an author of exceptional genius. Not only did he write the most sublime poetry, his powerful blank verse drama opened the way for everything Shakespeare subsequently achieved on the London stage. As Swinburne put it, 'After his [Marlowe's] arrival the way was prepared, the path made straight for Shakespeare.' In other words, Marlowe had skill and ability to have transitioned effortlessly into a writer of Shakespeare's calibre.

The only complication is that Marlowe, like Oxford, died too soon. In fact, he died before Shakespeare's name had been recorded on a single play or poem. This is the stumbling-block for Marlowe. His murder in 1593 was notorious at the time and has never been doubted since, at least not by mainstream historians. However, if Marlowe did somehow survive the extraordinarily fishy circumstances of his Deptford 'reckoning' in 1593, there is every reason to expect that he would have continued to write. Under those circumstances, he could only have done so by means of a *nom de plume*. A dramatic name like 'Shake-speare', and one that could be linked with a man working on the fringes of the theatre business to provide the necessary cover, might just have done the trick.

If this scenario is correct, it is hard to imagine Marlowe would be happy to disappear into the night and let a barely-literate bit-part actor take the laurels for his peerless writing. Marlowe was nothing if not ambitious, so I felt sure he would have been strongly motivated to leave a record for posterity about his 'posthumous' career. Confident that such a record must exist, I set myself the task of unearthing it.

What follows is a report of findings distilled from almost four decades of research. While this account has been written so as to be accessible to the general reader, the crucial evidence depends on numbers and the ratios of sacred geometry. Therefore, I must caution the presentation of this material may be taxing for those whose love of great literature is countered by a corresponding aversion toward anything involving numbers. To such gentle readers, I urge patience. The prize of discovering Shakespeare's true identity is worth a certain measure of mathematical discomfort.

When the evidence turns numerical, a calculator, pencil and paper is recommended as a means of verifying what is presented. In addition to this, the notes at the end of each chapter and the appendices are there to help the perplexed. Further supplemental information can be found on my website (Peter Bull's Research Site: https://shake-scene.com/).

As for the structure of the book, it is divided into three main sections. The first of these sets the scene and gives the background to my working hypothesis. It provides an overview of the 'Shakespeare authorship problem' and then presents the alternative candidacy of Christopher Marlowe. The second part examines the three different techniques that were used to incorporate hidden information in the *Sonnets*. While the first two are conceptually quite simple, the third – gematria – is less well known and understood, and it therefore requires a fuller explanation. To expand on this, I then include a 'proof of concept' chapter with demonstrations of gematria usage from the *Bible*, the 'Marlowe portrait' and the dedication to the *Sonnets*. These three case studies show how gematria can be practically employed to encode information within an otherwise unmarked piece of text. The third section is what Marlowe's hero Tamburlaine would call 'the slicing edge'. This is where I open up and dissect coded lines and verses in the *Sonnets* that reveal the identity of their great architect, Christopher Marlowe.

Part 1

The Protagonists

1
A Shakespeare Credibility Gap?

The notion that William Shakspere of Stratford-upon-Avon did not write the works of Shakespeare is unsettling. At face value, it seems to defy logic. Beneath the surface, it threatens a legend polished to a lustrous sheen by four-hundred years of ingenuous recital. The discomfort provoked by this apparent affront to England's greatest national treasure leads traditionalists to denigrate it as no more than a conspiracy theory. On the other side, those unimpressed by the legend will point out that conspiracies are not entirely unknown in human affairs, and were, in fact, almost a defining feature of the Elizabethan and Jacobean periods. If, for example, neither the Babington Plot against Queen Elizabeth nor the Gunpowder Plot against King James can be accepted as conspiracies, we would find ourselves living in a La-La Land of cotton-wool and double-speak. Political actors engage in deception as a matter of routine, and occasionally they do so as a matter of life or death.

One reason why doubts about Shakespeare's identity cannot be summarily dismissed is the quality of the doubters. These people are not lightweights or fools – in fact, quite the opposite: they include some of the most respected figures in the fields of literature, psychology and theatre. The writers who have doubted the Stratford man include Charles Dickens, Mark Twain, Henry James, Walt Whitman, Ralph Waldo Emerson and Daphne du Maurier. The psychologists with no faith in Mr. Shakspere's mind include William James and Sigmund Freud. From the world of theatre, the unconvinced include Charlie Chaplin, Tyrone Guthrie, John Gielgud, Orson Welles, Derek Jacobi, Mark Rylance and Jeremy Irons. These people are not only famous in their respective fields, they are those whose professional lives bring them into daily contact with the creative process. They have direct experience of inspiration and insight into whence it comes. Such first-hand knowledge is essential for a deeper understanding of Shakespeare's exceptional genius.

Henry James confessed that he was, 'Sort of haunted by the conviction that the divine William is the biggest and most successful fraud ever practiced on a patient world.' [1] On returning from a trip to Stratford, his brother William wrote:

> The absolute extermination and obliteration of every record of Shakespeare save a few sordid material details, and the general suggestion of narrowness and niggardliness which ancient Stratford makes, taken in comparison with the way in which the spiritual quantity 'Shakespeare' has mingled into the soul of the world, was most uncanny . . . [2]

What William James was referring to was the fact that the documentary evidence we have of the actor from Stratford points to a decidedly unexceptional individual; one whose greatest concerns were for material gain and social status. These are the instincts of a provincial businessman and are quite at odds with the mind that created 'Shakespeare'. By contrast, the author of the plays and poems made practically no attempt to profit from their publication in his lifetime and maintained a vanishingly low profile.

The indisputable facts we have about William Shakspere come almost entirely from a thin trail of legal paperwork: birth, marriage and death records, property deeds and a handful of minor court cases. On this basis, it can be established he was an actor, a theatre shareholder, a tax defaulter, a moneylender, a malt dealer, a malt hoarder in times of famine, a landlord, a petty litigant and a mostly-absent husband.

What cannot be found, as Diana Price has observed, is any evidence in his lifetime to connect him with the profession of writer.[3] Aside from title-page attribution, the only positive identification between the man and the work bearing his name came posthumously. This absence of documentation is disconcerting and lies at the root of what the distinguished lawyer Sir George Greenwood termed, 'the authorship problem'. [4] The lack of corroborating documentation is all the more surprising in the light of a point made by historian Hugh Trevor Roper:

> Of all the immortal geniuses of literature, none is personally so elusive as William Shakespeare. It is exasperating and almost incredible that he should be so. After all, he lived in the full daylight of the English Renaissance, in the well-documented reigns of Queen Elizabeth and King James I. Since his death, and particularly in the last century, he has been subjected to the greatest battery of organised research that has ever been directed upon a single person. Armies of scholars, formidably equipped, have examined all the documents that could possibly contain at least a mention of Shakespeare's name. One hundredth of this labour applied to one of his insignificant contemporaries would be sufficient to produce a substantial biography. [5]

This 'battery of organised research' has revealed a biography of such little substance Mark Twain famously observed, 'He is Brontosaur: nine bones and six hundred barrels of plaster of Paris.'[6]

No evidence remains of Shakspere's education. Literary historians assert he must have attended Stratford grammar school, and that this would have set him up with a solid education, well grounded in the classics. However, without documentation of any kind, this is no more than a hopeful guess. And, if Shakspere did attend the local school, there is no indication of what kind of a student he might have been. While fond imagination presents him as the outstanding scholar of the class and the apple of his teacher's eye, he may equally well have been ineffectual or disinterested in school work. Ben Jonson's famous put down that Shakespeare had, 'Small Latin and less Greek' does not lend any support to the theory of his fine education. The absence of evidence is more conclusive when it comes to the lack of a university education because Oxford and Cambridge both kept good records. That Shakspere attended neither institution is not doubted. Of course, this would not rule out a career in literature because some very fine contemporary writers, like Ben Jonson and Thomas Kyd, were in the same boat. However, the latter two, at least, are known to have attended excellent schools.

When it comes to Shakspere's correspondence, there is evidence: a single letter remains. Unfortunately, this was written to him, not by him, it was about money, and it wasn't delivered. Physical records are also disappointingly sparse for plays or poems written in his own hand. There aren't any.[7] In fact, the only evidence of his handwriting comes from six signatures, three of which are on his will, two from property deeds and one from a deposition to a court case. Even the signatures fail to inspire confidence. They are so varied it has been argued they were written by different hands. [8] For some, such as Professor Mortimer J. Adler, the palaeographic evidence was damning:

> Just a mere glance at [his] pathetic efforts to sign his name (illiterate scrawls) should forever eliminate Shakspere from further consideration in this question - he could not write. [9]

At least Shakspere managed better than his parents, both of whom were unambiguously illiterate and impressed their names on documents by means of a 'mark'. Shakespeare's much neglected wife Anne was equally challenged with a pen. His youngest daughter Judith maintained the family tradition of total illiteracy, and while the older daughter Susanna could just about manage a 'painful' signature, [10] although, she seems to have found reading a challenge because she was unable to recognise that a piece of writing with her name on it was written in her own husband's hand. [11]

Shakspere's family background comes as a rude surprise. Was the learned humanist such a hypocrite when it came to his own children's education that he wouldn't unclench his fist for the price of basic instruction in reading and writing? Or if the cost were too onerous for his means, would he not have taught them himself, or at least encouraged their literacy by reading and reciting poetry to them? How can such a mean-spirited embrace of ignorance be squared with the enlightened quality of his writing? In psychological terms, something is off.

At least, there was some recompense for his offspring in his will. They received the bulk of his estate, even at the expense of his clearly-unloved wife, who ended up with nothing more than his 'second best bed', and that only as an afterthought. It was probably no more than she expected as he had defaulted on a loan of forty-one shillings she had been forced to take out in his long absence from the family home. The will, which constitutes a meticulous inventory of mundane items, makes no mention of anything connected with a literary career. It is especially notable for its failure to mention a single book or manuscript. The other beneficiaries of his will include three actors and some local Stratford tradesmen and merchants. There is no indication he had friends among other writers, or emotional connections with intellectuals of any sort.

Reinforcing this lacuna is the fact there was a marked reticence, bordering on a total blackout, of contemporary references to him by his fellow writers. Ben Jonson, surely the closest rival Shakespeare ever had, never mentioned Shakspere in print during his lifetime. Three years after his death, in 1619, Jonson observed to William Drummond, 'Shakspeer wanted arte'.[12] Although another four years later, in his introduction to the *First Folio,* he contradicted himself and praised Shakespeare's art above all else. Michael Drayton ought to have known him too, not least because he frequently visited Stratford and was even a patient of Shakspere's son-in-law, Dr John Hall, but he never made a mention of the writer. Not a mouse stirring. Normally, the giants of literature and public entertainment attract attention to themselves. By contrast, the author Shake-speare was practically a non-entity.

Among recent scholars, Patrick Cheney has observed what he calls Shakespeare's, 'self-concealing authorship'. [13] He noted that when the author refers to himself, for example in *The Rape of Lucrece, Troilus and Cressida* and *Hamlet,* he contrives to keep invisible behind his pen. In *Lucrece,* he alludes to himself as the 'spear shaker' through the person of Achilles, but rather curiously makes this single character, from an otherwise clearly portrayed Trojan tableau, disappear from view:

> That for ACHILLES image stood his speare
> Grip't in an Armed hand, himselfe behind
> VVas left vnseene, saue to the eye of mind,
> A hand, a foote, a face, a leg, a head
> Stood for the whole to be imagined. *(Lines 1424-8)*

Cheney believes the Achilles stanza to have a critical bearing on the poet's presentation of himself in the role of author.

Another astonishing manifestation of his invisibility came with his death, for outside of provincial Stratford-upon-Avon, it went unnoticed. There was no recognition of any national loss. In fact, no one of any standing bothered to acknowledge the fact of his passing. Where was the elegiac poetry from his literary colleagues and admirers? Every other contemporary writer of consequence was eulogised in death, but not William Shakespeare. Where was the state burial in Westminster Abbey deemed appropriate for the likes of Edmund Spenser, Ben Jonson, Francis Beaumont and Michael Drayton? Beaumont died just a few months before Shakspere and got the full monty, but his vastly more accomplished colleague was totally ignored. Why? Why was William Shakspere allowed to slip unnoticed to his grave? Something is not right.

His disappearance was as mysterious as his sudden appearance in the plague year of 1593, when the long and courtly poem '*Venus and Adonis'* materialised from Richard Field's printing press. It was described as the, 'first heir of my invention'. Considering the lyrical sophistication and refinement of Shakespeare's prentice-piece, one wonders whether it was the poem or the name that was so freshly invented? For the credulous, this fully-formed birth, like Venus emerging out of a clam-shell, is all that is needed to confirm his divine genius; but for dispassionate observers it gets up the nose, like notes of *poisson* left in the sun.

It is almost impossible that *Venus and Adonis* could have emerged *ex nihilo*. Mainly for this reason, a vast and thorough history of Shakespeare's career prior to 1593 has been assembled. Hundreds of learned papers and scores of vastly erudite books have explored the details of his precocious childhood, his early teens – not sparing his first trials with masturbation, and his early ventures into play writing. Unfortunately, this magnificent historical reconstruction is not supported by one single documented fact. It is entirely made-up. The only evidence of any sort comes from some early references to plays, or versions of plays, that in some form made it into Shakespeare's *First Folio*, which was published more than 30 years later and seven years after his death. The name Shakespeare was not actually recorded as a playwright in any place until 1598.[14]

The single crumb of 'evidence' upholding the entire narrative of Shakespeare's existence as a writer prior to *Venus and Adonis* is the infamous reference in Robert Greene's *Groatsworth of Wit* (1592) to an 'upstart crow' who imagined himself the 'Only Shake-scene in a country'. Sadly for the faithful, this is not a reference to Shakespeare at all. It is very clearly an attack on the leading actor of the day, Edward Alleyn.[15] Shakespeare was completely unknown as a writer at that time.

The surprising attribution of *Venus and Adonis* to the new-named poet jarred on other writers. Satirists of the day made it plain that they had little faith in the 'Shakespeare' byline. Joseph Hall and John Marston entertained themselves and their readers with a character they called Labeo. In his '*Virgidemiarum*' (1597 and 1598), Hall made it plain that Labeo was a poet of quality using a common working man, who was no writer, to hide behind:

> FOr shame write better Labeo, or write none,
> Or better write, or Labeo write alone,

Nay call the Cynick but a wittie foole,
Thence to abiure his handsome drinking bole:
Because the thirstie swaine with hollow hand,
Conueied the streame to weet his drie weasand.
Write they that can, tho they that cannot, doe:
But who knowes that, but they that do not know. [16]

Labeo is letting a thirsty rustic take his place and drink from the waters of inspiration. This points to Shakespeare on account of the two lines from Ovid prefixed to the frontispiece of '*Venus and Adonis*', where the poet disdains vulgar tastes and calls for inspiration from a cup at the Muses' spring. Subsequently, in '*Pigmalion's Image*' (1598), John Marston affirms Labeo's identity more explicitly, in the following four lines:

So Labeo did complaine his loue was stone,
Obdurate, flinty, so relentlesse none:
Yet Lynceus knowes, that in the end of this,
He wrought as strange a metamorphosis. [17]

This can only identify Labeo with Shakespeare because it refers to a well-known line repeated twice in the latter's work. Most notably, it occurred in *Venus and Adonis*:

Art thou obdurate flintie hard as steele
Nay more then flint for stone at raine relenteth *(Lines 199-200)*

The line about a 'metamorphosis' alludes to the fact that Adonis changed to a flower at the end of Shakespeare's poem – just as the fine poet transformed himself into an unlettered rustic. The identification is further reinforced because '*Pigmalion's Image*' is a work very much inspired by, and imitative of, '*Venus and Adonis*'. [18]

The Autobiographical Sonnets

The issues of Mr. Shakspere's general unsuitability as an authorial candidate and the doubts of contemporary writers, are compounded by inexplicable autobiographical references in the *Sonnets*. Although creative and 'poetic' in character, they constitute a deeply personal testament to events and people in the writer's life. Unfortunately, these have no correspondence with anything known about William Shakspere. In fact, they are so at odds with the Warwickshire businessman's documented life, modern scholars have chosen to reduce the *Sonnets* to little more than an exercise in cerebral abstraction.

Helen Vendler elects to reframe the *Sonnets* in terms of, 'A writer's project invented to amuse and challenge his own capacity for inventing artworks'. [19] In other words, they amount to no more than an elaborate but essentially meaningless demonstration of verbal ingenuity. Her rationalisation of the soul-baring emotions on display is that they are merely, 'Aesthetically convincing representations of feelings felt and thoughts thought'.[20] Vendler's emotional evisceration of the *Sonnets* comes about because they seem to, 'exist to frustrate' any 'coherent psychological account' and 'do not fully reward psychological criticism . . .' [21] This frustration is scarcely surprising if the story is superimposed onto the prosaic circumstances of the Warwickshire grain dealer's life.

The issue of whether or not the *Sonnets* can be read as autobiography has always been quite clear to fellow poets. William Wordsworth was forthright in the belief that, 'With this key Shakespeare unlocked his heart'. More recently another great poet, W.H. Auden, reiterated the point with even greater force:

> What is astonishing about the Sonnets, especially when one remembers the age in which they were written, is the impression they make of naked autobiographical confession. [22]

Auden's friend Stephen Spender also rejected the notion that the story told in the *Sonnets* could be a fiction because, 'There are too many glancing references to people and events that must have existed – we feel sure that these are real'. [23]

It isn't just other poets who have been convinced of the factual basis of the *Sonnets*. Many of the most eminent

Shakespearean critics of previous years concurred with the view. F.J, Furnivall wrote, 'No one can understand Shakespeare who does not hold that his *Sonnets* are autobiographical'. [24] G.P.V. Akrigg stated that, 'The position generally held today is that *Shakespeare's Sonnets* are basically autobiographical'. [25] F.S. Boas believed that it was, 'Inconceivable that such intensity of passion as [the *Sonnets*] reveal . . . should spring from no solid basis in fact'. [26] For C.L. Barber the *Sonnets* were special because, 'They are the only poems we have which Shakespeare wrote out of his own life, in his own person'; and he went on to say that, 'They refer to complicated and very private relations'.[27] A.W. Schlegel thought, 'These *Sonnets* paint most unequivocally the actual situation and sentiments of the poet'. [28] E.K. Chambers believed that the order of the *Sonnets* was, 'An autobiographical one, following the ups and downs of an emotional relationship'. [29]

Therefore, it is true to say that, the ostriches of modern academia aside, there is a large and weighty body of testimony in favour of the view that the *Sonnets* are grounded in the actual story of Shakespeare's personal life.

One striking feature of the *Sonnets* is that they are extraordinarily opaque. Hotson speaks of them being, 'A maze, a labyrinth, the most intricate puzzle in Shakespeare', [30] and for G.B. Harrison they are, 'The most disputed of all collections of poetry in the English language'. [31] A.D. Wraight drew attention to a list of the 'seemingly unanswerable questions' they pose:

- To whom were they addressed and dedicated?
- To what events in the life of the author do they refer?
- When precisely, or even approximately, were they written?
- Whose hand was behind their arrangement - the author's or the publisher's?
- Why did Shakespeare, apparently never averse to any transaction that would financially benefit him, defer publication of his sonnet series until many years after the Elizabethan sonneteering vogue had spent itself? [32]

The autobiographical nature of the *Sonnets* provides a good reason for the obscurity. The collection of poems is an impassioned testament to private feelings and deep personal anguish. Such a revelation of the heart is unparalleled in any other writer of the period, and he was far, far ahead of his time. One problem this presented was that intimate relationships were involved. His friends and lovers were integral to his story, but he needed to protect them from tittle-tattle, slander or retribution – hence the obfuscation.

Whilst seeking to protect the identity of his friends is understandable, it is rather more perplexing that he should be so coy about his own identity. There are a number of sonnets with an explicit theme of self-revelation: for example, sonnets 71 to 76. These repeatedly refer to his name, but also warn of the dangers of its revelation:

71

Do not so much as my poore name reherse;
But let your loue euen with my life decay

72

My name be buried where my body is,
And liue no more to shame nor me, nor you.

76

Why write I still all one, euer the same,
And keepe inuention in a noted weed,
That euery word doth almost fel my name,
Shewing their birth, and where they did proceed

Why on earth should Shakespeare's name have been a source of shame, or mockery, had it been revealed? One also wonders why he kept his verbal 'invention' in a peculiar disguise (a 'noted weed'), and every word came close to exposing his real name. If this were Mr. Shakspere holding the quill, it is difficult to see why he needed to be so coy. These lines make sense only if the poet's real name was something other than 'Shakespeare'.

If one goes along with Hotson's view that the *Sonnets* constitute a four-hundred-year-old puzzle, the implication is that there must be a solution. Herein lies the challenge.

The Face that Launched a Thousand Quips

Aside from literary references, the visual evidence tying the actor Shakspere to the writer Shakespeare is equally problematic. The famous portrait adorning the *First Folio* of his plays, engraved by Martin Droeshout, has long been recognised as either a woeful botch-job, or else a pictorial cryptogram. For Hugh Trevor Roper, it depicted, 'the blunt face of a country oaf'.[33] Sir Edwin Durning Lawrence spotted that Shakespeare is drawn with two left arms, one facing forward, one facing back, and a face that is clearly an actor's mask.[34] Samuel Schoenbaum complained of the huge head surmounting an absurdly small tunic with oversized shoulder-wings, of the mouth being laterally displaced, and that the hair on both sides failed to balance.[35] It has also been noticed that Shakespeare has the unusual gift of two right eyes. In the light of these absurdities, it seems hardly surprising that Ben Jonson's lines composed to accompany the engraving do nothing to ease the reader's mind and actually serve to encourage the suspicion that the image should not be trusted:

> This Figure, that thou here seest put,
> It was for gentle Shakespeare cut;
> Wherein the Graver had a strife
> With Nature to out-doo the life:
> O, could he but have drawne his wit
> As well in brasse, as he hath hit
> His face; the Print would then surpasse
> All, that was ever writ in brasse.
> But, since he cannot, reader, looke
> Not on his Picture, but his Booke.

In similar fashion, the bust of Shakespeare adorning the monument in Holy Trinity Church, Stratford, is a very curious work. For Dover Wilson the image was not that of a great writer but brought more strongly to mind the impression of, 'A self-satisfied pork butcher'.[36] The original bust, prior to 'restoration work' initiated in the mid eighteenth century, showed an even rougher looking character with ape-like arms massaging an enigmatic sack.[37] Whether it contained fleeces relieved from Cotswold sheep or a judicious bushel of malt is not completely clear. What is quite apparent, though, is its total unsuitability as a container for his books, or the tools of a writer's trade. Overall, neither commodity-feeler nor country oaf seems any more kosher than the pork butcher.

Country oaf *Commodity-feeler* *Pork butcher*

Conclusion

The popular legend of Shakespeare and the hard, cold facts of William Shakspere's life are disconcertingly hard to reconcile. Whether true or false, there is a yawning credibility gap in the Stratford narrative, and it has long been recognised.

Chapter 1 Notes

---

[1] Henry James, in a 1903 letter to a friend. See, Lubbock, Percy, ed. *The Letters of Henry James*. 424-5.
[2] William James, 1902 letter to Charles Eliot Norton. *The Letters of William James*, Vol 2, 166.
[3] Diana Price, *Shakespeare's Unorthodox Biography.*
[4] Sir George Greenwood, *Is There a Shakespeare Problem?*.
[5] Hugh Trevor Roper, *Réalités*, 41-43.
[6] Mark Twain, *Is Shakespeare Dead?*
[7] It has been claimed that a fragment of the play Sir Thomas Moore is written in Shakespeare's hand (hand D), but this is unwarranted. There is no palaeographic case to be made because no adequate control sample of his writing exists. See Hays, M. L. (2016). Shakespeare's Hand Unknown in Sir Thomas More: Thompson, Dawson, and the Futility of the Paleographic Argument. *Shakespeare Quarterly*, 67(2), 180-203.
[8] The HMSO publication *Shakespeare in the Public Records* by David Thomas and Jane Cox (1985) states, "It is obvious at a glance that these signatures, with the exception of the last two, are not the signatures of the same man. Almost every letter in each is formed in a different way."
[9] Mortimer J. Adler (1902 – 2001) was a philosophy professor at the University of Chicago and a long-time Chairman of the Board of Editors of the Encyclopedia Britannica. This quotation comes from a letter to Max Weismann, Director, Center for the Study of The Great Ideas, November 7, 1997.
[10] The paleaographer E. Maunde Thompson described it as a "painfully formed signature, which was probably the most that she was capable of doing with the pen". In *Shakespeare's Handwriting: A Study*, 294. The three 'a's in her name were all differently formed, as were the two 'n's and the two final 'l's.
[11] An account of Dr James Cooke's interview with Susanna Hall (Shakspere) is found in Harriet Joseph, *Shakespeare's Son-in-Law: John Hall, Man and Physician*, 31. The episode is also discussed on Diana Price's website: http://www.shakespeare-authorship.com/resources/literacy.asp
[12] Ben Jonson, *Discoveries,* Vol V, 1-3.
[13] Patrick Cheney, *Shakespeare's Literary Authorship*, Ch. 1.
[14] This came in Francis Meres' *Palladis Tamia* (1598). The reference did include a backlist of a dozen plays, so it does show that those plays had been attributed to Shakespeare for some years prior to 1598. However, no firm conclusions can be drawn as to when this started. In the words of the orthodox scholar Arthur Acheson, "No atom of proof exists to show that, previous to the publication of "Venus and Adonis," Shakespeare had done any serious literary work". *Shakespeare and the Rival Poet*, 53.
[15] See two papers that I have written on this subject. Peter Bull (2020) Tired with a Peacock's Tail: All Eyes on the Upstart Crow, *English Studies*, 101:3, 284-311, https://doi.org/10.1080/0013838X.2020.1717829 . The follow-up paper 'In Quest of the Crow Maligned for the Unyarking of Robert Greene' is

available from my website: https://shake-scene.com/Academic.html . The case for Alleyn was also strongly argued in A.D. Wraight & Virginia F. Stern, *In Search of Christopher Marlowe*, pp. 187-213. Also, in A.D. Wraight, *Christopher Marlowe and Edward Alleyn,* 130-229.

[16] Joseph Hall, *Virgidemiarum*, Vol 1, Lib II, Sat1.

[17] John Marston, *The Metamorphosis of Pigmalions Image And Certaine Satyres*, C2.

[18] Marston's choice to quote line 199 of *Venus and Adonis* may well be strategic. The number 199 is emblematic of the poem as a whole because it is comprised of 199 stanzas. It also happens that this line has a value by gematria (see following chapters) of 1579, which is the same as the value of 'Christopher Marlowe'. None of the other 1194 lines of the poem has this gematria value. Since the other 1193 lines range in gematria from 539 to 6293, the chance of this occurring at random is less than one in five thousand.

[19] Helen Vendler, *The Art of Shakespeare's Sonnets*. 4.

[20] Vendler ibid., 16.

[21] Vendler ibid., 3.

[22] W.H. Auden, *'Introduction': Shakespeares Sonnets*, xxxiv.

[23] Stephen Spender, *'The Alike and the Other'*, 93.

[24] F.J. Furnivall, *'Introduction', The Leopold Shakespeare*, lxvi.

[25] G.P.V. Akrigg, *Shakespeare & the Earl of Southampton*, 228.

[26] F.S. Boas, *Shakespeare and His Predecessors*, 115.

[27] C.L. Barber, 'An Essay on the Sonnets', 7.

[28] A.W. Schlegel, *A Course of Lectures on Dramatic Art and Literature*, 352.

[29] E.K. Chambers, *Shakespearean Gleanings*, 120

[30] Leslie Hotson, *Shakespeare's Sonnets Dated*, 1-2.

[31] G.B. Harrison, 'Introduction'. *The Sonnets and A Lover's Complaint*, 13-14.

[32] A.D. Wraight, *The Story That The Sonnets Tell*, 1.

[33] Hugh Trevor Roper, op. cit., 41-3.

[34] Sir Edwin Durning-Lawrence, *Bacon is Shake-speare*, Ch. xi.

[35] Samuel Schoenbaum, *Shakespeare's Lives*, 11.

[36] J. Dover Wilson, *The Essential Shakespeare*, 6.

[37] For a more detailed examination of the early form of the monument, see Alexander Waugh's YouTube video 'Monkey Business at Stratford-upon-Avon', https://youtu.be/TRDX5wIx_8I .

2
The Marlowe Alternative

In 1994, the historian A. D. Wraight published her solution to the 'authorship problem' in, *The Story that The Sonnets Tell*.[1] Wraight's thesis is that Christopher Marlowe did not die in 1593 but that his 'murder' in May of that year was a ploy to help him escape imprisonment, torture and execution. She argued that after 1593 Marlowe must have gone into hiding but continued to write his plays and poems under the pen-name of 'William Shakespeare'. This idea of Marlowe's survival and authorship of Shakespeare's work is not original to Wraight, but this was the first time Marlowe's candidacy had been addressed in such a thorough, scholarly fashion.

The case for Marlowe described in this chapter is substantially informed by my reading of Wraight's work but also draws on the wider field of Marlovian research, which was pioneered by Wilbur Ziegler, Archie Webster and Calvin Hoffman, and which has more recently been advanced by the likes of Peter Farey, Daryl Pinksen, Donna Murphy and Ros Barber. [2]

Was Marlowe of the Right Stuff?

Marlowe's story is one of precocious talent and towering ambition. In 1587 he took the London theatre world by storm with *Tamburlaine the Great* and for six brief years thereafter he paved a trail of dramatic power, lyricism and great originality. There had been nothing like his plays before, and most of what Shakespeare was to achieve after him was built on his foundations.

Marlowe was highly admired by his contemporaries. Robert Greene addressed him as, 'Thou famous gracer of Tragedians',[3] while George Peele called him, 'Marley, the Muses Darling'.[4] Thomas Nashe, in reference to his unfinished poem *Hero and Leander,* extolled him as, 'A diuiner Muse than Musaeus'.[5] Henry Petowe, who in 1598 wrote a conclusion to the same poem, spoke of Marlowe's contemporary pre-eminence as a poet:

> Marlo admir'd, whose honney flowing vaine,
> No English writer can as yet attaine.
> Whose name in Fames immortall treasurie,
> Truth shall record to endles memorie, [6] (L*ines 59-62*)

Michael Drayton was also in awe of Marlowe's poetic gifts, and in a verse written to his friend Henry Reynolds in 1627 he wrote:

> Neat Marlow bathed in the Thespian springs
> Had in him those brave translunary things,
> That the first Poets had, his raptures were,
> All ayre, and fire, which made his verses cleere, [7] (L*ines 105-110*)

Writers of subsequent generations have been equally fulsome in Marlowe's praise. For Algernon Swinburne:

> Marlowe is the greatest discoverer, the most daring pioneer, in all our poetic literature. Before Marlowe there was no genuine blank verse and genuine tragedy in our language. After his arrival the way was prepared, the path made straight for Shakespeare. . . [8]

Leigh Hunt opined in 1844:

> If ever there was a born poet, Marlowe was one . . . his imagination, like Spenser's, haunted those purely poetic regions of ancient fabling and modern rapture . . . Marlowe and Spenser are the first of our poets who perceived the beauty of words [9]

His power as a playwright was no less considerable, and Charles Lamb viewed the death-scene of Edward II as, moving,

'Pity and terror beyond any scene, ancient or modern, with which I am acquainted'.[10]

Nor have literary critics shied away from placing Marlowe shoulder to shoulder with Shakespeare. In the nineteenth century James Broughton thought that Dr Faustus's, 'last impassioned soliloquy of agony and despair', is 'surpassed by nothing in the whole circle of the English Drama".[11] George Saintsbury felt that the, "riot of passion and of delight in the beauty of colour and form which characterises his version of "Hero and Leander" has never been approached by any writer'.[12] In consideration of Marlowe's standing as a playwright, A. W. Ward wrote:

> As the author who first introduced blank verse to the popular stage he rendered to our drama a service which it would be difficult to overestimate . . . Marlowe [is] worthy to be called not a predecessor, but the earliest in the immortal company, of our great dramatists. [13]

In twentieth century, the critic Edward Dowden viewed him unequivocally as Shakespeare's equal:

> If Marlowe had lived longer and accomplished the work that lay clearly before him, he would have stood beside Shakespeare. [14]

Marlowe's famous biographer, Dr John Bakeless, was of a similar opinion and noted that, as a writer, Shakespeare was massively indebted to Marlowe. In fact, he pointed out that Shakespeare's work is replete with quotations, echoes and allusions to Marlowe:

> That Shakespeare knew Marlowe's works is plain enough. Several of their characters can be paired off, one against the other, Shakespeare having obviously borrowed from Marlowe, since he had barely begun to write for the stage at the time of Marlowe's murder. Thus Barabas and Shylock; Abigail and Jessica; Edward II and Richard II, Kent in *Edward the Second* and Kent in *King Lear;* Young Mortimer and Hotspur; the Duke of Guise and Aaron; the murderers of the two little princes and the murderers of Edward

> II show many points of close resemblance. If Marlowe had never conceived these characters as he did, Shakespeare's characters would have been quite other than they are. [15]

To this list one could also add the extraordinary number of parallels and allusions noted by Eric Brown between *Dr Faustus* and *Love's Labor Lost*.[16] The latter play provides an alternative treatment of very similar themes raised in the former and seems to have an organic relation to it.

The parallelisms between the two outstanding dramatists of the Elizabethan age are so close that an earlier generation of literary critics identified several of the plays included in Shakespeare's *First Folio* as attributable to Marlowe's pen. For example, a representative selection would include *Titus Andronicus, Richard II, Richard III, 1 Henry VI, 2 Henry VI & 3 Henry VI.* Some others actually believed Marlowe to have been the pen-name of the young Shakespeare. [17] Even a stalwart of the Stratfordian orthodoxy such as Sir Sidney Lee described how Shakespeare's, 'early tragedies often reveal him in the character of a faithful disciple' [18] of Marlowe, and he was also moved to comment, 'All the blank verse in Shakespeare's early plays bears the stamp of Marlowe's inspiration'. [19]

One point that needs to be made clear is that everything Marlowe wrote was but the product of his youth, for he died at the age of twenty-nine. Bakeless explained:

> Marlowe died in his immaturity, still an experimenter . . . he used a form once – and dropped it. . . Marlowe's reputation rests wholly on the work of his prentice hand. He lived to do no other; and what he did, he did almost without models . . . [20]

If it is understood that his was early work, then the kneejerk reaction of distancing Marlowe from Shakespeare by claiming that the former's works are irreconcilable with the latter's in being less mature and more impetuous is short-sighted. Writers develop and mellow as they grow older and settle into their vocation.

The objection also fails to take account of the fact that Marlowe's brush with arrest and bail by the Privy Council, imminent torture, likely execution, staged murder and miserable exile had been radically life-changing experiences. Given the scenario of his survival, Marlowe would for the rest of his life have been looking over his shoulder. His psychological outlook would have shifted, and it would be natural for him to be much more cautious in his writing. Furthermore, it is a fact that dramatic genres were in a process of rapid evolution at that time, and so had Marlowe's career not terminated in May of 1593, his writing style would have continued to move with the times.

Stylometrics

The phenomenon of change over time is one that needs to be born in mind when making stylometric comparisons between Marlowe and Shakespeare.[21] One early study by Thomas Mendenhall examined word length frequency in a number of writers of the period. The results caused something of an upset because Mendenhall discovered that, 'In the characteristic curve of his plays Marlowe agrees with Shakespeare about as well as Shakespeare agrees with himself'.[22] All other writers in Mendenhall's detailed survey had distinctly independent profiles. Mendenhall's methods have recently been reapplied in a digital analysis of the works of 36 writers and over five million words: the result was that no pairing of writers showed a stronger correlation than Shakespeare and Marlowe.[23]

Since then, there have been several attempts to refute Mendenhall's unwelcome conclusions. One of these was carried out by Gary Taylor, where he looked at the frequency of ten 'function words' in Shakespeare and some of his contemporaries, with the aim of 'fingerprinting' each writer.[24] He believed he was able to prove the author of *Tamburlaine* (Marlowe) couldn't possibly have written any of Shakespeare's work. However, a study by Peter Farey showed Taylor's conclusions are undermined by his failure to consider the way writers develop over time.[25] In fact, Farey was able to show Taylor's figures actually reveal a smooth continuum between the writing of Marlowe and that of Shakespeare (see fig.1 below). In Farey's words [with my emphasis], 'Wherever a trend can be established for Shakespeare, Marlowe is **always** to be found where one might have expected a **young** Shakespeare to be, had he written anything at all before his late twenties'.

TREND OBTAINED FROM GARY TAYLOR'S FIGURES

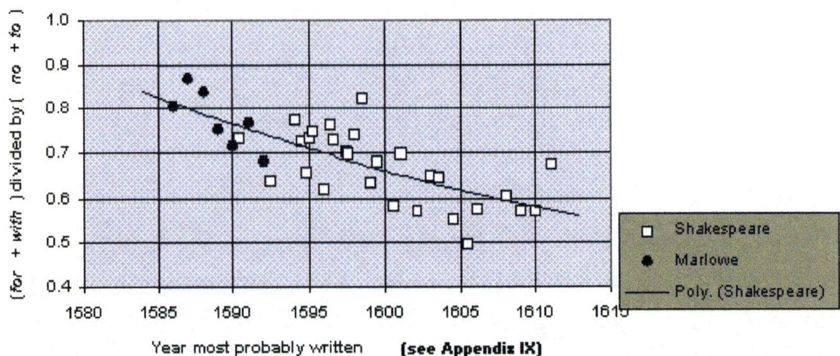

Fig.1 reproduced from Peter Farey's (mirrored) website [26]

Synchronicities

There is a remarkably neat transition between the careers of the two great writers. Marlowe 'died' on 30th May 1593 and Shakespeare made his first documented appearance as a writer with the publication of *Venus and Adonis* less than two weeks later: it was out by 12th June. This poem, to which Marlowe's unfinished *Hero and Leander* seems to be a sequel – for it refers explicitly back to that work[27] – was entered in the Stationers' Register on 18th April without recording the author's name. The printed version, which appeared in mid-June, contained a dedication and authorial attribution on a page that had been separately printed and subsequently interleaved with the main text, as if as an afterthought.

What is especially noteworthy about the title page of the poem is the Latin quotation from Ovid's *Amores* chosen as an epigraph:

Vilia miretur vulgus: mihi flauus Apollo
Pocula Castalia plena ministret aqua.

This immediately brings Marlowe to mind, because he had recently made the first translation of these lines into English:

Let base conceited witts admire vilde things,
Faire Phoebus lead me to the Muses springs.

The subtle part about this choice of couplet would have been appreciated only by those familiar with the Castalian springs from which the poem flowed, for it proceeds with a rousing summons to the deceased poet's resurrection and afterlife.

About my head be quiuering mirtle wound,
And in sad Louers heads let me be found.
The Liuing, not the Dead can enuie bite,
For after Death all men receiue their right.
Then though Death rakes my bones in funeral fire,
Ile liue, and as he puls me downe mount higher.

Thus, a very clear message resides in this choice of passage. It is extraordinary how neatly the circumstances of Shakespeare's literary debut dovetail with the theory of Marlowe's survival.

One Minute to Midnight

If Marlowe had the poetic genius and mastery of drama to have been Shakespeare's doppelgänger, the critical issue is his untimely 'death' on 30th May 1593. His candidacy abuts this one, seemingly insuperable, obstacle.

The background to his 'murder' is that the Archbishop of Canterbury, John Whitgift, had recently fallen into a paroxysm of rage against critics of the Church, and several Puritan intellectuals had already been dispatched to, and at, the gibbet. There was also a fresh outbreak of plague in England, and as a result most forms of public entertainment had been banned. Fear, resentment and frustration began to build among the population and, with tensions rising, foreign immigrants frequently became cast as scapegoats. It wasn't long before posters began to appear pasted onto walls around London vilifying foreigners and attempting to stir up mobs of apprentices to riot and attack them. The tipping point of this campaign occurred when an inflammatory poster appeared on the Dutch Churchyard in Broad Street on the night of 5th May 1593. It was signed by one calling himself 'Tamberlaine' and contained allusions to some other of Marlowe's plays. Apparently, the author of this poster wished to link Marlowe with the incendiary libels it contained.

A couple of days later the Privy Council ordered the Lord Mayor's commissioners to round up and coerce confessions from those suspected of involvement:

> . . . after you shal have examined the persons, if you shal finde them dulie to be suspected and they shal refuze to confesse the truth, you shal by aucthoritie hereof put them to the torture in Bridewel, and by th'extremitie thereof, to be used at such times and as often as you shal thinck fit, draw them to discover their knowledge concerning the said libells.[28]

One of those arrested and tortured in Bridewell was Marlowe's colleague, the playwright Thomas Kyd. Undergoing the aforesaid, extremity and prolongation of torture, Kyd implicated Marlowe as the source of a supposedly atheistic tract found in his lodgings. Immediately thereafter, an arrest warrant was issued for Christopher Marlowe. He was summoned to the Star Chamber, but put on bail and required to appear before their Lordships each day following. In the meantime, Marlowe's arch-enemy, an informer called Richard Baines, was paid to assemble a list of slander and innuendo about Marlowe – centred on his suspected atheism.

Marlowe had been under suspicion of holding unapproved views for a long time. He was prominent in a group of free-thinking scientists, explorers, poets and Hermeticists that gathered around the Earl of Northumberland and Sir Walter Raleigh. These men, among whom were some of the most brilliant minds of that generation, would have privately discussed matters – scientific, philosophical and theological – that were beyond socially accepted norms. Rumours about their activities began to garner unwelcome attention.

Whilst Marlowe was on bail and Baines compiling his list of dirty laundry, the clock was ticking away – and Marlowe's friends would have known it. His predicament was not entirely dissimilar to that of Faustus on the last day of his twenty-four year contract with the devil:

> Now Faustus let shine eyes with horror stare
> Into that vaste perpetuall torture-house,
> There are the Furies tossing damned soules,
> On burning forkes: their bodies broyle in lead.
> There are liue quarters broyling on the coles,
> That ner'e can die: this euer-burning chaire,
> Is for ore-tortur'd soules to rest them in.

The reality awaiting Marlowe, in the care of her majesty's chief torturer, Richard Topcliffe, would have filled his mind with similar fears – and not without good reason. With the days, hours and minutes ticking away, Marlowe and his friends must have grown quite desperate:

> O Faustus,
> Now hast thou but one bare houre to liue,
> And then thou must be damn'd perpetually.
> Stand still you euer mouing Spheares of heauen,
> That time may cease, and midnight neuer come.
> Faire natures eye, rise, rise againe and make
> Perpetuall day: or let this houre be but a yeare,
> A month, a weeke, a naturall day,
> That Faustus may repent, and saue his soule.
> O lente currite noctis equi:
> The Stars moue still, Time runs, the Clocke will strike.
> The deuill will come, and Faustus must be damn'd.

It was at just this point in the story, on the tenth day of his bail – 30th May 1593 – and just three days after Baines' long list of dirt had been submitted to the Privy Council, that something extraordinary happened in a house on Deptford Strand. The official story, as documented in the coroner's inquest, is that Christopher Marlowe was murdered in a fight over a bill for a meal amounting to a few pennies. The official story is, however, a can of worms.

Before examining what is reported to have happened, it is worth considering Marlowe's support network. It is your friends you turn to in times of need. When Marlowe was arrested, he was staying at the manorial home of Thomas Walsingham, cousin to the late Sir Francis. It is clear that Thomas Walsingham was both a friend and a patron to Christopher Marlowe. Like Marlowe himself, Thomas Walsingham had worked for the state on a number of occasions as an intelligence agent. With his background, Thomas Walsingham had all the resources and all the contacts necessary to plan and execute a rescue operation for his friend – England's pre-eminent playwright and poet.

Aside from personal friends, Marlowe had some very powerful statesmen on his side, and none more significant than Lord Burghley. Although he was getting on in years and not in good health, Burghley remained the most powerful man in the country. Marlowe had clearly been working for Burghley as an intelligence agent. This work had put him in some very awkward situations, but, each time he got into trouble, Lord Burghley moved in to clear up the mess. As an example, Burghley got Marlowe off the hook in 1592 when he was arrested in the garrison city of Flushing (Vlissingen). Marlowe had been informed on by his *bête noire,* Richard Baines, for 'coining'. This was a treasonous crime. When Marlowe was returned under arrest to Lord Burghley, he should have been executed or at least jailed, but he walked away as if nothing had happened.

Given this level of official protection the previous year, why not again in May 1593?

The Murder

Christopher Marlowe's last day on earth was curiously spent. According to the coroner's report, he passed the day 'talking in quiet sort' with three very distinctive men: Robert Poley, Nicholas Skeres and Ingram Frizer. These three had shared interests. Firstly, they were all highly proficient in the arts of deception and subterfuge. Secondly, they had all used their skills working under the direction of Thomas Walsingham. This is significant because Walsingham was Marlowe's close friend and literary patron. Moreover, Marlowe was staying as a guest at his house, Scadbury Manor near Chislehurst, from the time of arrest to the time of his 'murder'.

The leader of the trio was Robert Poley. He was the most skillful and also the most infamous agent in the Elizabethan secret service. He played the leading role in uncovering the 'Babington Plot' to murder Queen Elizabeth. During this operation Thomas Walsingham was Poley's contact with his cousin the spymaster Francis Walsingham. They knew each other well and had worked together over a period of years. For the Deptford operation, Poley had been summoned in haste from the Hague where he was performing, 'secret affayres of great importaunce', for her Majesty. Nicholas Skeres had also worked on the Babington plot and had performed diverse duties for Thomas Walsingham. The third member of the trio was Thomas Walsingham's private servant and financial agent, Ingram Frizer. Frizer and Skeres were also adept in the dubious Elizabethan practice of 'conny-catching' – duping the credulous out of their assets (by means which were not necessarily illegal).

It seems obvious this team of operators had been assembled for a purpose that required their particular skill-set. There is no innocent explanation as to why Marlowe would have chosen to spend the last day of his life, before being transferred to Bridewell, talking quietly and dining with them. There is also no straightforward explanation as to why they would spend this day secreted away from all outside company in a private house in the town of Deptford.

Contrary to popular tradition, the house in question was not a tavern or a brothel. It belonged to Dame Eleanor Bull, who was a respectable woman: a widow and a cousin of the Queen's 'nanny' Blanche Parry. Since Lord Burghley was also a cousin to Parry and both Burghley and Dame Eleanor were beneficiaries of Parry's will, it can be said that Dame Eleanor was a relative of Burghley's. Eleanor's late husband Richard had been a bailiff of the Clerk of the Greencloth, a job which involved supplying imported goods to the royal household. In this office lies another connection to Marlowe which seems to indicate that Dame Bull's house may have been 'home territory' for him. The reason, as Richard Wilson informs us, is that the sole agent of the Muscovy Company, the most profitable international trading company of Elizabethan times, which was based in warehouses at Deptford, was one Anthony Marlowe.[29] Marlowe, who held this important and immensely profitable post from 1576 to 1599, has long been identified as a distant relation of Christopher Marlowe. He has also been posited as the source of much of the otherwise highly secret information on the arms covertly supplied to Ivan the Terrible and the latter's atrocities which found their reflection in the Tamburlaine plays. Anthony Marlowe was also related to the Walsingham family and he worked for Sir Francis Walsingham. Anthony Marlowe's family had close connections with the Bull family over at least three generations, and Anthony would have known Richard and Eleanor Bull very well.

Therefore the 'murder scene' was not what it appeared to the outside observer and could scarcely have been chosen more propitiously to ensure Christopher Marlowe's safe disappearance. This secure location permitted the four men to go about their clandestine business on apparently neutral territory and far away from prying eyes. In the circumstances, the only business that makes much sense is a faked murder. Having a 'hit' team of three ensured that there would be one 'killer' and two witnesses. That was the minimum required under law to corroborate the killer's story that he acted in self-defence. On the other hand, if a real murder was on the cards, there would be no need for any such elaborate plan. In the latter scenario, it would be far more desirable to kill Marlowe anonymously and for the killer to flee.[30] It would be neater and far less risky for those involved. The only reason the plan would require a self-confessed killer and two witnesses is if all three were required to testify about the identity of the deceased, and the two witnesses were to corroborate the killer's plea of self-defence.

Aside from Deptford providing a safe house with strong connections to both the Marlowe and Walsingham families, it had many other advantages for a rescue plan. Firstly, it was a port with regular sailings to a variety of destinations, thus allowing Poley to arrive from the Low Countries and Marlowe to slip away quietly. Secondly, it does not seem to be a town where Marlowe was generally known, so the inquest jury would almost certainly be reliant on Marlowe's three companions to identify the corpse. Thirdly, it has to be noted that the most eminent and powerful inhabitant of the town, with a large house on the Green, was none other than the Lord Admiral, who was the patron of the theatrical company for whom Marlowe was the leading writer. He might have proved another extremely useful contact to pull strings and smooth over proceedings locally. Fourthly, Deptford seems to have been chosen because it fell, on that day, within the 'verge', and hence the peripatetic jurisdiction of the coroner to the Royal Household, William Danby.

Wraight argues that there are grounds for thinking that the Queen herself would have been aware of such a plot and would have been ready to lend tacit support for it. Thomas Walsingham was a young man well known to Elizabeth and highly trusted by her. She sent him, for example, in 1582 as her special envoy to the Duke of Anjou, who had been courting her, and thence to King Henry III - with the message that the envoy was totally in her confidence and could answer all Monsieur's questions as if she were speaking herself. He remained high in her affections and was knighted at his own home, Scadbury Manor, when Her Majesty paid him a private visit in 1597. In 1593 he would have known well that the Queen hated nothing more than to be deceived and that she insisted on being kept abreast of everything going on around her. He would also have known that she was not above a little intrigue herself.

One has to wonder if the Queen, who loved the theatre, would be happy to see England's greatest playwright put to 'th'extremitie of torture' and then put to death. Elizabeth had no time for religious fanaticism or doctrinal inquisitions. It is also to be wondered if she could bear the consequence of Marlowe's testimony, under torture, indicting her erstwhile favourite Sir Walter Raleigh and the whole group of brilliant young men that gathered around him: they not only constituted some of England's finest minds, they also held the keys to the nation's maritime and colonial future.

If this scenario is correct, and the Queen secretly informed, then the coroner Danby, who was also an old acquaintance of Burghley's, could be taken care of. Additionally, there would be future support from the highest authority in the land for preserving what would become the secret of Shakespeare's identity. This latter is unlikely to have been a consideration in the crisis days at the end of May 1593, but it perhaps explains why, in later years, Shakespeare's contemporaries were so cautious about saying anything that might let the cat out of the bag.

The murder scene played out after supper when Marlowe and Frizer apparently argued about *le recknynge,* a bill which amounted to 'a sum of pence'. In the fracas that followed, Marlowe was apparently lying on a bench behind the dining table and grabbed for Frizer's knife but was himself overpowered and stabbed with it above the right eye; from which wound he immediately died.

This is a story that rings more of contrivance than credibility. For one thing, no one has a ferocious argument and starts a knife fight lying down on a bed while their opponent is sitting with their back to them. That is quite incredible. This detail only really makes sense to explain away blood stains on a victim who had clearly been lying in a prone position. Either Marlowe had been held down and murdered, or an already prone (pre-deceased) 'corpse' had been dressed with animal blood and an impressive wound. None of these men were short of money, as all were in employment and Marlowe in particular had no reason to worry about a 'sum of pence'. Moreover, the whole occasion was likely organised and financed by Thomas Walsingham. Frizer received two small cuts on the scalp – just enough to show that he had acted 'in self-defence'. Marlowe, by contrast had a most improbable wound. Forensic testimony records that it is virtually impossible to push a knife through the thick part of the skull above the eye, especially in the rough and tumble of a fight and even more unlikely because Frizer was sat on a bench wedged between Poley and Skeres.

It seems on reflection the spectacular head-wound, with perforated cranium, would create such a bloody mess as to distort the face and thereby disguise the owner's identity. This is just what would be required if the corpse did not belong to the supposed victim. In *Measure for Measure* Shakespeare refers to the same trick when the Provost and the Duke discuss how to pass off Barnadine's corpse as Claudio's:

> Oh, death's a great disguiser, and you may adde to it; Shaue the head, and tie the beard, and say it was the desire of the penitent to be so bar'de before his death: you know the course is common. (*Act iv*, 2)

Was the bard writing from personal experience?

Two days later, on Friday 1st June, the inquest took place before Coroner Danby. This was irregular. Research by Peter Farey uncovered the fact the Queen's coroner had no jurisdiction to act alone when performing an inquest 'within the verge', but was legally bound to do so jointly with the local coroner.[31] Therefore, in legalese, the non-involvement of the Deptford coroner amounted not just to a suspicious circumstance, but potentially rendered the inquest, 'erroneous and void'.[32]

The verdict of this dubious report, based entirely on the testimony of the three professional liars, was that Frizer had acted in self-defence and therefore was not guilty of murder. With the desired result attained, the corpse was summarily buried in an unmarked grave in the churchyard of St. Nicholas, Deptford.

In the immediate aftermath, two interesting things happened. The first was that Frizer received his royal pardon in less than a month. This was astonishingly quick for such cases. Normally those involved in homicide languished in a fetid gaol for many months before being either pardoned or hung. Secondly, on the day after his release from prison, Frizer, along with Skeres, is on record as being involved in a business matter with his master Thomas Walsingham. Frizer had not only gone straight back into the service of Walsingham, but he continued to be his assistant for many years afterwards. This loyal service would have been unthinkable if he had just knifed his master's brilliant friend in a drunken brawl. There can be no doubt that the events which occurred on 30th May 1593 were orchestrated by Marlowe's patron, Thomas Walsingham.

As to whether Walsingham's plans involved the elimination or the salvation of his friend, one piece of evidence for the latter appeared a few years later when Edward Blount dedicated Marlowe's poem *Hero and Leander* to Sir (as he then was) Thomas. Blount made it abundantly clear that Walsingham had been personally very close to the poet:

> I suppose my selfe executor to the vnhappily deceased author of this Poem, vpon whom knowing that in his life time you bestowed many kinde fauours, entertaining the parts of reckoning and worth which you found in him, with good countenance and liberall affection: I cannot but see so far into the will of him dead, that whatsoeuer issue of his braine should chance to come abroad, that the first breath it should take might be the gentle aire of your liking:

It would have been grotesquely disingenuous to frame the dedication in such terms if the most recent of Sir Thomas's 'kinde fauours' had included assembling a team of hit men to murder him. Sir Thomas would certainly have welcomed neither the poem nor its dedication. It seems Marlowe was held in as dear affection in

1598 as he was when invited to stay at Scadbury in May 1593. Thus, there is every reason to suppose Walsingham acted to save him.

The wording of the Queen's pardon of Frizer is also interesting in that it effectively prevented any further investigation of the case. The key Latin sentence translates as, "*provided nevertheless that the jurisdiction remain in our court if anyone should wish to speak against him concerning the above mentioned death*".[33] This, although not unique to Frizer's pardon, suggests that the Queen had an interest in closing the lid on the many irregularities which transpired on that day.

The Story in The Sonnets

The primary source used in Wraight's argument lay in the testimony of the *Sonnets*. While William Shakspere fits the author's profile like a square peg in a round hole, the *Sonnets* actually make perfect sense if understood as the anguished testament of Christopher Marlowe living an 'afterlife' in hiding.

Key scenes from Marlowe's life and death are well described in specific sonnets. The most spectacular of these are sonnets 71 to 74, which describe his death.

72

My name be buried where my body is,
And liue no more to shame nor me,nor you.

74

BVt be contented when that fell arest,
With out all bayle shall carry me away,

So then thou hast but lost the dregs of life,
The pray of wormes,my body being dead,
The coward conquest of a wretches knife,
To base of thee to be remembred,

The shame and the ignominy that Marlowe must have felt in the aftermath of what happened in Deptford is obvious. The circumstances of that death can only have been galling for him:

29

VVHen in disgrace with Fortune and mens eyes,
I all alone beweepe my out-cast state,
And trouble deafe heauen with my bootlesse cries,
And looke vpon my selfe and curse my fate.

34

VVHy didst thou promise such a beautious day,
And make me trauaile forth without my cloake,
To let bace cloudes ore-take me in my way,
Hiding thy brau'ry in their rotten smoke.
Tis not enough that through the cloude thou breake,
To dry the raine on my storme-beaten face,
For no man well of such a salue can speake,
That heales the wound, and cures not the disgrace:

121

TIS better to be vile then vile esteemed,
When not to be, receiues reproach of being,

If the name of Shakspere had ever become so deeply mired in scandal and opprobrium, history would have turned up some hint of what it had been. Neither taking potshots at the local squire's deer, getting a neighbouring farmer's daughter pregnant, being an absent husband and negligent parent, tax dodging nor hoarding malt in times of famine seem to be sufficient cause for such depth of anguish.

Marlowe, on the other hand, was truly 'vile esteemed' in the aftermath of his 'murder'. Religious bigots from every corner of the land found it a perfect opportunity to gloat and moralise. Take, for example, the Puritan fanatic Thomas Beard in his *Theatre of God's Judgements* (1597):

> . . . *Marlin,* by profession a scholler, brought up from his youth in the Vniversity of Cambridge, but by practise a playmaker, and a poet of scurrilitie . . . But see what a hooke the Lord put through the nose of this barking dogge: . . . The manner of his death being so terrible (for he even cursed and blasphemed to his last gaspe, and togither with his breath an oth flew out from his mouth) that it was not onlie a manifest signe of God's iudgement, but also an horrible and fearfull terrour to all that beheld him. [34]

The tidal wave of sanctimonious odium that descended on Marlowe's name was unprecedented. In the words of Charles Norman, author of a Marlowe biography:

> The outburst of Puritan wrath against Marlowe is without parallel in literature. No vile epithet was too vile for his detractors to use, yet most of them wrote only from hearsay, or merely embroidered one another's accounts, hardly one able to contain his gloating.[35]

Unfortunately, the scribes, Pharisees and hypocrites of yesteryear set a precedent of calumny that carries right through to the present day. Some modern scholars and critics, who should know better, persist in denigrating Marlowe as a reprehensible transgressor of all the moral boundaries they imagine themselves to be the guardians of. Might they be more profitably employed reckoning up their own abuses?

A.D. Wraight was undoubtedly correct in choosing the *Sonnets* as the bedrock of her case for Marlowe. They tell a story that is coherent and logical for an ever-living Christopher Marlowe. By contrast, they leave the devotees of Mr. Shakspere scraping the barrel for explanations.

A Big Hint Dropped in a Play

Drama is a far less appropriate genre for dropping in autobiographical references, but that doesn't mean the author felt no inclination to vent his private feelings in certain dramatic contexts. One place where personal frustations emerged is in the comedy *As You Like It*. In this play, even the most hidebound of traditionalists accept Shakespeare is referring to Marlowe. In Act 3, scene 5, the love-sick Phoebe quotes verbatim from *Hero and Leander* and refers to its author:

> Dead Shepheard, now I find thy saw of might, [36]
> Who euer lov'd, that lou'd not at first sight?

In the original *Hero and Leander* Marlowe had written:

> Where both deliberat, the loue is slight,
> Who euer lou'd, that lou'd not at first sight?

For Wraight, the scenes in *As You Like It* involving the marriage plans of Touchstone, Audrey and the rival William serve to perform an 'allusive revelation' about the author's identity. The name Touchstone implies the alchemists' stone used for telling true gold from fool's gold. Marlowe is Touchstone and the rustic William is the actor Shakspere. Touchstone touches William:

> **Clo.** Giue me your hand: Art thou Learned?
> **Will.** No sir.
> **Clo.** Then learne this of me, To haue, is to haue. For it is a figure in Rhetoricke, that drink being powr'd out of a cup into a glasse, by filling the one, doth empty the other. For all your Writers do consent, that ipse is hee: now you are not ipse, for I am he. (V, i)

Touchestone is saying that it is he *ipse* – 'himself' – that is the writer who fills William's glass from his own cup. This is the truth revealed when he touches the 'fool's gold' – simple William. Touchestone and William are rivals for the love of the Audiences of the plays – Audrey. The vicar who was going to couple Touchstone with Audrey was Sir Oliver Mar-text - whose name alludes to text which has been 'marred' by ambiguity, or 'Marlowe's text'. If Mar-text had actually performed the marriage, the audience would know that the play constituted Marlo's text, not William's.

When Touchstone greets Audrey, she comments that he is strangely invisible to her:

> **Clo.** Come apace good Audrey, I wil fetch vp your
> Goates, Audrey: and how Audrey am I the man yet?
> Doth my simple feature content you?
> **Aud.** Your features, Lord warrant vs: what features?
> (III, iii)

If Touchstone is featureless, then he must be hiding his true features from the audience. And immediately after this come the anguished words revealing the true identity of Touchstone:

> **Clo.** When a mans verses cannot be vnderstood, nor a mans good wit seconded with the forward childe, vnderstanding: <u>it strikes a man more dead then a great reckoning in a little roome</u>: truly, I would the Gods hadde made thee poeticall. (III, iii)

Here Marlowe's frustration seems to boil over, and he refers explicitly to his 'death' in a small room over 'le recknynge'. He is also saying that the audience's lack of understanding of his cryptic lines was even more frustrating than 'death'.

As You Like It was entered in the Stationers' Register on 4th August 1600. However, its publication was 'staied' and it didn't see the light of day again till printed in the *First Folio* twenty-three years later. Wraight suggests the only reason it was 'staied' was because in printed form its references to Marlowe's authorship were dangerously obvious.[37]

Small Hints Concealed in a Play

A substantial section of Wraight's book was devoted to *Twelfth Night*, and hinged on Leslie Hotson's discovery that the play had been written to celebrate the visit of Don Virginio Orsini, Duke of Bracciano, to Queen Elizabeth on Twelfth Night 1600/1. She postulated this would mesh with Marlowe's discrete return from an exile in Italy. If he had enjoyed the hospitality of Orsini in Italy, then the writing of the play would have been a way to thank both him and the queen, as well as to cement a new political entente.

One thing that Wraight didn't pick up on in the play is how the pivotal role that Viola/Cesario plays, uniting Orsino and Olivia, mirrors the role Marlowe may have played bringing together the real Orsini and Elizabeth. This is especially apposite as much of the force of the play depends on the confusion of identities resulting from Viola's disguise. Obviously, Marlowe could no more put his true name to the play than he could attend its first night without being in disguise himself.

Two hints of a connection between Viola/Cesario and a revenant Marlowe appear in Act 2, scene 4. The first is relatively slight, but its presence triggers the astute reader's attention to that which follows. The duke, after conversing with Cesario about transience and death, calls for the clown to sing a song about death:

> **Du.** O fellow come, the song we had last night:
> **Marke it** Cesario, it is old and plaine;

The two words in red form the very obvious short anagram of the author's name **Kit Mar.**, and they do this in a way that associates them with Cesario. The context of a song about death is suitable, too, for the 'dead' writer.

However, a mere 70 lines later something even more interesting turns up. Viola, disguised as Cesario, tells the duke a tale of her sister, who loved a man but kept her love hidden:

> **Vio.** . . . My Father had a daughter lou'd a man
> As it might be perhaps, were I a woman
> I should your Lordship.
> **Du.** And what's her history?
> **Vio.** A blanke my Lord: she neuer told her loue,
> But let concealmen**t like a worm**e i' th budde
> Feede on her damaske cheeke: she pin'd in thought,
> And with a greene and yellow melancholly,
> She sate like Patience on a Monument,
> Smiling at greefe . . .

When the Duke then asks if her sister died of her grief, Viola replies enigmatically that it is her own story but she cannot answer the question:

> **Du.** But di'de thy sister of her loue my Boy?
> **Vio.** I am all the daughters of my Fathers house,
> And all the brothers too: and yet I know not.

It is apparent something associated with dying but not dying lies hidden in these very cloudy words; and this is linked to Viola's hidden identity. Is it too much to suppose the thing concealed in her blank and untellable history might reside in the letters picked out in red? These are a perfect anagram of our undead author, **Kit Marlowe**. And if we further include the next seven letters, we find '**Kit Marlowe - but hid(e)**': a 'concealed man', smiling at grief.

Conclusion

The scenario Wraight and others have presented is certainly credible. It provides a good fit with the known facts and also has a sound ring of psychological truth. The only thing that is lacking is hard evidence. So, where might this be found?

From clues sprinkled in *As You Like It, Twelfth Night* and the *Sonnets,* it is apparent the author wanted to set the record straight. However, if he couldn't reveal the truth openly, it follows he would have employed the kind of covert communication techniques he was familiar with from his time as an intelligence agent. In the next section, three cryptographic techniques suitable for use in a work of literature will be explored.

Chapter 2 Notes

---

[1] A.D. Wraight, *The Story That The Sonnets Tell* (1993).
[2] See for example, Wilbur Ziegler, *It Was Marlowe: A Story of the Secret of Three Centuries* (1895); Archibald Webster, 'Was Marlowe the Man?', *National Review* 82 (1923); Calvin Hoffman, *The Murder of the Man who was Shakespeare.* (1955). Peter Farey's material was located on his own website until his death in 2020. The website is currently (February 2023) mirrored at: https://marloweshakespeare.info/farey/index-2.html . Daryl Pinksen, *Marlowe's Ghost: The Blacklisting of the Man Who Was Shakespeare, 2008.* Donna Murphy, *The Marlowe-Shakespeare Continuum: Christopher Marlowe, Thomas Nashe, and the Authorship of Early Shakespeare and Anonymous Plays (2013).* Ros Barber, from her website*:* http://rosbarber.com/home/marlowe .
[3] Robert Greene, *Greenes Groats-worth of Witte,* E4v.
[4] George Peele, *The Honour of the Garter*, prologue.
[5] Thomas Nashe, *Lenten Stuffe*, 42.
[6] Henry Petowe, *The Second Part of Hero and Leander Conteyning Their Further Fortunes.*
[7] Michael Drayton, *To My Most Dearely-loved Friend Henery Reynolds Esquire – Of Poets and Poesie*. London.
[8] A.C. Swinburne, *Letters on the Elizabethan Dramatists*, 16-17.
[9] Leigh Hunt, *Imagination and Fancy*. 1844. Cited in Millar MacLure, *The Critical Heritage, Christophe Marlowe*, 89-91.
[10] Charles Lamb, *Specimens of English Dramatic Poets*. 1808. Cited in MacLure, 69.
[11] James Broughton, 'Life and Writings of Christopher Marlowe'. *Gentleman's Magazine*, 1830.
[12] George Saintsbury, *A History of Elizabethan Literature*, 1887. Cited in MacLure, 163.
[13] A.W. Ward, from *A History of English Dramatic Literature*, 1887. Cited in MacLure, 120-121.
[14] Edward Dowden, *The Tragedies of William Shakespeare*, Introduction.
[15] John Bakeless, *The Tragicall History of Christopher Marlowe*, Vol II, 208.
[16] Eric Brown (2003), 'Shakespeare's anxious epistemology: Love's Labor's Lost and Marlowe's Doctor Faustus.' *Texas Studies in Literature and Language,* 45/1, Spring 2003. University of Texas at Austin.
[17] William Taylor, in *The Monthly Review*, 1819.
[18] Sidney Lee, *A Life of William Shakespeare*, 61.
[19] Sidney Lee, essay on Marlowe in *The Dictionary of National Biography* 1917.
[20] Bakeless, op. cit., 3-4.
[21] Stylometrics is a term for a range of statistical and analytical methods designed to identify an author's characteristic patterns of word usage and written style.
[22] T.C. Mendenhall, 'A Mechanical Solution to a Literary Problem'. *Popular Science Monthly*, 1901, 9, 97-105.

---

[23] Peter Farey, *A Deception in Deptford*, Ch. 8. Online: https://marloweshakespeare.info/farey/chap8.html
[24] Gary Taylor, 'The canon and chronology of Shakespeare's plays', pp.81-2, in Stanley Wells and Gary Taylor (et al), *William Shakespeare, a textual companion.*
[25] Peter Farey, *A Deception in Deptford*, Ch. 8
[26] Peter Farey, *A Deception in Deptford*, App. V. Online: https://marloweshakespeare.info/farey/appx5a.html
[27] John Baker, *On the Likelihood of Marlowe's Authorship of Venus and Adonis*, essay entered for 'Calvin and Rose G. Hoffman Prize', 2001.
[28] Letter issued by the Starr Chamber, on Friday, 11th of May, 1593. See, Arthur Freeman, "Marlowe, Kyd, and the Dutch Church Libel." *English Literary Renaissance* 3, 1973, 44-52.
[29] Richard Wilson, 'Visible Bullets: Tamburlaine the Great and Ivan the Terrible'. *ELH* 62.1 (1995), 47-68.
[30] Just as Black Will suggested to Shakebag in the contemporary play *Arden of Faversham*: "Greene and we two, will dogge him through the faire, And stab him in the croud, and steale away."
[31] See Peter Farey's internet essay *"Was Marlowe's Inquest Void" https://marloweshakespeare.info/farey/inquest.html*
[32] Farey also discovered that the leader of the jury, a gentleman by the name of Nicholas Draper, was not from the Deptford area, but he was a close neighbor, and probable acquaintance of Thomas
[33] See Constance Brown Kuriyama, *Christopher Marlowe: A Renaissance Life*, 233-4.
[34] Thomas Beard, *TheTheatre of Gods Iudgements . . .*, 147-8.
[35] Charles Norman, *The Muses Darling*, 243.
[36] In Elizabethan times, poets were frequently alluded to as shepherds. In Marlowe's case, this was especially appropriate as he was very widely known for his beautiful short poem *The Amorous Shepherd.*
[37] A.D. Wraight, op cit., 342.

Part 2

The Means

3
The Shakespearean Ciphers Explained

Any researcher seeking to prove that Shakespeare included secret messages in his writing has one great advantage and one even bigger disadvantage. Both of these influences come thanks to a single book written by two of the most celebrated cryptographers of the twentieth century. In 1957, William and Elizebeth Friedman published *The Shakespearean Ciphers Examined.*[1] This was a comprehensive and meticulous examination of all the ciphers that had been claimed to exist in Shakespeare's plays and poems up to that time. The Friedmans, who were responsible for some of the most critical breakthroughs in cryptanalysis of the Second World War,[2] were unable to find that any of the claimed solutions for alternative authors were valid.

The advantage of the Friedmans' study is that it addressed 'the Shakespearean ciphers' with great seriousness. In so doing, it set out the ground rules for detecting and proving the presence cryptograms in works of historical literature. These ground rules remain as true today as they were in 1957. Thus, when it comes to secret messages in Shakespeare's writing, their book can be taken as the touchstone of cryptographic gold.

The colossal disadvantage of the Friedmans' opus derives from its systematic refutation of every claimed solution. Their work clinically dissected the mistaken assumptions and flawed methodologies of dozens of determined attempts to 'decode' Shakespeare. These efforts, which at that time were predominantly aimed at demonstrating the hidden hand of Francis Bacon, covered a spectrum from the potentially credible to the unambiguously deluded.

Within the wider field of cryptography, the project was seen to provide an object lesson in the perils of untrained amateurs sticking their noses into the preserve of elite professionals. When David Kahn came to write his celebrated history of cryptography, *The Codebreakers,* he chose to précis the Friedmans' work in a chapter entitled *The Pathology of Cryptology*. This offered an interval of comic relief in his grand chronicle, and Kahn had a field-day poking fun at the infelicities of the bard's would-be decipherers. He coined a new name, 'enigmatologists', and made a laughing stock of them. The effect of this characterisation has been to push all subsequent attempts to uncover Shakespeare's secrets far beyond the pale of serious cryptology. Consequently, the gatekeepers of the profession today only need to mention the dread names 'Friedman' or 'Kahn' to provoke a chuckle and dismiss any new approaches without the necessity of paying the slightest attention to them.

The current state of affairs would actually have saddened the Friedmans. Their careful study betokened a deep and personal interest in the 'Shakespearean ciphers'. This stemmed from the time they had both been employed by Colonel George Fabyan at Riverbank Laboratories, where they assisted Elizabeth Wells Gallup hunt for Baconian biliteral ciphers in the Shakespeare's plays. Having been caught up in the action themselves, they believed all investigators should be accorded a measure of due respect:

> They must be given something more than derision, if only to reassure them that they are not the victims of a merely emotional reaction on the part of those who often have a material interest in the affair. They are entitled to a courteous and – wherever possible – a scientific examination of their arguments.[3]

The Friedmans' concern for a scientific methodology is initially manifested through an outlining of the terminology and principles of cryptology that need to be understood before any attempt at a 'Shakespearean decryption' can be properly evaluated.

The Science of Covert Communication

At the start of their chapter 'Cryptology as a Science', a distinction is made between codes and ciphers. In code systems, the elements making up the cryptogram are understood to represent something else (the plain-text solution) with no algorithmic relationship between the two. For example, a picture of a cat may represent 'yes' and a picture of a dog 'no'. This must be agreed between both parties in the communication beforehand.

In a cipher, however, the elements of the cryptogram bear a uniform relationship to the elements of the message. A simple example of a cipher can be found in the number sequences 25-05-19 and 14-15: these can represent 'yes' and 'no' when the letters are substituted for their ordinal positions in the alphabet. Ciphers work by either *substituting* the elements of the message for something else and/or by *transposing* the order of the elements. Anagrams represent simple unstructured transposition ciphers. For example, 'yes' can be transposed to 'esy'. A more sophisticated system would transpose a substitution cipher in a structured way, for example it would encode 'yes' by reversing the order of the substituted letters seen above: 19-5-25.

An additional consideration is the distinction between open ciphers and those which are hidden. In a *concealment* cipher, the presence of the cryptogram is masked, so the innocent viewer will be unaware of its existence. This is sometimes called steganography. A common example is a 'null cipher', where the letters of the cipher message are hidden amongst those of an apparently unrelated text. The most familiar version of this is an acrostic message, where the message is made from the first letter of every consecutive line in a poem.

To be sure the deciphered message is the same as the message originally encrypted, the process of conversion must have its rules; and these need to be followed systematically. The rules will come in the form of a *general system* of operation combined with a *specific key* (or keys). The general system could, for example, specify a one-for-one substitution of letters and the key could be a table showing which letters of the plain-text correspond to those of the cipher-text.

When encountering issues of potential doubt, there are three critical considerations.[4] Firstly, the plain-text solution (the decrypted 'message') must make sense, be grammatical and mean something relevant. Secondly, the general system and the specific key must be rational and consistent, so they can be used reasonably, precisely and without ambiguity. In other words, there must be no possibility of arbitrary steps or decisions. Once these requirements have been satisfied, there is a final consideration:

> The mathematical theory of probability can be applied, and the chances calculated exactly. If the cryptanalyst finds a certain key and (on the basis of the way it is built up) he calculates that the chances of its appearing by accident are one in one thousand million, his confidence in the solution will be more than justified.[5]

Throughout the process, the Friedmans emphasised the importance of adhering to scientific principles. Thus, code-breaking should follow the scientific method of observation, deduction/induction, hypothesis formation, experimentation and analysis of findings. If a genuine cipher exists, the end result must be a solution that is unambiguous, unique and vastly improbable by chance.

What the Friedmans Did Not Say

While there can be no question *The Shakesperean Ciphers Examined* settled the issue of those ciphers which had been claimed up to that time, it could not be expected to address all future possibilities. In addition, it was written with a limited mandate of informing the educated layman.

One area the Friedmans judiciously avoided was that of complexity. In real life, successful codes and ciphers are seldom as straightforward as an introductory guide might lead the lay-reader to believe. A casual browse through William Friedman's classic paper '*The Index of Coincidence*' will very quickly drive home the mind-bending complexity of the decryption process for polyalphabetic transposition and substitution ciphers of even a hundred years ago. The presence of complexity is inevitably correlated with the resilience and security of codes and ciphers. On this basis, it would be a logical deduction that any cryptogram undetected after 400 years in one of the most intensely scrutinised works of world literature is likely to embody some measure of complexity.

It will be seen in due course that the creator of *Shakespeares Sonnets* did leave an extraordinary number of concealed messages, and at least one cryptogram in his work. None of these are simple. Only a couple have ever been detected. The cryptogram comes in the form of an acrostic message embedded in a grid. This is a fairly straightforward method of double-encryption. It is the kind of technique that could be successfully taught to any schoolchild of moderate intelligence. The only difficulty for decryption would be knowing where to look and what to look for. Those obstacles should not be underestimated, but with many bright minds applied to the task, they would be quickly overcome.

Shakespeare's artistry was to take the gridded-acrostic and give it a subtle-distorting-twist, to make it break the strict rules of acrostic formation, and thereby escape detection. Technically, this qualifies as triple-encryption. The subtle-distorting-twist was something novel and entirely of his own devising. It amounts to a new cryptogram, one of incredible beauty and precision, built out of the acrostic message. It is this artful design that validates the way the acrostic has been modified. The cryptogram, which is numerical and geometric in form, makes use of an ancient form of letter-number substitution called gematria.

It follows that in order to understand the message in the *Sonnets*, it will be necessary to take a closer look at the techniques of acrostics, letter-grids and gematria. Of these, acrostics and letter-grids are well-established features in the cryptography of the period; however, gematria, despite having a far older pedigree, is dismissed by historians of cryptology today because they have no understanding of the ways it can be exploited in a work of poetry. For them, the mysteries of Renaissance literature are terra incognita.

Acrostics

Among possible techniques for claiming authorship of a literary work produced under a pen-name, or anonymously, acrostics come near the top of the list. The Friedmans noted they have unquestionably been used to establish claims to authorship in the past. Acrostic writing was very popular among Elizabethan poets and had, for example, been overtly used in a poem to honour of the head of the Elizabethan secret service, Sir Francis Walsingham – for whom Marlowe seems to have worked. Another example cited by the Friedmans was one that cropped up in an apparently anonymous Latin work printed in 1616. The anonymity of this piece, however, lasted only as long as the reader did not put together the consecutive initial letters of each of the fifty-three sections into which the book was divided. If she did, then the phrase, 'Franciscus Godwinvvs Landavensis Episcopus hos conscripsit', was revealed: this translates as, 'Francis Godwin, Bishop of Llandaff, wrote these'.[6]

One benefit of an acrostic is that the message is integral to the text in which it appears, and therefore one can be sure that it cannot have been placed after the fact by a meddling editor or printer:

> . . . in the case of acrostics, any message found must have been inserted by the man who wrote the open text; and to change or insert any hidden message would be impossible without changing the open text itself. If, therefore, any genuine messages of this kind exist, they must be taken as conclusive. [7]

In addition to this, the Friedmans highlighted the strength of an acrostic, lies in a combination of the grammatical integrity of the solution and the inflexible method by which its letters are selected. These two factors make it 'enormously improbable' the message just happened to be there by accident.[8]

While acrostic messages can provide definitive evidence of the author's involvement, their great popularity at the time rendered them insecure as a serious form of cryptography. The basic premise is so simple and unsophisticated it is not unfamiliar to primary school reading and writing classes today. Therefore, if Shakespeare wanted to encode sensitive information on which his life and the security of his friends depended, he would have needed additional layers of security. One way to mask the appearance of an acrostic is to require the text be reassembled in a grid formation. By this means, the spacing of the target letters remains hidden until the text is set out correctly. An example of an acrostic in a letter-grid comes from the curiously worded dedication to the *Sonnets*.

TO.THE.ONLIE.BEGETTER.OF.
THESE.INSVING.SONNETS.
Mr.W.H. ALL.HAPPINESSE.
AND.THAT.ETERNITIE.
PROMISED.

BY.

OVR.EVER-LIVING.POET.

WISHETH.

THE.WELL-WISHING.
ADVENTVRER.IN.
SETTING.
FORTH.

T. T.

Letter Grids

It has long been suspected that the dedication to the *Sonnets* is a cryptogram. The phrasing and the layout are so contrived they can hardly be taken at face value:

Leslie Hotson, who was a brilliant, albeit maverick, scholar, started the ball rolling when he squared up the 12 lines of text in a grid. From lines 3, 4 & 7, he happened upon the name 'Mr. W. Hatliv', which he believed to be a shortened form of William Hatcliffe.[9] He proposed that Hatcliffe was the 'begetter of the sonnets', Mr. W. H., and therefore Shakespeare's beloved friend, as eulogised in the poems. Unfortunately, this solution was not one of Hotson's finest moments, and few have given it credence.

Thirty-three years later, in 1997, a retired physicist called John Rollet, found a different candidate by similar means.[10] He noticed that the characters making up the dedication sum to the significant total 144. When Rollet put the letters in a grid with sixteen columns and nine rows, he was startled to find the name HENRY jumping out at him in a diagonal line:

T	O	T	H	E	O	N	L	I	E	B	E	G	E	T	T
E	R	O	F	T	**H**	E	S	E	I	N	S	U	I	N	G
S	O	N	N	**E**	T	S	M	R	W	H	A	L	L	H	A
P	P	I	**N**	E	S	S	E	A	N	D	T	H	A	T	E
T	E	**R**	N	I	T	I	E	P	R	O	M	I	S	E	D
B	**Y**	O	U	R	E	V	E	R	L	I	V	I	N	G	P
O	E	T	W	I	S	H	E	T	H	T	H	E	W	E	L
L	W	I	S	H	I	N	G	A	D	V	E	N	T	U	R
E	R	I	N	S	E	T	T	I	N	G	F	O	R	T	H

Realising that this was more than a little anomalous, Rollett tried some other grid arrangements in the hope of finding HENRY's other name. In a grid of eighteen columns and eight rows he found what he was looking for. The long and unusual name 'Wriothesley' can be seen divided up into three blocks WR IOTH ESLEY. Whilst it would be more gratifying to see it in one piece, the division does not render the result invalid. This method of splitting an important name is found in the rituals of Freemasonry, where passwords are routinely disguised by being delivered 'lettered' or 'halved'.[11] It adds security without significantly impeding communication.

T	O	T	H	E	O	N	L	I	**E**	B	E	G	E	T	T	E	R
O	F	T	H	E	S	E	I	N	**S**	U	I	N	G	S	O	N	N
E	T	S	M	R	W	H	A	L	**L**	**H**	A	P	P	I	N	E	S
S	E	A	N	D	T	H	A	T	**E**	**T**	E	R	N	I	T	I	E
P	R	O	M	I	S	E	D	B	**Y**	**O**	U	R	E	V	E	R	L
I	V	I	N	G	P	O	E	T	W	**I**	S	H	E	T	H	T	H
E	**W**	E	L	L	W	I	S	H	I	N	G	A	D	V	E	N	T
U	**R**	E	R	I	N	S	E	T	T	I	N	G	F	O	R	T	H

With the name 'Henry Wriothesley', Rollett had found one of the two most commonly postulated candidates for Shakespeare's beloved youth. Wriothesley, who was the 3rd Earl of Southampton, was the dedicatee, and putative patron, of Shakespeare's two earlier long poems *Venus and Adonis* and *The Rape of Lucrece*. In some ways this was a perfect match and sealed by the fact that, in Rollet's estimation, the chances against the name cropping up in this manner were 320,000,000 to 1 against.

I cannot see any reason to doubt Rollet's conclusion that the name 'Henry Wriothesley' is encoded in the dedication. Whether or not one concurs with his probability calculation, it is extremely unlikely this particular name could have occurred in the dedication in this manner by chance.[12] The more pressing question raised is how it should be interpreted. Wriothesley was Shakespeare's earlier patron of choice, so it is perfectly possible he was the 'fair youth' eulogised in the *Sonnets*. However, there is as yet no other evidence to confirm this.

One reason why Wriothesley's name might have been placed within the dedication is to serve in some way as a warning.

As a peer of the realm, the Earl of Southampton was not someone for commoners to trifle with, and so he may have been 'riding shotgun', and serving to keep interlopers out. If he happened to be a Freemason, he would be performing the role of a *tyler*, a 'brother mason' who stands as a sentry to guard the door of the lodge.[13]

A small clue that a Masonic theme could be present here can be gained by tracing a counter-diagonal at ninety degrees to the name HENRY in the first grid and spotting the reversed name HIRAM.[14] To the initiated, for whom a nudge is as good as a wink, this is a fairly significant clue. Hiram Abif was the legendary master builder slain, buried and then resurrected as the archetypal Master Mason. For the Marlovian, it is curious that the name MARLO can also be found interlaced with that of Hiram. Would it be unduly speculative to reverse the two elements Hi and Ram, to end up with Lo and Mar – the slain Marlo mysteriously compounded with the archetypal figure of Hiram? At this stage, it is pure conjecture.

T	O	T	H	E	O	N	L	I	E	B	E	G	E	T	T
E	R	O	F	T	**H**	E	S	E	I	N	S	U	I	N	G
S	O	N	N	**E**	T	S	**M**	R	W	H	A	L	L	H	A
P	P	I	**N**	E	S	S	E	**A**	N	D	T	H	A	T	E
T	E	**R**	N	I	T	I	E	P	**R**	**O**	M	I	S	E	D
B	**Y**	O	U	R	E	V	E	R	**L**	**I**	V	I	N	G	P
O	E	T	W	I	S	H	E	T	H	T	**H**	E	W	E	L
L	W	I	S	H	I	N	G	A	D	V	E	N	T	U	R
E	R	I	N	S	E	T	T	I	N	G	F	O	R	T	H

Gematria

Gematria is a system of substituting the letters of a word or name for numbers. The origins of the practice are disputed. Some believe it began as a method of scriptural exegesis in Judaism, while others claim the Jewish mystics adopted a pre-existing practice of the ancient Greeks. In fact, it must have begun before either of them because the earliest known reference to gematria comes from an 8th century BCE Assyrian inscription counting the name of King Sargon II.[15]

The method arose quite naturally because in many languages of antiquity there was no independent system of notation for numbers: instead, numbers were signified by letters of the alphabet. It followed that every name, word or phrase had a numeric value. This was powerful because numbers have always had symbolic and magical significance.

The simplest way to use an alphabet as a counting system is to give each letter an ordinal value. This practice is manageable for very simple mathematics, but it has a disadvantage that its highest number is limited to the extent of the alphabet. For example, in the Hebrew alphabet there are only 22 letters, so there is no number with a higher value than 22. Therefore, in languages such as Hebrew, Syriac, and Greek the practical system of numeration used 9 units, 9 tens and 9 hundreds with a slightly modified alphabet. Latin was exceptional in merely using a small selection of letters as numerals.

In Renaissance Europe, rumours about the practices of Jewish Cabalists excited a great deal of interest. And when Christian scholars began to examine the scriptures in their original languages of Hebrew and Greek, they were astonished by what they found. It became immediately obvious there were sophisticated numerical patterns hidden within the texts. They realised these patterns contained information that had been hidden for thousands of years – concealed by the use of gematria. And this wasn't any information: it was insider knowledge of the Divine mind – the most sacred information of all. This discovery marked the beginning of a major intellectual movement in Europe, which became known as Christian Cabala. It elevated gematria to exalted status, and it also gave a massive boost to the ever-popular study of numerology.

It had always been appreciated that God worked with numbers. In the *'Wisdom of Solomon'* (11:21) it was stated that the divine architect had created the universe out of measure, number and weight:

> "omnia in mensura, et numero, et pondere disponsuisti."

This was regarded as an axiomatic truth in the Medievel and Renaissance periods. Thus, the very highest form of theology was not literal and scriptural but resided in numbers.

The universities taught the seven liberal arts, of which the upper level, the 'quadrivium', was entirely devoted to numbers. Arithmetic dealt with number in the abstract, Geometry addressed number in space, Music examined number in time, and Astronomy was concerned with number in space and time. That was the mainstream view. However, forward thinkers took the numerical philosophy even further. Pico della Mirandola, one of the foremost scholars of Christian Cabala, made the following claim, in John Dee's inimitable translation, about the astonishing power of number science:

> "By Numbers, a way is had, to the searchyng out, and understandyng of every thyng, hable to be knowen." [16]

Among the esotericists, it was understood the magical power of numbers rested on the harmonious accord between the microcosm of man and the macrocosmic vastness of all else that exists. It followed that the philosopher must understand the operation of these numbers in both worlds if he was to plumb the mysteries of Creation. Henry Cornelius Agrippa put it thus:

> 'Seeing man is the most beautiful and perfectest work of God, and his image, and also the lesser world; therefore, he by a more perfect composition, and sweet harmony, and more sublime dignity doth contain and maintain in himself all numbers, measures, weights, motions, elements, and all other things which are of his composition . . .

> From hence all the ancients in times past did number by their fingers, and showed all numbers by them; and they seem to prove that from the very joints of man's body all numbers, measures, proportions, and harmonies were invented; hence according to this measure of the body, they framed, and contrived their temples, palaces, houses, theatres; also their ships, engines, and every kind of artifice, and every part and member of their edifices, and buildings, as columns, chapiters of pillars, bases, buttresses, feet of pillars, and all of this kind. [17]

Numbers and numerology thus formed the corner-stone of science, art and religion.

One place where a reverence for numbers found a natural home was in literature. Professor Alistair Fowler describes how:

> Numerology . . . was widely used by Latin authors, common to the best medieval and renaissance poets and almost universal in the period 1580 to 1680, when it reached its greatest height of sophistication. [18]

Poets were particularly concerned with numbers. While this had its root in their natural concern for metre, it expanded to the formal organization of every element that could be used to structure a poem. Using numerical patterns to add value to poetry, and especially subtleties concealed from the casual reader, reached its peak in the sonnet vogue of the last two decades of the sixteenth century.

Analysing *Shakespeare's Sonnets* for structural and numerical patterns, Professor Fowler was not disappointed:

> "Of all Elizabethan (sonnet) sequences, indeed, with the exception of that of Spenser, his rival, Shakespeare's is the most complex formally." [19]

The work of Fowler shows that Shakespeare designed his *Sonnets* with great attention to esoteric number symbolism – numerology – but that this remains obscure to the eye of the uninitiated. It raises the question as to what other means he may have used to encode his sonnets with hidden meaning. If he chose to employ gematria, it would be fully in keeping with the spirit of the age.

It is known that some writers of Shakespeare's generation openly espoused gematria. Henry Reynolds, who was a close friend of Michael Drayton and born in the same year as Marlowe and Shakespeare, outlined the practice in a tract called *Mythomystes.* Here, he explained how the sages of antiquity, such as Pythagoras and Plato, communicated their occult doctrines to 'sublime wits' but at the same time safeguarded this knowledge from the 'unworthy vulgar':

> Now, from this meanes that the first auncients vsed, of deliuering their knowledges thus among themselues by word of mouth; and by successiue reception from them downe to after ages, That Art of mysticall writing by Numbers, wherein they couched vnder a fabulous attire, those their verball Instructions, was after, called Scientia Cabalae, or the Science of reception . . . A learning by the auncients held in high estimation and reuerence and not without great reason; [20]

When he speaks of the 'Art of mysticall writing by Numbers', Reynolds is referring to numerical Cabala, otherwise known as gematria.

Modern cryptographers are quick to dismiss this as vacuous nonsense. They have no time at all for the subtleties of gematria and regard it as a historical aberration unworthy of a moment's attention. The problem, as they proclaim it, is that names, words, phrases or chunks of text end up with a number that is simply the sum of the component letter values. It doesn't tell you what the letters or words were, and a random number can have a great many different significations. In other words, it doesn't do what they want it to do, so it is summarily dismissed.

Unfortunately, that is the attitude of a pig squatting in a manger. It reminds me of unlovely Jaques in *As You Like It*:

Jaques: Rosalind is your love's name?

Orlando: Yes, just.
Jaques: I do not like her name.
Orlando: There was no thought of pleasing you when she was christen'd.

In parallel fashion, there was no thought of pleasing the likes of William Friedman or David Kahn when the book of *Genesis* was written, or when The Word was made flesh. These things were recorded in words and numbers, both of which can still be read and understood today. The knowledge is perfectly preserved and still as fresh as the day it was written. The practice of gematria ensures its astonishing longevity.

As we will see shortly, the first seven words of the *Bible* present the informed reader with a group of seven numbers with startling implications. They do this because they were not pulled out of a hat at random. They form patterns according to their intrinsic numerical properties and according to ratios of geometric proportion that do not, and cannot, vary across the breadth of the cosmos nor through aeons of time. It is through the deliberate and meticulous patterning of numbers that gematria conveys its covert information. Understanding those patterns and recovering that concealed information is the role of the cabalist.

Gematria Codes

The dual counting systems of Hebrew and ancient Greek are well established in the historical record. While technical names exist, for convenience I will label the plain, ordinal method the Short code (S-code), and the tiered, or hierarchical method the Long code (L-code). The latter was the default system for recording numbers and for counting gematria values.

The two codes of Hebrew look like this:

Hebrew Short Code

א	ב	ג	ד	ה	ו	ז	ח
1	2	3	4	5	6	7	8
ט	י	כ	ל	מ	נ	ס	ע
9	10	11	12	13	14	15	16
פ	צ	ק	ר	ש	ת		
17	18	19	20	21	22		

Hebrew Long Code

א	ב	ג	ד	ה	ו	ז	ח	ט
1	2	3	4	5	6	7	8	9
י	כ	ל	מ	נ	ס	ע	פ	צ
10	20	30	40	50	60	70	80	90
ק	ר	ש	ת	ך	ם	ן	ף	ץ
100	200	300	400	500	600	700	800	900

With the Hebrew alphabet, there are only 22 letters, so the final five letters of the L-code are taken by five existing letters, but only when they come as the final letter of a word. These are called 'sofit' letters and they have an elongated shape. Purists, and those adhering to the classical (pre-Medievel) tradition, do not use the five extra values.

The two Greek codes are similar:

Greek Short Code

α	β	γ	δ	ε	ζ	η	θ
1	2	3	4	5	6	7	8
ι	κ	λ	μ	ν	ξ	ο	π
9	10	11	12	13	14	15	16
ρ	σ/ς	τ	υ	φ	χ	ψ	ω
17	18	19	20	21	22	23	24

Greek Long Code

α	β	γ	δ	ε	F/στ	ζ	η	θ
1	2	3	4	5	6	7	8	9
ι	κ	λ	μ	ν	ξ	ο	π	ϙ
10	20	30	40	50	60	70	80	90
ρ	σ/ς	τ	υ	φ	χ	ψ	ω	ϡ
100	200	300	400	500	600	700	800	900

The 24 letter Greek alphabet was originally supplemented by three other characters, *digamma* (6), *koppa* (90) and *sampi* (900) for counting purposes, but these were not part of the literary alphabet. Only the *digamma* was put into occasional use as a substitute for the ligature στ (*sigma-tau* – known as *stau*). This practise is post-classical and arose during the Byzantine period. The famous example is the word Σταυρος, meaning a cross. Normally it is valued at 1271, but when the first two letters are counted as *digamma* (*stau*), its value reduces to 777.[21]

If Shakespeare were to have used gematria to encrypt information in his poetry, he obviously would have had to employ the gematria system of English. In his day, the English alphabet had 24 letters, and there is a traditional S-code based on that alphabet, running from A = 1 to Z = 24. This has a well-established provenance. An early demonstration appears in the following medieval poem, spelling out the name 'IHESUS' by means of numbers: [22]

8 is my trew love;	H
do beffore 9;	I
put therto 5;	E
so well it wil beseme;	
18 twyse told,	S
20 betwen.	U

In the 24-letter alphabet, which was based on Latin, no distinction was made between an 'i' and a 'j', or between a 'u' and a 'v'. They were written according to conventions of spelling and typography largely indifferent to variations in pronunciation.[23] The English language has always embraced idiosyncratic quirks. This S-code was formally recorded in Selenus' famous cryptographic tome *Cryptomenytices et cryptographiae* (1624). [24]

Short Code

a	b	c	d	e	f	g	h
1	2	3	4	5	6	7	8
i/j	k	l	m	n	o	p	q
9	10	11	12	13	14	15	16
r	s	t	u/v	w	x	y	z
17	18	19	20	21	22	23	24

Finding the L-code for English presents a tougher problem for the researcher because the English alphabet was never used as a counting system. What is more, the L-code seems to have been used by certain secret societies as a means of concealing high-value information and was thus a closely guarded secret. It only seems to have been published in two books, and it took me many years of searching before I stumbled upon it.[25] As far as I can establish, the place it first appeared was in the 20th chapter of the second of Heinrich Cornelius Agrippa's *Three Books of Occult Philosophy* (1531). This compendium of esoteric lore was written in Latin and thus the code is applicable to all the European languages based on Roman script.

CXLIIII. DE OCCVLTA PHILOSOPHIA,

Valentinianus nominibus: deinde hi & hu conſonantes aſpiratæ, ut in Hieronymus & Huilhelmus, licet Germani pro hu aſpirato, duplici w utantur, Itali uero & Galli in ſuo uulgari g cum u coniunctum loco eius ponũt, ſic ſcribentes, Vuilhelmus & Guilhelmus.

1	2	3	4	5	6	7	8	9	10	20	30	40	50	60	70	80	90
A.	B.	C.	D.	E.	F.	G.	H.	I.	K.	L.	M.	N.	O.	P.	Q.	R.	S.

100	200	300	400	500	600	700	800	900
T.	V.	X.	Y.	Z.	I.	V.	HI.	HV.

Long Code (Agrippa)

a	b	c	d	e	f	g	h	i
1	2	3	4	5	6	7	8	9
k	l	m	n	o	p	q	r	s
10	20	30	40	50	60	70	80	90
t	u	x	y	z	j	v	*hi*	w
100	200	300	400	500	600	700	*800*	900

It will be seen that the code naturally terminates at z = 500, but additional letters such as 'j', 'v' and 'w' were recognised as sufficiently well-established to make up the shortfall. The 'hi' letter didn't really catch on in English, but it's something like the soft 'j' sound in 'Hierusalem' (Jerusalem).

A Simple Example of Gematria

The Elizabethan magus John Dee was a keen follower of Agrippa, and he owned several copies of his *Occult Philosophy*. Dee's biographer, Peter French, states that he used the book 'constantly'.[26] He was also an ardent cabalist, so he would have been extremely familiar with Agrippa's gematria code.[27] By this system, the seven letters of his name sum as:

$$600 + 50 + 8 + 40 + 4 + 5 + 5 = 712$$

While there is nothing wrong with it, the number 712 is not especially noteworthy. It seems this was one reason why Dee liked to present himself as, 'Doctor John Dee', even though he lacked the requisite qualification. The benefit of the title 'Doctor' is that it lifted the value of his name to the supremely auspicious figure of 999. Among other things, this represents the 9 units, 9 tens and 9 hundreds of the complete gematria system – all numbers. Even better still, when Dee's favourite number, 7, was divided by 999, it produced his esoteric signature, 0.007007007007 . . . *ad infinitum*. Therefore we can understand the iconic 007 codename belonging to England's most famous spy owes its existence to Dee's use of Agrippa's gematria code.

Gematria and Geometry

The word Gematria derives from the Greek word Γεωμετρια – 'Geometria', and it implies geometry and the laws of geometrical proportion play a central role in the way the numerical patterns are structured and interpreted. In terms of its doctrinal base, the Cabala is intimately tied up with speculation about, and observation of, the cosmos. As God's creation, the universe was believed to be a harmonious piece of architecture and constructed according eternal principles of 'sacred geometry'.

A simple demonstration of the geometric patterning of language occurs in the first trinity of names recorded in *Genesis*. These are related by the square root of three and therefore can be represented in the proportions of the vesica piscis.

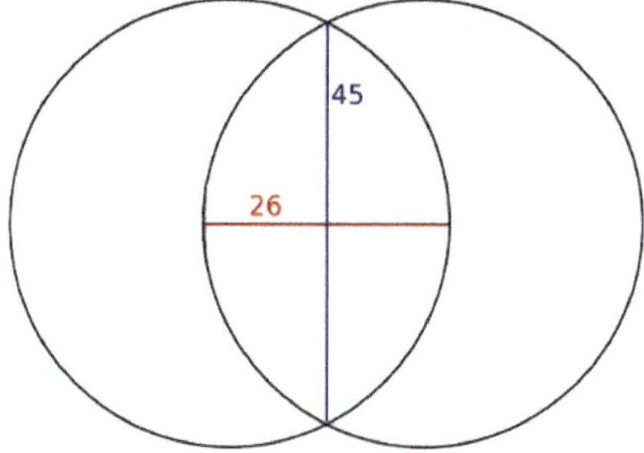

The name יהוה - 'Yahweh', has a value of 26 by Hebrew gematria and if this measures the width of a vesica piscis, the height of the vesica will be 45. 45 provides the gematria value of, אדם – 'Adam'. The difference between the two is 19, which gives the value of, חוה - 'Eve'. In this way the sacred vesica measures the relationship between the creator and the 'man' created in his likeness.

This method of transmitting arcane information ensured that the rules of geometry were known and preserved by initiates. No secret knowledge could be apprehended without a thorough grounding in geometry and the related algebra. This helps us understand why Plato had the words, 'Let none unskilled in geometry enter here', written above the doorway to his Academy.

Gematria Shorthand – Notarikon

Aside from gematria, there is also a form of cabalistic shorthand called notarikon. As a counting method, this simply uses the first letter of each word. By this method, the value of '**D**octor **J**ohn **D**ee' is the sum of three numbers only, and thus reduced to: 4 + 600 + 4 = 608. Notarikon has the advantage of being easier for a writer to engineer, and disadvantages of being less flexible and easier to detect. It is of subordinate status to gematria.

Conclusion

This chapter has introduced the cryptographic techniques

of acrostics, letter-grids and gematria. The main focus of attention has been on gematria because it is less well known than the other two, and its mode of operation is conceptually harder to grasp, especially for modern cryptographers. To further clarify how gematria can be used effectively as a technique to secretly record information, the next chapter will look at three case studies.

Chapter 3 Notes

[1] William F. and Elizebeth S. Friedman, (1957) *The Shakespearean Ciphers Examined.*
[2] William Friedman has been lauded as the greatest cryptologist of all time. See, David Kahn. *The Codebreakers: The Story of Secret Writing*. New York: Macmillan, 1967, p. 393.
[3] W. & E. Friedman, xvii.
[4] W. & E. Friedman, 20.
[5] W. & E. Friedman, 21.
[6] W. & E. Friedman, 100.
[7] W. & E. Friedman, 92.
[8] W. & E. Friedman, 100.
[9] Leslie Hotson. *Mr W. H.,* 153-7.
[10] Announced in *The Times* 31st December 1997 and published in *The Elizabethan Review* Autumn 1997 edition.
[11] See for example, the Fellow-Craft Ritual as set out in *Duncan's Masonic Ritual and Monitor* (1866), 69, 76 etc.
[12] The general rule for cipher solutions is that they should have a minimum of 25 letters before they can be regarded as unambiguous. However a 16-letter name appearing as an acrostic in a text of only 144 letters is a non-standard example. See Claude Shannon. 'Prediction and Entropy of Printed English'. *Bell System Technical Journal*, Vol. 30/1 (1951), 50-64.
[13] The myth that Freemasonry began in 1717 with the founding of the United Grand Lodge of England is demonstrably false. There are literary references to some kind of intellectual 'masonic' fraternity in late Elizabethan pamphlets; and more clearcut documentation such as the Schaw Statutes from Scotland in 1598 and 1599. The earlier history is more murky. The Grand Lodge at York traces its history all the way back to 926 A.D., in the reign of King Athelstan. This would be hard to believe were it not for odd documents such as the Cooke manuscript (c.1450), which describes King Athelstan: "For of speculatyfe he was a master, and he lovyd well masonry and masons, And he bicome a mason himself."
[14] My gratitude is due to Art Neuendorffer for pointing this out to me.
[15] https://archeologie.culture.gouv.fr/khorsabad/en/new-city
[16] Dee, John (1570) *Mathematicall Praeface to The Elements of Geometrie by Euclid of Megara*, 4th page.
[17] Henry C. Agrippa, *Three Books of Occult Philosophy*, Book II, Ch. 27.
[18] Alistair Fowler, *Triumphal Forms - Structural Patterns in Elizabethan Poetry*, ix.
[19] Fowler, *Triumphal Forms*, 183.
[20] Henry Reynolds, *Mythomystes*, 33-34.
[21] See Kieren Barry, *The Greek Qabalah*, 217.
[22] Balliol College, Oxford, ms. 354. See R. Robbins, *Secular Lyrics of the XIVth and XVth Centuries*, 253.
[23] Another potential point of confusion for modern readers is that there were two forms of the letter "s" (as there are in Greek). In lower case letters, the long

'medial S' looked like the letter "f"without a cross stroke and was more frequently used, while the modern "s" only consistently appeared at the end of words.
[24] Book 4, Chapter 6.
[25] See the following page on my website: https://shake-scene.com/Masonry%20and%20Cabala.htm The second location where it may be found is in: Petrus Bungus, *Numerorum Mysteria*, Bergama, 1591. p.625.
[26] Peter French, *John Dee – The World of an Elizabethan Magus*, 90.
[27] In the preface to his *Monas Hieroglyphica* (1564), Dee hints at his use of Agrippa's book when he alludes to putting gematria and notarikon into contemporary language. He distinguishes 'real Cabala' from 'vulgar Cabala', and it seems telling that 'Realis Cabala' has a value equal to that of 'Gematria' by Agrippa's code – 233.

4
A Proof of Concept: Three Case Studies

The manner in which gematria can be employed in practice is best understood by looking at a trinity of real-life examples. The first verse of the *Bible* makes for an original starting point. A second example will show how a witty student of late-Tudor England put the gematria of his mother-tongue to use on his portrait. This refers to the inscription on a painting found hidden behind a false wall in Christopher Marlowe's alma mater, Corpus Christi College, in Cambridge. Finally, the words of the dedication and cover page(s) of *Shakespeare's Sonnets* are subjected to a close reckoning by means of letter-counting.

Case Study 1 – Numerical Patterns in The Beginning

"In the beginning God created the heaven and the earth". All around the world and in almost every tongue, the opening words of the *Bible* are familiar. However, these words were first written in Hebrew, and it is to the original Hebrew one must go if a deeper understanding of their significance is sought. Gematria analysis of the seven words from which the sentence is constructed reveals a numerical plan with profound implications.

[In the explanation that follows, I make no claims to originality. I am indebted to the late mathematician Vernon Jenkins for bringing to my attention much of the information presented] [1]

The Number 2701

In Hebrew the seven words of the first verse look like this:

בְּרֵאשִׁית בָּרָא אֱלֹהִים אֵת הַשָּׁמַיִם וְאֵת הָאָרֶץ

The words, which can be transliterated (in a right-to-left text direction) as 'BRAShITh BRA ALHIM ATh HShMIM VATh HARTz', have gematria values of 913 + 203 + 86 + 401 + 395 + 407 + 296 = 2701. This total, 2701, is a very special number. Firstly, it is a triangular number. This means it can be represented as an equilateral triangle with 73 'pebbles' along the base and 73 rows of progressively decreasing width, up to a top row with a single unit: for this reason, it is known as the 73rd triangular number.

2701 also constitutes the product of 73 and its mirror 37. The latter is another very important number. 37 can be considered as one of the fundamental building blocks of creation[2] and is one of only two *trifigurate* numbers in existence – the other being 91. The word *trifigurate* means that 37 units (or 'pebbles') can be arranged in the form of three different symmetrical geometric figures. These are the second octagon, the third hexagram and the fourth hexagon. The number 73 is also figurate, representing the fourth hexagram. The virtue of figurate numbers devolves from their total independence of language or the units of measurement employed. As universal constants, they are potentially as comprehensible to residents of the far-distant Tadpole Galaxy aeons ago as they are here on Earth today.

The 2701 pebble triangle has some important properties. Its perimeter of pebbles can be calculated as base 73, left side 72 and right side 71, making 216 pebbles in all. 216 can be thought of as 6 x 6 x 6, and in this context, it is important to remember that the universe was 'created in six days'. It is also noteworthy that the cube of side 6 is geometrically unique because its surface area and its volume are the same number: they are both 216. The pebble triangle may be subdivided into three smaller triangles of 666 and a central one of 703.

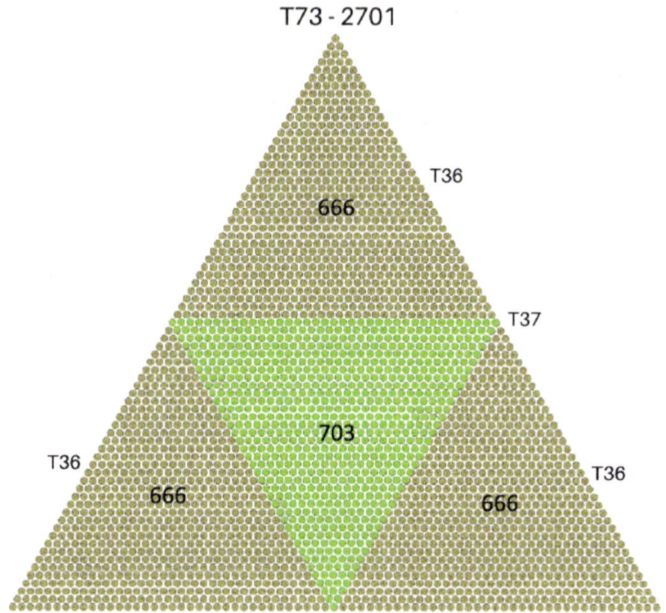

666 is the 36th (or 6 x 6th) triangular number (T36) and can also be considered as (6 + 6 + 6) x 37.[3] 703 is the 37th triangular number (T37) and the product of 37 and 19. [4]

Another connection between 37, 666 and 2701 accrues through the geometry of a six by one rectangle, the proportions of which are found in Noah's Ark.[5] This rectangle has a diagonal measurement amounting to the square root of 37 (6.08276). When scaled up to a 666 by 111 rectangle, the diagonal becomes 675.187: this is (practically) the side of a 2701 perimeter square. Similarly, the number 73 is connected to 666 via the geometry of a square. A square with an area of 666 has two diagonals summing to 73.

The Makeup of 2701

The foregoing is all well and good, the critic may say, but the occurrence of 2701 in the first line of the Bible may be a fluke. The reason why this cannot be so, as Vernon Jenkins demonstrated, lies in the value of the seven words that make up the 2701 total. These are:

913 203 86 401 395 407 296

The first five numbers, representing the initial phrase of the sentence, sum to 1998 and the last two make 703. This represents the basic structural division of the 2701 pebble triangle:

$$1998 + 703 = 666 + 666 + 666 + 703$$

It can also be noticed that word values allow the figure of 1998 to be halved to produce two instances of 999 (27 x 37):

$$913 + 86 = 999 \quad \text{and} \quad 203 + 401 + 395 = 999$$

This fact leads on to the consideration of another regular arrangement of the 2701 'pebbles', whereby a central triangle of 703 is flanked by two parallelograms, each 27 wide and 37 high, hence 2 x 999 in total. This produces a trapezium, and one whose dimensions make it a figure unique to geometry; for it has a base of 91, sides of 37 and a top platform of 55, and these numbers represent 8 symmetrical figures. 91 provides the thirteenth triangular number, the sixth hexagon and the sixth pyramid (the sum of consecutive squares). 37 gives the second octagon (after 1), the third hexagram and the fourth hexagon. 55 embodies the tenth triangular number and the fifth pyramid.[6] The perimeter of the trapezium is 91 + 55 + 35 + 35 = 216, and as seen above, 216 is 6 x 6 x 6.

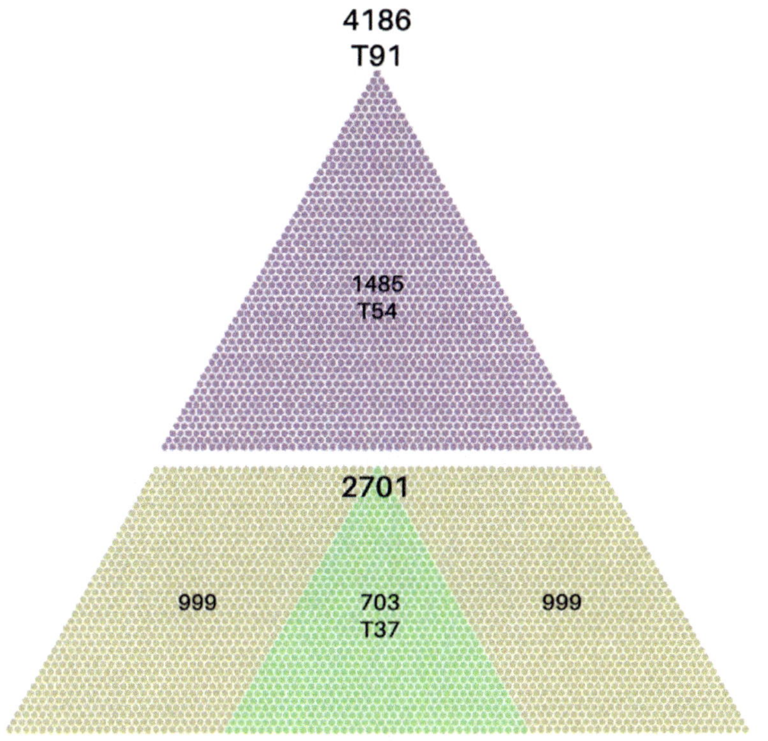

Finally, the 2701 trapezium may be converted to a 4186-pebble triangle by the superposition of a base 54 triangle (T 54 with a total of 1485 units). 4186 is the 91st triangular number (and 91 is made up of 54 and 37).

Aside from geometric considerations, the numbers can be manipulated by purely arithmetical means to produce some astonishing results. Adding 2701 to its mirror, 1072, produces 3773, which is comprised of 37 and 73: the mirrored factors of 2701. Subtracting 296 (the 7th word) from 1998 produces 1702, another transposed version of 2701. Subtracting 1702 from 2701 produces 999. Subtracting 296 from 407 (the 6th word) produces 111. Subtracting 407 from 999 produces 2 x 296. Subtracting 296 from 999 produces 703. The reason for so many interconnections of this nature is due to the remarkably high frequency of the building number 37.[7] This factor is further emphasized when the digits of the seven numbers are added:

913	9 + 1 + 3 = 13 = 1 + 3	= 4
203	2 + 0 + 3	= 5
86	8 + 6 = 14 = 1 + 4	= 5
401	4 + 0 + 1	= 5
395	3 + 9 + 5 = 17 = 1 + 7	= 8
407	4 + 0 + 7 = 11 = 1 + 1	= 2
296	2 + 9 + 6 = 17 = 1 + 7	= 8
		37

While 'mystical numerology' is widely used as a term of disparagement for the soft-headed in pursuit of the imaginary, this is the real deal. If further confirmation is needed, one only has to multiply the seven numbers together. The product forms 6 groups of three digits which, when added together, returns to the sum of the numbers:

913 x 203 x 86 x 401 x 395 x 407 x 296 = 304,153,525,784,175,760
304 + 153 + 525 + 784 + 175 + 760 = 2701

It can also be seen that adding the digits of the product gives a total of 73, the mirror of 37, and its partner as a factor of 2701:

3 + 0 + 4 + 1 + 5 + 3 + 5 + 2 + 5 + 7 + 8 + 4 + 1 + 7 + 5 + 7 + 6 + 0 = 73

In addition to this, Jenkins found something else remarkable happens if the zeros are cancelled in the seven figures and the resultant numbers added together:

913 + 23 + 86 + 41 + 395 + 47 + 296 = 1801

1801 can be regarded as 2701 minus 900 (30^2). 1801 is also the 25th hexagonal number. This 1801 hexagon is the hexagon at the heart of the 2701 triangle. [8]

The number 1801 also arrives independently when adding the last four words of Genesis 1:1 to the first word of Genesis 1:2 –

'VHARTz' – 'And the earth'. That word has a value of 302, so the sum is: 401 + 395 + 407 + 296 + 302 = 1801.

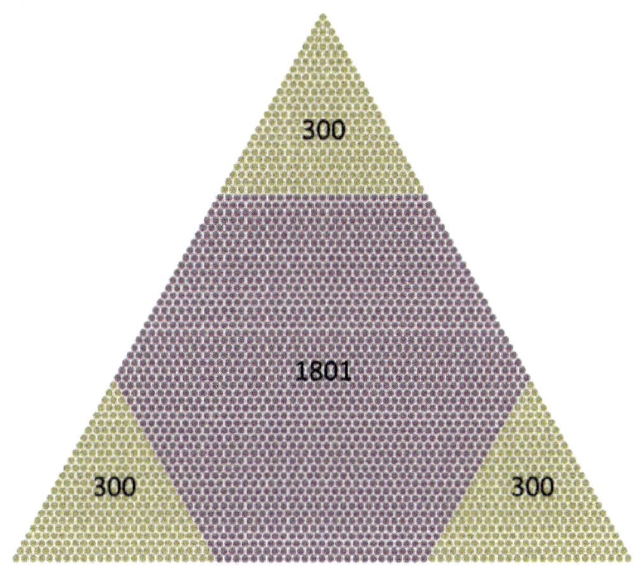

When added to 2701, 302 also serves to generate the 77th triangular number 3003. This is an extremely interesting number, especially in relation to 6 – the 'number of creation'. It was seen above (*note* 2) that 3003 multiplied by 37 produces 111111 - six ones. If this number is squared, the result is a beautifully symmetrical homage to the number six – 12345654321. 3003 cubed also produces a remarkable number 27081081027 – and the sum of the digits of this number is 6 x 6, while the sum of the four two-digit groups is 6 x 6 x 6.

The first words of Genesis open the door to numerical mysteries in scripture of a most intriguing nature. Whether understood in terms of divine architecture or cold mathematics, it demonstrates that, in acting as a bridge between words and numbers, gematria provides a means for communicating greatly more than 'the vulgar eye seeth'.

Case Study 2 – The 'Marlowe' Portrait

There has been much debate about whether the iconic portrait found in 1953 by builders behind a false wall in the Old Court of Corpus Christi College, Cambridge is in fact Marlowe's. While the picture has become the *de facto* image of the poet, the identity of the sitter has never been confirmed.

The painting is of a type called an *impresa,* and these were in fashion in England during the last two decades of the sixteenth-century. The distinguishing feature of an *impresa* is that it included a carefully crafted personal motto. According to William Camden, 'The body [picture] must be of fair representation, and the word [motto] in some different language, wittie, short, and answerable thereunto neither too obscure nor too plaine'.[9] In the parallel field of emblems, Geffrey Whitney drew attention to their puzzling nature. He said they should have, 'some wittie deuise expressed with cunning woorkemanship, somethinge obscure to be perceiued at the first, whereby, when with further consideration it is vnderstood, it maie the greater delighte the behoulder.'[10] Thus, an *impresa* gave a subject the opportunity to express his or her personality through a combination of visual and verbal 'conceits'.

If the portrait below was commissioned by Marlowe at the age of 21, it would represent a characteristically ambitious exercise in self-promotion. University students, especially those reliant on scholarships, would normally have neither the funds nor the self-belief for such an investment. However, we know that around this time he had several periods of absence from college, and it may indicate he had started working for the state on 'secret affairs'. If so, it is likely he would have received some form of payment. The sitter's unusual pose with folded arms could signify a 'keeper of secrets'. If it wasn't from a secret service pay-off, another possible source of income would have been his pen. Of his extant plays, Marlowe is thought to have written *Dido Queen of Carthage* while at university and he may have recieved payment for other plays and poems, too.

If the painting is viewed as an announcement to the world

of a brilliant poet's arrival, one would expect the 'word' to be deeply layered with personal significance. However, aside from noting the age of the sitter in 1585, I am unaware of any but tangential attempts to pair the inscription with a youthful Kit Marlowe.[11]

For those unfamiliar with Latin, the words 'ANNO DNI' are short for 'Anno domini', meaning 'The year of the Lord' (1585), and 'ÆTATIS SVÆ 21' literally means, 'of his age 21'. The latter is ambiguous and could mean he was either 20 or 21 years old at the time.[12]

The message, 'Quod me nutrit me destruit', means, 'That which nourishes me destroys me.' It is a unique and personal adaptation of the well-known motto, 'Qui me alit me extinguit', which accompanied an emblem showing a torch inverted and thereby being extinguished by its own fuel dripping down.[13] It most likely refers to desire, 'whose sweet torments nourish the mind, but which consumes the body unto death'. This original motto later appeared in Shakespeare's play *Pericles* as the 'word' of the fourth knight in the jousting contest in the second act.[14]

The inverted torch symbolism is ideal for a man named Marlowe as it constitutes a straightforward pun on his name. The verb 'mar' means to spoil, and the old Scottish noun 'lowe' signifies a flame. Thus, the literal meaning of Mar-lowe is 'Spoil-flame'.

While the concept is simple, the real artistry lies in the precise wording and layout of the inscription. Given his interest in esoteric philosophy, and in particular the 'forbidden bible' of that subject written by Henry Cornelius Agrippa,[15] it lies somewhere between the probable and the inevitable he would have turned to Agrippa's gematria code to tailor the numerical properties of his motto. He would also have been familiar with its more prosaic cousin the 'S' code.

It must be born in mind, the whole purpose of the 'word' was to express the character and wit of the subject. Gematria provides the perfect means for doing this. It permits a huge expansion in the amount of information carried through the literal signification of the words. Moreover, it does this in a completely concealed way – like those modern secret codes which hide a message in the pixels of an image file.

Marlowe would not have been alone in thinking along such lines. A very similar *impresa* motto was adopted by Mary of Lorraine, the mother of Mary Queen of Scots. This was an image of a phoenix accompanied by the words, En ma Fin gît mon Commencement – 'In my end lies my beginning'.[16] Assuming the words were not chosen on a lucky whim, it seems likely the selection was predicated with consideration to Agrippa's code. Their value of 708 by this means equates them unerringly with, η Φοινιξ – 'the Phoenix'.[17]

A further elaboration may come from the breakdown of the two phrases, En ma Fin and gît mon Commencement. Their values of 131 and 577 align with two prophetesses, Πελεια – 'Peleia' and Κασσάνδρα – 'Cassandra'. Peleia would be one of the Pleiades – the 'dove' priestesses of the oracle at Dodona, who tended the eternal flame. It could also hint at Mary's connection with the sixteenth century French literary circle La Pléiade. The founder of the group, Pierre de Ronsard, was a page in the Scottish court when King James V married Madeleine of Valois. On Madeleine's death in 1537, Mary of Lorraine became James' second wife. Thus, there is a direct line of connection between Mary and Ronsard. Cassandra was the Trojan priestess who foresaw, amongst other things, the catastrophe of the Trojan Horse: she tried to destroy it with a flaming torch, but was thwarted by the citizens of Troy because no one ever believed her oracles. The 'prophetess' angle would add significantly to the meaning of Mary's *impresa* motto, although this component would be discretely veiled from casual readers. Had Mary Queen of Scots been aware of the Cassandra connection, it would surely have played on her mind as she embroidered her mother's *impresa* and its motto while in the Tower of London awaiting her execution. She may also have considered her title to the unique role of phoenix more deserving than that of her cruel cousin Elizabeth.

The words on Marlowe's motto amount to a value of 1511 by Agrippa's code. There is a good chance this was chosen because it equates the subject with the title, 'Master Kit Marlowe'. Being at Cambridge at that time and having recently received his bachelors' degree, his academic title in Latin would have been 'Dominus', and this translates to 'Master' in English.

Q	u	o	d	M	e	N	u	t	r	i	t	M	e	D	e	s	t	r	u	i	t	
70	200	50	4	30	5	40	200	100	80	9	100	30	5	4	5	90	100	80	200	9	100	**1511**

M	a	s	t	e	r	K	i	t	M	a	r	l	o	w	e	
30	1	90	100	5	80	10	9	100	30	1	80	20	50	900	5	**1511**

Another clue to the sitter's identity comes in the form of a rebus – a pictorial puzzle. The initial hint resides in the layout of the top two lines, where it seems the year, 1585, has been arbitrarily placed. Looking more closely, the second 5 appears slightly askew: it is smaller and shallower than the first, and inclined on a sharper angle. The overall effect is to place this subtly 'defective' number plumb beneath the *æsch* ligature of ÆTATIS.

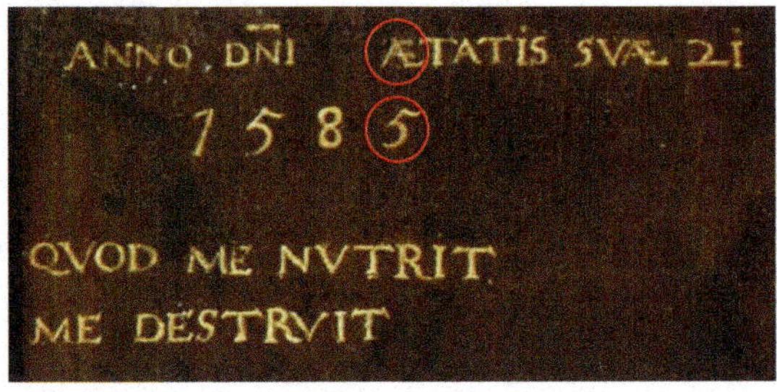

If the value of 'Æ', which is 6, is docked from 1585, the remainder is 1579. This counts the value of 'Christopher Marlowe'.[18]

C	h	r	i	s	t	o	p	h	e	r	M	a	r	l	o	w	e	
3	8	80	9	90	100	50	60	8	5	80	30	1	80	20	50	900	5	**1579**

There are two further clues pointing to this distinctive number. Firstly, it will be noticed, the two antonyms 'Nutrit' and 'Destruit' sum as 529 + 588 = 1117. This turns out to be 1579 divided by the square root of two. By contrast, the first and last words, 'Quod' and 'Destruit' sum as 324 + 588 = 912. This gives 1579 divided by the square root of three. In a motto of this significance, it seems reasonable to conclude the presence of these two numbers, derived by related means, might point to something more than coincidence. I believe the reason for this is to be found in the implied geometry. The two numbers serve to limn the name 'Christopher Marlowe' by means of the square and compass.[19]

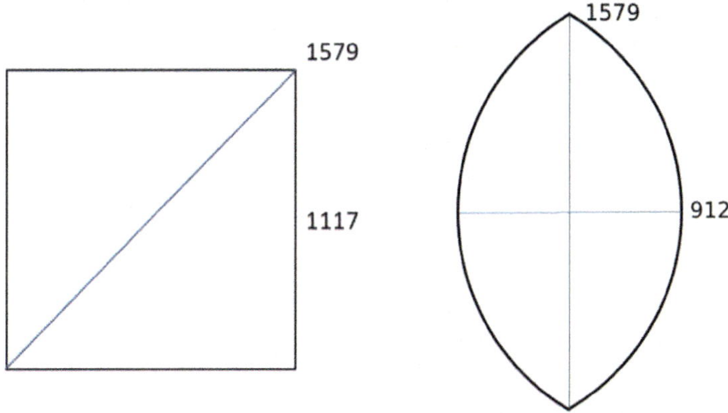

It is possible a vesica was chosen rather than the more obvious figure of a circle on account of its perimeter. Being well grounded in geometry, Marlowe would have known the perimeter of this vesica measures 3819.[20] Having an equally thorough background in Christian scripture, he may also have understood 3819 is equated with these resonant words from *1 Corinthians* 3, 13: ἑκάστου τὸ ἔργον ὁποῖόν ἐστιν τὸ πῦρ δοκιμάσει – 'The fire shall try every man's work of what sort it is'.[21]

A second rebus may be indicated by the prominent gold buttons on the sitter's doublet. A count reveals there are 33, of which 30 are complete and 3 partial. By gematria, the initials 'C. M.' are counted 3 + 30 = 33.

Whilst on the subject of the doublet, it can be noticed the effect of the bright orange silk revealed through the pinked slashes in the outer velvet gives the impression of red-hot embers. Added to this, the sitter's bouffant auburn hair has a passing resemblance to flames streaming from the body of a firebird. It would not be possible for the cobbler's son to show himself in that guise explicitly because the phoenix was thought a royal bird, and Queen Elizabeth had already claimed sole title to it (at least south of the Scottish border). Marlowe may have been impetuous and at times rash, but no one who valued their neck would openly try to displace the old bird from her fragrant nest.

On the other hand, the layout of the motto could be interpreted as a touch risqué. It has been divided up in two lines with the result there are four letters starting or finishing lines: Q, M, T and T. The value of these letters (by Agrippa's code) is: 70 + 30 + 100 + 100 = 300. By the alternative 'S' code, this provides the value of, 'Christopher Marlowe Phoenix':

C	h	r	i	s	t	o	p	h	e	r	M	a	r	l	o	w	e	P	h	o	e	n	i	x	
3	8	17	9	18	19	14	15	8	5	17	12	1	17	11	14	21	5	15	8	14	5	13	9	22	**300**

If this was intentional, he would presumably be banking on the fact that conflating two codes introduces a measure of plausible deniability. In this case, he would perhaps be assisted in his defence by virtue of the name 'Kit Marlo' being assayed at 300 by Agrippa's code.

Another rebus may be present on account of the typographical convention of writing the letter 'U' as a 'V' and vice-versa.[22] By this means, the words of the motto have the visual appearance of including three 'V's. If taken as such, it would increase the gematria total from 1511 to 3011. This number supplies the value of Μαστηρ Χριστοφερ Μαρλω, which transliterates as, 'Master Christopher Marlowe'.[23] It pairs very neatly with 'Master Kit Marlowe' coming at 1511, even though the meaning of Μαστηρ is 'seeker' or 'searcher'. Despite this difference, the literal meaning cannot be discounted for the poet who wrote the following gloriously self-referential lines in his play *Tamburlaine The Great*:

> Nature, that fram'd us of four elements
> Warring within our breasts for regiment,
> Doth teach us all to have aspiring minds:
> Our souls, whose faculties can comprehend
> The wondrous architecture of the world,
> And measure every wandering planet's course,
> Still climbing after knowledge infinite,
> And always moving as the restless spheres,
> Will us to wear ourselves, and never rest,[24]

The inclusion of the *aesch* ligatures in ÆTATIS SVÆ may have significance, too. If these are counted as single letters rather than pairs, the overall letter count of the inscription is 38. This is the 'S' code value of 'Kit'. If 38 is multiplied by six – to represent the number of digits in his age and the date, we find 38 x 6 = 228. In English, 228 gives the value of, 'A Firebrand'; while in Greek, it equates with Ναϱθηξ – 'Narthex', which was the giant fennel stalk Prometheus used to conceal and carry away the fire of the gods.

A	f	i	r	e	b	r	a	n	d	
1	6	9	80	5	2	80	1	40	4	228

Ν	α	ρ	θ	η	ξ	
50	1	100	9	8	60	228

The actual name Πϱομηθευς – 'Prometheus' has a gematria value in Greek of 912. We saw this number above as the value of the terminal words in the motto, 'Quod' and 'Destruit'. Prometheus was chained up and had his liver eternally destroyed by an eagle sent by Zeus as a punishment for his theft of fire.

A grand total for the inscription can now be calculated from a combination of the top line of text, the age, the date and the motto: 786 + 21 + 1585 + 1511 = 3903.

A	N	N	O	D	N	I	A	E	T	A	T	I	S	S	U	A	E	
1	40	40	50	4	40	9	1	5	100	1	100	9	90	90	200	1	5	**786**

3903 is 1301 x 3, and it can thereby represent the name Κιτ Μαϱλω –'Kit Marlowe' in the form of an upright equilateral triangle – the alchemical symbol of fire.

K	*i*	*t*	*M*	*a*	*r*	*l*	*owe*	
Κ	**ι**	**τ**	**Μ**	**α**	**ρ**	**λ**	**ω**	
20	10	300	40	1	100	30	800	**1301**

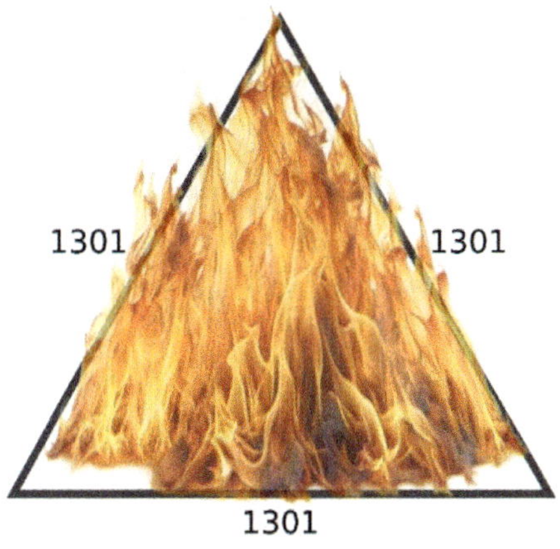

Finally, our grand total can be made a touch grander by the addition of 3. In this case, the 3 would stand for the three invisible letters indicated by the line over 'dni' – domini. The new total of 3903 + 3 = 3906 provides the value of the title, Χϱιστοφεϱ Μαϱλω Πυϱσος. This translates as, 'Christopher Marlowe Firebrand'.

Ch	r	i	s	t	o	ph	e	r	M	a	r	l	owe	
Χ	ρ	ι	σ	τ	ο	φ	ε	ρ	Μ	α	ρ	λ	ω	
600	100	10	200	300	70	500	5	100	40	1	100	30	800	**2856**

P	y	r	s	o	s		
Π	υ	ρ	σ	ο	ς		
80	400	100	200	70	200	**1050**	**2856 + 1050 = 3906**

By all of these means, the symbolism detected in the inscription helps reinforce the identification of Christopher Marlowe as the sitter. Every feature of it is congruent with this interpretation and there is no redundancy: the portrait fits him like a glove. In strict cryptological terms, the absence of a ciphered message means there is no final proof of this conclusion. However, it should be understood, that this is not a flaw because the *impresa* was never designed for such a purpose. Those who saw the painting hanging on the wall of his lodgings would have been well aware whose face it revealed. The numerical and verbal designs were intended as puzzles of 'cunning woorkemanship' for the entertainment of his friends: 'somethinge obscure to be perceiued at the first, whereby, when with further consideration it is vnderstood, it maie the greater delighte the behoulder'.

Overall, I feel confident that if Marlowe had an *impressa* painted while studying at Cambridge, he would have found it challenging to come up with a design that more aptly expresses his remarkable wit and ambition. Could anyone do better?

Case Study 3 – Gematria Codes in *Shakespeare's Sonnets*

Sceptics may concede that numerical symbolism of that kind might sometimes be encoded in mottos or lines of poetry, but they will argue it is inconsequential because it can never be proved – not unless the author were to state explicitly that it had been done. This is not likely to happen because the whole rationale of the technique was to evade the scrutiny of vulgar eyes. However, as was seen in *Genesis* 1, 1, there are some examples of gematria employment which generate patterns so anomalous, in terms of their numerical properties and statistical improbability, they do amount to proof of intentional placement. The context may also make the interpretation such patterns inescapable. Therefore, it is most fortunate that Shake-speare himself supplies clear examples of gematria usage in English, and he does so in the very best possible place: the front-matter to the original edition of his *Sonnets*.

The dedication prefixed to these poems is so weird in form and phraseology it is universally acknowledged to constitute some type of cryptogram. That is the conclusion of all scholars who have ever racked their brains trying to crack it. My gambit was to approach it as a puzzle of numerical Cabala.

Since I wasn't sure if Shakespeare would have used the 'S' code or the 'L' code, I decided to count the words by both. Also, to cover all eventualities, I counted the full gematria value of the words and the first letter values only – the technique of notarikon. With two codes and two techniques, this entailed four separate counting steps. I was excited to see if any interesting or unusual patterns would emerge.

The table below gives line totals counted by S-code notarikon, S-code gematria, L-code notarikon and L-code gematria, respectively:

S Not	S Gem		L Not	L Gem
68	216	TO. THE . ONLIE . BEGETTER . OF.	302	747
46	244	THESE . INSUI NG . SONNETS.	199	1018
50	188	M^{r}. W.H. ALL . HAPPINESSE.	947	1427
25	166	AND . THAT . ETERNITIE.	106	607
15	94	PROMISED.	60	328
2	25	BY.	2	402
34	220	OUR. EVER-LIVING. POET.	115	2120
21	88	WISHETH.	900	1120
40	165	THE . WELL-WISHING.	1000	2121
10	143	ADVENTURER . IN.	10	1264
18	90	S E TT I NG.	90	351
6	64	FORTH.	6	244
335	1703		3737	11749
		17524		

Initially, the numbers and the totals for each method do not look in any way interesting. They seem to be exactly what one would expect from a random distribution. Not wishing to give up so soon, I reflected on the matter, and after some thought, I saw a problem. There are two words, 'Ever-living' and 'Well-wishing', which are hyphenated. When these are valued by notarikon, I only counted the first letters. But what if the hyphenation implies not a single word in two parts but two separate words? In that case, the 'L' of 'living' and the 'W' of wishing would need to be counted, too. Might this factor yield the breakthrough I was hoping for? I decided to count again.

S Not	S Gem		L Not	L Gem
68	216	TO. THE . ONLIE . BEGETTER . OF.	302	747
46	244	THESE . INSUI NG . SONNETS.	199	1018
50	188	M ^{r}. W.H. ALL . HAPPINESSE.	947	1427
25	166	AND . THAT . ETERNITIE.	106	607
15	94	PROMISED.	60	328
2	25	BY.	2	402
45	220	OUR. EVER-LIVING. POET.	135	2120
21	88	WISHETH.	900	1120
61	165	THE . WELL-WISHING.	1900	2121
10	143	ADVENTURER . IN.	10	1264
18	90	S E TT I NG.	90	351
6	64	FORTH.	6	244
367	1703		4657	11749
		18476		

When I saw the new results, I was again disappointed. The totals appeared to be no less devoid of significance than the first time. I was about to move on and look for some more gratifying angle of research when a new thought occurred to me. I wondered what might happen if I were to add the two grand totals for each method. When I did so, my eyes opened wide:

17,524 + 18,476 = 36,000

Now, there was one big round number that didn't look random at all. I wasn't quite sure what to make of it, but it clearly looked interesting.

It was sometime later that another nagging thought rose up into consciousness. There was something missing. The initials 'T.T.' stand very prominently in large font at the bottom of the dedication, and I hadn't counted them. Could they be part of the scheme, too? It has always been assumed, they represent the initials of Thomas Thorpe, the putative publisher of the *Sonnets*. However, even if that is correct, it wouldn't prevent them being used for a dual purpose. With 'T' counted at 19 by the S-code and 100 by L, the pair of them sum to 238. However, this needs to be doubled to 476 because each 'T' must be counted by notarikon and gematria.[25]

I very soon realised that 'T.T.' was a key because when 476 is added to 17,524, it produces 18,000 and when it is taken away from 18,476, it produces 18,000. These two 18,000s are therefore independent of each other. What is more, their combined total of 36,000 is distinct from the original 36,000 because it is completely dependent on the 'T.T.' initials. This seems too much of a coincidence to indicate anything other than a design feature.

At this point I knew I was on to something: the code was beginning to crack. While it was exciting, I soon ran in to a dead end. It didn't seem to go any further. Discovering the next piece of the puzzle eluded me for many months and involved a lot of profitless head-scratching. After endlessly playing around with the numbers, I found it. Some door-locks have a feature whereby the key can be turned a second time in the barrel to extend the bolt further and more securely into the receiving plate. Likewise, I discovered the 'T.T.' key may be turned twice to amplify its effect.

When its value of 476 is added to both figures of 17,524 and 18,476, a new total of 36,952 appears. To the casual observer, this looks like another haphazard scattering of digits. However, appearances can be deceptive, especially in the hands of a skillful cabalist. 36,952 is an interesting number on account of its factors. An investigation of these reveals it is divisible in eight different ways. The significance of this dawns when all of its factors are summed because they come to a grand total of exactly 72,000. One doesn't need to be a mathematician to realise this is double 36,000 and four times 18,000. Bingo!

Dedication	
17524	
18476	36000

Dedication		T.T.	Total	
17524	plus	476	18000	
18476	minus	476	18000	36000

Dedication		T.T.	Total	
17524	plus	476	18000	
18476	plus	476	18952	36952

36952	1	
18476	2	
9238	4	
4619	8	
1192	31	
596	62	
298	124	
248	149	72000

These are very significant round numbers, and they come in a perfect sequence. There is nothing random about them. On the contrary, the numerical structure is the product of an incredibly precise construction. There is an artful designer at work here: a genius, even, with a thorough knowledge of mathematics.

This discovery has several important implications. The numbers demonstrate that Shake-speare was using both gematria codes of English, the L-code and the S-code. They also show he counted letters by means of gematria and notarikon. Furthermore, they prove that he used all four counting methods in combination. As an added refinement, he made use of hyphenation to double the number of possible outcomes and then he combined these, too. In the Cabala, it is axiomatic that every tiny feature carries significance. That is why Jesus said, 'Till heaven and earth pass, one jot or one tittle shall in no wise pass from the law, till all be fulfilled.'[26] Thus, the calculations above require eight separate counts of the words – anything less than this and the result will be no better than chaff.

Apart from the two critical hyphens, the 'T.T.' initials are another essential feature: an authentic cryptographic key. A further implication is that the spelling cannot be haphazard, as it might appear to be to the unenlightened reader, but highly precise. Shake-speare used the orthographic malleability of the language to calculated effect. A related consequence is disproval of the long-held assumption that the *Sonnets* could have been printed as a pirated edition and thus in a disordered sequence. Their printing was meticulous, and it can only have been overseen by the author as its architect.

Meaning?

The next obvious question is, 'What do the numbers mean?' While their patterns are marshalled by the inflexible rules of mathematics, their intended meaning can only be symbolic. As such, the interpretation falls into the realm of the 'language of numbers'. In the twenty-first century, this is unfamiliar territory, but in Shake-speare's day the meaning of numbers was a branch of knowledge so extensive and so well-developed it was almost a universal science.

The safest guide to the meaning of number patterns is context. In the case of *Shakespeares Sonnets,* which were mostly composed in the 1590s, the context is the literature and esoteric philosophy of Western Europe in that period. For this purpose, it is fortunate there is a closely parallel piece of numerological symbolism coming from the one contemporary poet even more celebrated than Shakespeare for the systematic structuring of his poetry, Edmund Spenser. The line count for the 1590 Part 1 edition of his *Faerie Queene* was precisely 18,000. Furthermore, Professor Alastair Fowler, the world's leading authority on number-symbolism in early modern literature, believed the overall target was precisely four times that amount:

> The line-total of 18,000 for Part 1 implies a grand line-total for the completed *Faerie Queene* in twelve books, of 36,000 x 2. Thus, the

> numerological movement of the whole poem would have corresponded to two Great Years, and embraced Plato's two cycles – each of a Great Year in duration – the peaceful progressive cycle of Uniformity, and the discordant retrogressive cycle of Dissimilarity.[27]

By this reckoning, the numbers refer to inordinate time scales. Effectively, they launch the poems into eternity and deliver immortality to the poet, his friends and lover(s).

A second possible reference is closely related. It delves far back into the sands of time. Professor Fowler noted that the structure of the sonnets is built on triangular and pyramidal numbers, which imply that, "Shakespeare designed the sequence to function as a monument . . . and the pyramid seemed the monumental form *par excellence*."[28] If Shakespeare had wished his poetic edifice to truly stand proud, he might have considered incorporating design elements from the one surviving representative of the Seven Wonders of the World – the Great Pyramid of Giza. If so, it might be relevant to note the 9th century Persian geographer Abu Zayed al-Balkhi reported inscriptions on the side of the Great Pyramid to the effect that, 'These two pyramids were raised when the Eagle was in conjunction with Gemini.' In the fifteenth century, the commentator Al-Maqrizi worked out that, 'The time that had elapsed from that time until the Hegira of the Prophet was twice 36,000 solar years, that is to say 72,000 solar years."[29] Could Shakespeare have been aware of Al-Maqrizi's writing, which was only recorded in Farsi and Arabic? Whether he was or was not, a double 36,000 seems to be best explained as referring to a double 'Great Year'.

If the Egyptian connection seems a touch too speculative, an alternative monument from antiquity rears into view. In *1 Kings* chapter 6, verse 2, we learn that, 'The house which king Solomon built for the LORD, the length thereof was threescore cubits, and the breadth thereof twenty cubits, and the height thereof thirty cubits.' A simple mathematical calculation reveals that the volume of Solomon's Temple must have been 36,000 cubic cubits. In context, it may be noted the rebuilding of Solomon's Temple on the spiritual plain is a task not unfamiliar to the brethren of Freemasonry.

Almost as a footnote, and on an entirely personal grounds, the round figure of 36,000 would be enormously propitious if the author of the *Sonnets* were an ever-living Christopher Marlowe. A great circle with an area of 36,000 will be found to have a diameter of 214, and therefore it can be neatly contained within a square with sides of 214. The area of this square is 45,796. If then the *master key* 'T.T.' were to be used to divide the total – using its 'S'-code valuation of 2 x 19 = 38 – the result would be the fractional number 1205.1579. From a Marlovian perspective, this is more than slightly propitious because:

1205 is the gematria value of 'Kit Marlowe'
1579 is the gematria value of 'Christopher Marlowe'
214 is the 'S'-code gematria value of 'Christopher Marlowe'
38 is the 'S'-code gematria value of 'Kit'

How probable is it that by squaring the circle of the *Sonnets* dedication and turning the 'T.T.' key, it could throw up a perfect sequence of eight digits, split by a correctly placed decimal point, to give the value of the two common forms of his name – moreover, with both counted by the two codes of English gematria? If Marlowe didn't write the *Sonnets*, this an outrageous coincidence. However, if he did write them, it is exactly the kind of numerical signature he would have sought to include at the outset of his autobiographical masterwork.

The Sonnets Cover Pages

Shortly after discovering the numerical key to the dedication, I came across the work of Alan Green. Amongst many other extraordinary discoveries, Alan has demonstrated the cover page of the *Sonnets* is type-set with great precision and constitutes a geometric master-plan based on a series of right-angled triangles nested in a circle.[30] Alan's work got me to thinking that maybe the cover page, too, could be cabalistically structured.

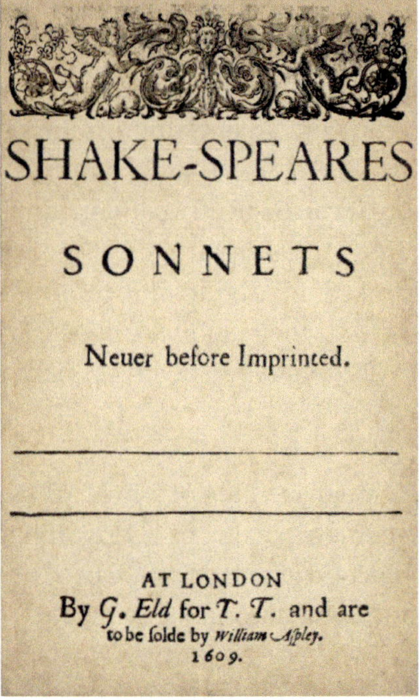

SHAKE-SPEARES

SONNETS

Neuer before Imprinted.

AT LONDON
By *G. Eld* for *T. T.* and are
to be solde by *William Aspley.*
1609.

Putting the cover page through the same counting process as the dedication threw out another highly improbable round number:

S Not	S Gem		L Not	L Gem	
18	121	**SHAKE-SPEARES**	90	445	
18	100	**SONNETS**	90	415	
24	212	Neuer before Imprinted.	51	1315	
12	89	AT LONDON	21	305	
60	168	By G.Eld for T. T. and are	222	905	
63	264	to be solde by William Aspley.	1095	2293	
		1609.			
195	954		1569	5678	8396

S Not	S Gem		L Not	L Gem	
36	121	SHAKE-SPEARES	180	445	
18	100	**SONNETS**	90	415	
24	212	Neuer before Imprinted.	51	1315	
12	89	AT LONDON	21	305	
60	168	By G.Eld for T. T. and are	222	905	
63	264	to be solde by William Aspley.	1095	2293	
		1609.			
213	954		1659	5678	8504

8,396 + 8,504 = 16,900

16,900 is not just a number rounded to the nearest hundred, it is also a square number – 130^2. What is even more interesting is that it fits together with 36,000 to make a second square number. 16,900 + 36,000 = 52,900. This is 230^2. Obviously, these numbers are related by more than just being large, round and square: 130^2 and 230^2 are identical apart from their separation by 100. Geometrically, they can be drawn like this:

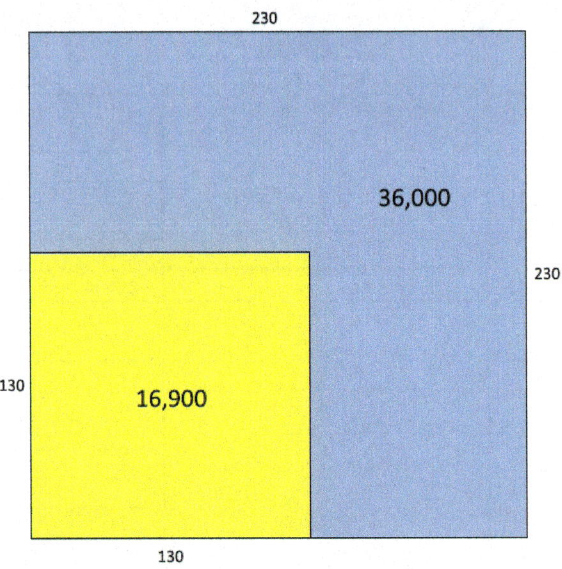

Delving in my numerological database, I was able to find one potentially relevant connection between the numbers 130 and 230. In *Genesis* 5, 3, it is written, "Nowe Adam liued an hundred and thirtie yeeres, and begate a childe in his owne likenes after his image, and called his name Sheth." That is from the Masoretic text, specifically the *Geneva Bible* of 1560.[31] However, in the *Septuagint*, an alternative age is given: "And Adam lived two hundred and thirty years, and begot a son after his own form, and after his own image, and he called his name Seth."

Could the two figures of 130^2 and 230^2 be a reference to Seth? Who was Seth? As the third child of Adam and Eve, Seth was born to take the place of Abel, who had been murdered by his brother Cain. Unlike Cain and Abel, Seth was born 'in the likeness of Adam', and in the Cabalistic tradition, he helped redeem the (original) sin of his father. In the *Zohar*, Seth is accounted 'the first of the righteous' and, as a wisdom teacher, is regarded the starting-point of the Cabalistic tradition.[32] According to Josephus, his descendants recorded their secret knowledge on two pillars and placed these in Egypt to outlast catastrophic floods and fires that had been prophesied.[33] Later authors conflated Seth with the Egyptian god of wisdom, Thoth. In early Freemasonry, there was a tradition that Seth was the founder of the order, and it was only during the seventeenth century that he became supplanted in that role by his descendent Enoch.[34]

Another indicator towards Seth comes because the name Seth - שת – has a value of 700 in Hebrew gematria.[35] It happens that 700 is the exact number of computations made to achieve the count of 36,000 in the dedication:

Gematria:	144 letters x 4	= 576
Notarikon 1:	28 letters x 2	= 56
Notarikon 2:	30 letters x 2	= 60
T.T.	(2 codes & 2 counts)	= 8
		700

If Freemasonry is on the horizon, an intriguing albeit entirely speculative, suggestion might be in order. It involves a prominent piece of stonework in Egypt. Taking the gematria total of 72,000 from the dedication, it is possible to make a construction that bears a striking resemblance to the original entrance to the Great Pyramid:

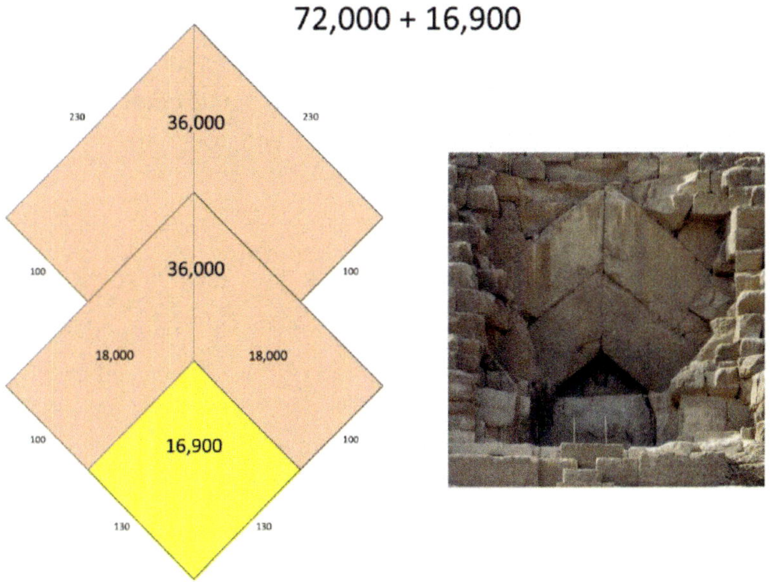

Do the cover and dedication to the *Sonnets* mark its entrance? Could the *Sonnets* be deliberately modelled on the Great Pyramid? If so, these numbers constitute an intriguing addition to the theory.

As to how the author might have known about such matters, there are several possibilities. For example, there is a tradition Leonardo da Vinci visited Egypt and surveyed the pyramids for the vizier of Cairo.[36]. If so, the information he acquired could have been passed down to others – through a secret-society lineage. It also seems that John Dee's friend the cartographer Gerhard Mercator visited the pyramid in 1563.[37] Another possibility concerns the Venetian explorer Prospero Alpini, who made a close inspection of the pyramid in 1591: if Shake-speare ever had traffic with Venice, he may have come across Alpini's journals. Whatever the truth of the matter, it is very likely that early Freemasons and their antecedents would have had a strong interest in the design of the Great Pyramid.

Seeing Double

It is a little-known fact that the *Sonnets* came out in two, almost completely identical, first editions in 1609. The one which is most familiar was sold by William Aspley, but there was also one sold by John Wright. This raises a question, 'Was the Wright edition purely a marketing stratagem, or might it have been designed to contribute a third element to a numerical master-plan?'

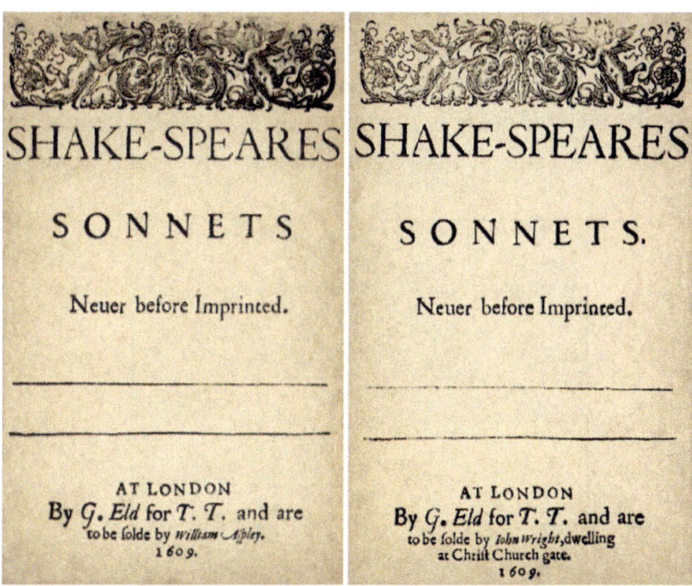

SHAKE-SPEARES

SONNETS

Neuer before Imprinted.

AT LONDON
By *G. Eld* for *T. T.* and are
to be solde by *William Aspley*.
1609.

SHAKE-SPEARES

SONNETS.

Neuer before Imprinted.

AT LONDON
By *G. Eld* for *T. T.* and are
to be solde by *Iohn Wright*, dwelling
at Christ Church gate.
1609.

It was with some anticipation that I set about counting its gematria and notarikon:

S Not	S Gem		L Not	L Gem	
18	121	**SHAKE-SPEARES**	90	445	
18	100	**SONNETS**	90	415	
24	212	Neuer before Imprinted.	51	1315	
12	89	AT LONDON	21	305	
60	168	By G. Eld for T. T. and are	222	905	
75	323	to be solde by John Wright,dwelling	1698	3535	
14	185	at Christ Church gate.	14	806	
		1609.			
221	1198		2186	7726	11331

S Not	S Gem		L Not	L Gem	
36	121	**SHAKE-SPEARES**	180	445	
18	100	**SONNETS**	90	415	
24	212	Neuer before Imprinted.	51	1315	
12	89	AT LONDON	21	305	
60	168	By G.Eld for T. T. and are	222	905	
75	323	to be solde by John Wright,dwelling	1698	3535	
14	185	at Christ Church gate.	14	806	
		1609.			
239	1198		2276	7726	11439

11,331 + 11,439 = 22,770

22,770 is less 'round' than the previous numbers and it is not square. However, it is divisible by 230, and because of this it can be fitted into the overall geometric scheme:

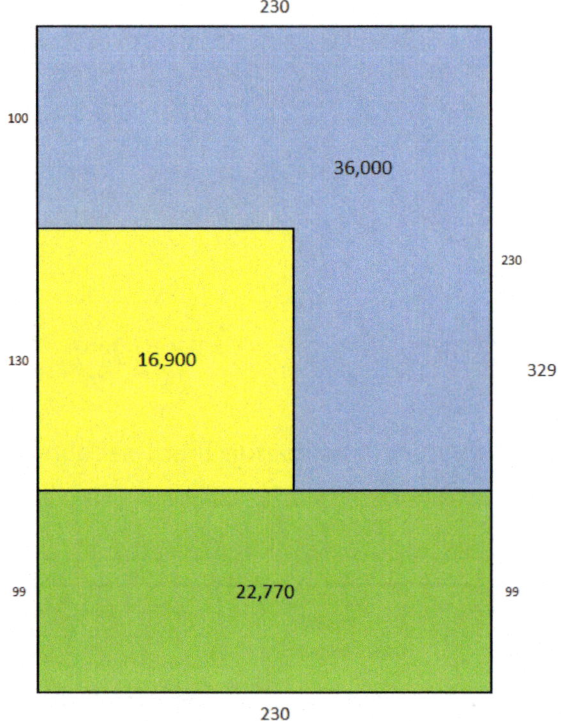

What was immediately noticeable is that at 99 x 230, it is just a fraction short of an obvious target. Had it been 100 x 230, the overall length of the construction would have been 330, and thus there would be a perfect sequence of 130 – 230 – 330. Could this tiny shortfall constitute an artful omission? If so, what could the purpose be?

Expected	Actual
130	130
230	230
330	329
690	**689**

690 is the gematria value of the Hebrew word – סלם (*sullam*).[38] This usually means a ladder, but it can also be used figuratively to describe a pyramid. It is particularly interesting because if the final letter (Mem) is counted at its regular evaluation (rather than as a 'sofit'), it takes the value 130. [39] If a pyramid is what it refers to, that pyramid is incomplete – just like the most famous pyramid of all.[40]

There are other ways in which the numbers seem to play on a theme where 69 represents a state of completion that has not been reached. If 329 is divided by 330, it produces the imperfect fraction 0.99696969696. However, if 230 were to be divided by 330, it would yield the perfect version 0.6969696969. We also notice 22770 divided by 330 is 69.

There may be more completely worked-out explanations thrown up in due time to explain the figures of 36,000, 16,900 and 22,770 arising in the front-matter of the *Sonnets*. What can't be changed, though, is the mathematical certainty they could not have arrived there by any other means than numerical engineering using the two codes of English gematria.

Summary

The three examples given here show gematria has a provenance stretching from when the book of *Genesis* was written to at least 1609, when *Shakespeare's Sonnets* was published. The longevity of the technique and the prestige of the texts in which it has been found are surely indications of the high regard in which it was held, by those who understood it, as a method of covert communication. While the cabalistic tradition is predicated on the oral exposition of these mysteries, the patterns revealed by gematria can allow the well-informed investigator to probe their secrets and gain insight into the meaning.

For such *profane* interpretations of gematria to be credible, there are two guiding principles. Firstly, while single numbers appear everywhere at random, distinct numerical patterns are far less likely to be random: they have probabilistic implications which render them susceptible to analysis. An equally critical factor is provided by context. This includes everything from the linguistic content of the encoded text to the wider symbology of 'the language of numbers'. Pattern-analysis and context-matching are not exclusive to cabalistic analysis: they form the basis of every code-breaking methodology known to the field of cryptology.

Chapter 4 Notes

---

[1] Vernon was a retired mathematics and engineering lecturer from South Wales. Unfortunately, Vernon's website went offline after his death in 2020. However, a collection of some of his most important papers can be found on the Academia website: https://cardiff.academia.edu/VERNONJENKINS

[2] 37 in combination with the 'divine' number 3 also proves to be one of the keys to the decimal system of numeration, as the following examples show:

$3 \times 37 = 111$ $3 \times 3 \times 3 \times 37 = 999$ $999 + 111 = 1110$

$3 \times 3 \times 3 \times 3 \times 37 = 3000 - 3$

$(3000 + 3) \times 37 = 111111$ $3003003 \times 37 = 111111111$

$111111111^2 = 12345678987654321$ and (the sum of these digits is 3^4)

$1/37 = 0.027027027027$ $27 = 3 \times 3 \times 3$ $2 + 7 = 9 = 3 \times 3$

$1/27 = 0.037037037037$ $1/(3 \times 3) = 0.111111111$

$1/(3 \times 3)^2 = 1/81 = 0.012345679012345679 0 \ldots$

[3] The sum of the first 36 numbers is 666. The sum of the first 36 triangular numbers is 8436 – or 12 x 703. The sum of the first 36 squares is 16206 – or 6 x 2701.

[4] 19 is the denary mirror of 91, which is the only other trifigurate number in existence. The numbers 19, 37, 61 and 91 are all related by the cube: $3^3 - 2^3 = 19$ $4^3 - 3^3 = 37$ $5^3 - 4^3 = 61$ $6^3 - 5^3 = 91$

Additionally, a cube made from smaller cubes with sides of 3 has a maximum of 19 visible units, a cube with sides of 4 has 37, a cube of 5 has 61 and a cube of 6 has 91.

[5] *Genesis*, 6,15.

[6] It can be seen that there are not only the only pair of trifigurate numbers in existence, but also a very rare pair of numbers that are simultaneously triangular and pyramidal.

[7] Martijn Valk has calculated the 7 numbers can be combined in different ways to produce 23 different multiples of 37. See Vernon Jenkin's paper 'A statistical analysis of the residue values of Gen. 1:1 modulo 37' at https://cardiff.academia.edu/VERNONJENKINS

[8] The 1801 hexagon is very unusual in that its side is 5^2, the number of rows is 7^2, and its perimeter is 12^2.

[9] William Camden, *Remaines of a greater worke,* 158.

[10] Geffrey Whitney, *A Choice of Emblemes and Other Devises*, Leyden, 1586. 'To The Reader'.

[11] In a recent article in the *London Review of Books,* Mark Rowe has shown a connection between the source of the motto and one of Marlowe's main sources for his play *Tamburlaine*. This lies in George Whetstone's *Heptameron* (1582). Mark Rowe, *But was it Marlowe?*, https://www.lrb.co.uk/blog/2025/october/but-is-it-marlowe

[12] If it meant he was in the 21st year of his life, most people today would consider him 20. However, that reading is not prescriptive. For one thing, it is a matter of semantics, and there is also the issue of whether the Julian or the Gregorian calendar was referred to. Marlowe was born in February 1564

according to the Gregorian calendar we use today, and which was in use in some countries on the continent. But in England at that time the Julian calendar was used, so the year 1564 began on 25th March (Lady Day), which is a month after his baptism. We also need to remember that the concept of recording a 'date-of-birth' is far more rigid today than it ever was in Elizabethan England. At that time people did not celebrate birthdays, and most had no idea of the day on which they were born.

[13] Whitney, *Choice of Emblems*, 1583, 183. There is also an intermediate version of the motto in French, 'Qui me nourit, me destruit'. This appeared in George Whetstone's *Heptameron of Civil Discourses* (1582), where it alluded to the image of a song thrush snared by glue while feasting on the berries of a holly tree. See the article by Mark Rowe 'But was it Marlowe' cited above.

[14] Pericles 2, ii. The motto is often printed with 'Quod' as the first word rather than 'Qui', but the latter is found in the earliest extant quarto of the play (1609).

[15] *Three Books of Occult Philosophy* (1531). We know that Marlowe was particularly interested in Agrippa and his *Occult Philosophy* because the character of Faustus is partially modelled on him. See for example, Frances Yates, *The Occult Philosophy in the Elizabethan Age*, p. 137.

[16] This was recorded in a letter from William Drummond of Hawthornden to Ben Jonson, on 1 July 1619.

[17] Φοινιξ is one of those rare words which can be either masculine or feminine, so take either ο or η as the definite article.

[18] A discussion of why Marlowe would have chosen this spelling of his name in a gematria context can be found on my website: https://shake-scene.com/Spelling-Christopher-Marlowe.html

[19] The diagonal of a square is the side-length multiplied by the square root of two. The height of a vesica piscis is the width multiplied by the square root of three.

[20] Multiply the width by 4/3 π (4.18879).

[21] See Appendix 3 for the way this line (and other extracts of New Testament Greek) is counted.

[22] While it was standard practice at the time, as reflected in the early-modern 24-letter alphabet, Agrippa's gematria code of 1531 shows it was well recognized the two letters were phonologically distinct.

[23] When counting Μαστηρ, the στ digraph needs to be counted as digamma, 6, rather than the standard 200 + 300 of *sigma* and *tau*. See the explanation of this feature of Greek gematria in Chapter 3.

[24] Act 2, vii.

[25] The 'pointing' (full-stops) indicates word breaks in the dedication.

[26] Matthew 5, 18.

[27] Alastair Fowler, *Spenser and the Numbers of Time*, 40-1.

[28] Alastair Fowler, *Triumphal Forms,* 188-9.

[29] This quotation is reported in Chapter 40 of *Al-Khitat* (*A Topographical and Historical Description of Egypt*), which is an anthology of ancient Arab writings

collected by Ahmad Al-Maqrizi (1364-1442 CE). It was translated into French by Urbain Bouriant in 1895-90: the quotation is from p. 332.
[30] Alan's work can be viewed on his website at https://tobeornottobe.org/the-sonnets/ and his YouTube channel: https://www.youtube.com/c/TheBardCode
[31] Unless otherwise stated, I quote from the Geneva edition of the *Bible*, as this was the version most commonly used by Shakespeare.
[32] *Zohar*, Bereshit B, 371-2. In verse 377, it is written that when Moses received the law and the covenant on Mount Sinai, he was only able to do so because Seth had preserved the prelapsarian wisdom from total loss. Seth's role as originator of the Cabala is more explicitly stated by Du Bartas in the *Divine Weeks* – Week 2, Day 2 'The Columns'.
[33] Antiquities, Book 1, Ch. 2, 68-71. As a word, ShTh (Seth) means a pillar. It may also be relevant that 130 is the gematria value of AaMVDI – pillars, and 230 the value of NTzIB MLCh – a pillar of earth.
[34] The history of Freemasonry in the sixteenth and seventeenth centuries is murky and complex. There are hints of Seth's role in the tradition; for example in Andrew Marvell's poem, *The Loyal Scot* (1669), where he writes, "Seth's pillars are no antique brick or stone; But of the choicest modern flesh and bone."
[35] There are a great many other potentially significant correspondances to 700 in Hebrew (and Greek) gematria.
[36] Codex Atlanticus, ref. 1336, 1337.
[37] Mercator left his graffito inscribed in the very heart of the pyramid, on the side wall of what later became known as 'Davison's Chamber'. Peter Tompkins. *Secrets of the Great Pyramid*, 38.
[38] *Sullam* is written סלם , but there is an alternate spelling סולם . The latter has a gematria value of 696, which may be relevant to pattern of repeated inverse digits.
[39] The letter 'Mem' is usually valued at 40 by gematria, but when it comes as the terminal letter of a word, it can be counted as 600.
[40] Possible support for this interpretation comes from Greek gematria, where 690 gives the value of Ο τελειος – The perfect one.

Part 3

The Evidence

5
Sonnet Number 1

We now have the keys to start exploring the subterranean landscape of the *Sonnets*. We must start by stripping off the top-soil of purely linguistic meaning and bring to light the hidden strata of numbers. Then, if anomalous patterns begin to emerge, we can try to make sense of them.

Initially, there will be two quite modest goals. The primary aim is to get a feel for how the poet works with symbolic numbers. This will be unfamiliar territory for everyone these days; and, for lovers of literature, the numerical aspects may reawaken the psychological traumas of lessons in arithmetic and geometry at school, so we need to get our bearings by taking small steps. For those more actively curious about the number patterns, I recommend approaching the remaining chapters armed with a pen, paper and calculator. In Appendix 1, you will find the gematria codes for English, Greek and Hebrew set out, and in Appendix 2 there is a guide to the main geometric ratios that are required. There is nothing too complex involved, and you will soon get the hang of using them. As I see it, the important thing is that everyone is able to verify any of the numerical claims I make to their own satisfaction and so need take nothing on trust.

The second aim is to start looking for numerical patterns or anomalies that allude to and potentially identify real people – including the author himself. This will be a search similar to that undertaken in the analysis of Marlowe's *impresa* portrait in the previous chapter. In these early stages there should be no expectation of finding any kind of hard evidence or definitive proof to upset the history books. Instead, we will be looking for puzzles of 'cunning workmanship' that are obscure at first but give delight to the beholder when understood. The credibility of those solutions proffered will simply rest on the steady accumulation of coincidences. If these are too frequent and too appropriate to have arisen by chance, they should be there for a reason. It is not illegitimate to consider what that reason might be.

The method

FRom faireſt creatures we deſire increaſe,
That thereby beauties *Roſe* might neuer die,
But as the riper ſhould by time deceaſe,
His tender heire might beare his memory:
But thou contracted to thine owne bright eyes,
Feed'ſt thy lights flame with ſelfe ſubſtantiall fewell,
Making a famine where abundance lies,
Thy ſelfe thy foe,to thy ſweet ſelfe too cruell:
Thou that art now the worlds freſh ornament,
And only herald to the gaudy ſpring,
Within thine owne bud burieſt thy content,
And tender chorle makſt waſt in niggarding:
Pitty the world,or elſe this glutton be,
To eate the worlds due,by the graue and thee.

In this faithful reproduction of Sonnet 1 in its original form, you will have to get used to the long 'medial S' that looks like an 'f' and the interchangeble printing of 'u' and 'v' letters. All letters should be counted according to standard value rather than the initially confusing typography.

When looking at a sonnet, there are four ways of counting each line (assuming there are no hyphenated words). Here is an example showing the count for line 1:

	FRom	fairest	Creatures	We	desire	increase	
Long notarikon	6	6	3	900	4	9	**928**
Short notarikon	6	6	3	21	4	9	**49**

	F	R	o	m	f	a	i	r	e	s	t	c	r	e	a	t	u	r	e	s	w	e	d	e	s	i	r	e	i	n	c	r	e	a	s	e	
Long gematria	6	80	50	30	6	1	9	80	5	90	100	3	80	5	1	100	200	80	5	90	900	5	4	5	90	9	80	5	9	40	3	80	5	1	90	5	**2352**
Short gematria	6	17	14	12	6	1	9	17	5	18	19	3	17	5	1	19	20	17	5	18	21	5	4	5	18	9	17	5	9	13	3	17	5	1	18	5	**384**

At first glance, this fourfold count seems worryingly complex. However, there is overwhelming evidence it was the system Shake-speare employed in the *Sonnets*, so any attempt to simplify it and thereby reduce the cognitive load is not a legitimate option. The virtue of having four separate counts in any line is that it greatly increases the scope for the poet to engineer more sophisticated numerical patterns, especially in situations where just a single line is counted.

In recording line scores, I adopt a format whereby the 'S' numbers are set out to the left, along with the line number, and the 'L' numbers set to the right:

S-not	**S-gem**	**Line**		**L-not**	**L-gem**
49	384	*1*	FRom fairest creatures we desire increase,	928	2352

In regard of interpretation, it should be emphasized the 'L' values carry the primary symbolic weight because this is the main gematria code, from Agrippa, and it is these that I give priority to.[1] The 'S' values serve a secondary purpose: they display direct symbolism less frequently and are used principally as an adjunct to the 'L' values.

The process of cabalistic analysis is one of firstly identifying any numerical patterns that are either anomalous or potentially significant in the context where they are found. Secondly, these patterns need to be explained by means of 'the language of numbers'. It is my experience that a sound sense of intuition is the most important guide to interpretation. If the results don't fit together in a way that feels right, they almost certainly aren't right. It takes a large investment of time and effort to reach a point where one's instincts start to generate credible leads and to unearth the lode-bearing ore. By way of a warning, I should point out it is a field which offers almost unlimited scope for fools to rush in and excavate shiny stones of no worth. While this renders it unsuitable for humdrum cryptographic purposes, it does not preclude the excavation of genuine nuggets of gold by those with patience, persistence and sobriety. Let's see if that is possible.

Exegesis

As with the previously examined example from *Genesis*, the very first line of Sonnet 1 is a suitable place to begin. This not only marks the start of the complete sequence, it also comes as the beginning of the first of three major groups in the *Sonnets*. This is a collection of 17 sonnets characterised by exhortations to a young man to marry and procreate. By this means, the sparkling beauty and vigour of his youth will be preserved against the ravages of time.

It has long been suspected these seventeen sonnets were written to mark the seventeenth birthday of Shake-speare's 'go-to' patron, Henry Wriothesley, the seventeenth Earl of Southampton. That felicitous day fell on 6th October 1590. At that time, Lord Burghley, his guardian, was earnestly engaged in a scheme to get him 'straightened out' and married off to his own granddaughter, Elizabeth Vere. However, the young squib was putting up spirited resistance. It is thought the old statesman commissioned his *tame* sonneteer, the one who later adopted the soubriquet 'Shake-speare', to come up with some suitable verses to jolly the youth along and nudge him in the direction of family responsibilities.

There is a potential reference to Wriothesley in the first line. It comes via the gematria value 2352. If this marks the circumference of a circle, the pentagon which may be drawn inside it will have a perimeter of 2200 (for the geometry, see Appendix 2). This is the exact value of, 'Henry Wriothesley'.

H	e	n	r	y	W	r	i	o	t	h	e	s	l	e	y	
8	5	40	80	400	900	80	9	50	100	8	5	90	20	5	400	**2200**

A poetic rationale for this geometrical arrangement is that it would present Wriothesley in the guise of a discretely hidden Tudor rose.

The pronunciation of Wriothesley was either 'Roseley', or else could be inflected that way with poetic licence, and a rose is prominently mentioned in the second line.

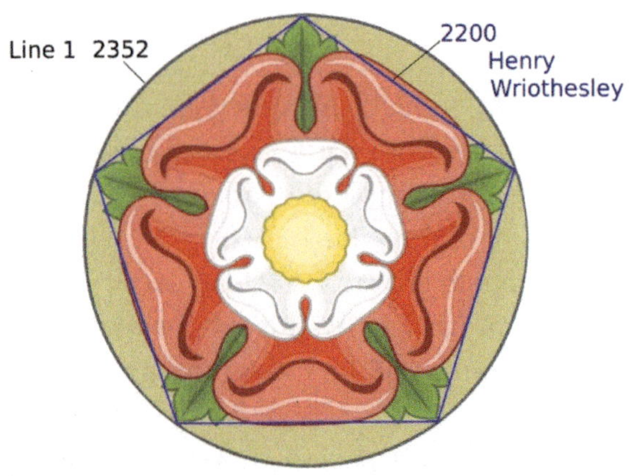

While it should be added that a single number like 2352 can be interpreted in many different ways and so proves nothing, this interpretation is concordant with the sonnet's widely recognized theme, so it is worthy of consideration. We will later see a second piece of symbolism connected to 2352 – one that fits a different pattern. Both interpretations may be correct as in Shakespeare's poetry many different layers of meaning often intersect. The *Sonnets* are particularly rich in this way.

If the hypothesis that Marlowe wrote the *Sonnets* and encoded his name in them is correct, it is likely he would have wanted to start the process at the very beginning. A subtle hint of this may appear in the first line using the same geometric design as just seen. A pentagon with sides of 928, which is the line's notarikon score, may be contained within a circle of diameter 1579: this is the value of 'Christopher Marlowe'. By this means, the poet would 'compass', or span, the unfolded contents.

While single numbers in single lines can do no more than establish 'congruency' with *a priori* theories, number patterns are more prescriptive and therefore carry greater weight. When all fourteen lines in the first sonnet are counted, some obvious anomalies emerge. I have added colour to make these easier to identify.

S-not	S-gem	Line	1	L-not	L-gem
49	384	*1*	FRom fairest creatures we desire increase,	928	2352
86	392	*2*	That thereby beauties *Rose* might neuer die,	356	2448
82	341	*3*	But as the riper should by time decease,	379	1771
69	345	*4*	His tender heire might beare his memory:	186	1397
83	453	*5*	But thou contracted to thine owne bright eyes,	362	3059
105	517	*6*	Feed'st thy lights flame with selfe substantiall fewell,	1218	3786
52	274	*7*	Making a famine where aboundance lies,	958	1657
158	480	*8*	Thy selfe thy foe,to thy sweet selfe too cruell:	779	3615
112	458	*9*	Thou that art now the worlds fresh ornament,	1297	3530
86	344	*10*	And only herauld to the gaudy spring,	356	2034
80	438	*11*	Within thine owne bud buriest thy content,	1157	3761
78	367	*12*	And tender chorle makst wast in niggarding:	1083	2020
102	418	*13*	Pitty the world,or else this glutton be,	1224	2817
116	371	*14*	To eate the worlds due,by the graue and thee.	1319	3198

On an initial glance, the most striking feature of the line scores is the curious doubling of 356 in lines 2 and 10. It doesn't look accidental. In fact, it looks more anomalous when we notice the corresponding 'S' values of 86 make an identical pair, too. Statistically, there's only a 1/100,000 chance of a particular 5-digit sequence appearing by chance, so roughly a 1 in 7692 probability of the same 5 digits appearing in one of the 13 other lines in a sonnet. It's not impossible, but it is eye-catching. It looks like the paired numbers define a group of nine lines, with line 6 as its focal point.

The first explanation I could think of for the group being bounded by the pair of 356s is that it might name the subject. Bearing in mind there are 9 lines in the group, I multiplied 356 by 9 to get 3204. That provides the exact value of the name, 'Henry Wriothesley the Earl of Southampton'. It might be a coincidence, but it could follow on from the potential identification in the first line and fit the sonnet's theme.

H	e	n	r	y	W	r	i	o	t	h	e	s	l	e	y	
8	5	40	80	400	900	80	9	50	100	8	5	90	20	5	400	2200

t	h	e	E	a	r	l	o	f	S	o	u	t	h	a	m	p	t	o	n	
100	8	5	5	1	80	20	50	6	90	50	200	100	8	1	30	60	100	50	40	1004
																				3204

Procreation

The next question is why the group should be centred on line 6. In numerology, 6 has powerful symbolism. Most obviously, it is known as the first 'perfect number' and thus was called the 'number of perfection'.[2] However, in the context of Henry Wriothesley, it would appear to have greater relevance as the 'marriage', or 'procreative' number.[3] It acquires this signification through being the product of 2, the first 'female' number, and 3, the first 'male' number. Simultaneously, it also appears as the number of days God took to create the universe. Procreation is the theme of the first 17 sonnets in general and Sonnet 1 in particular.

It may be that the pair of 86s allude to the age at which the previously childless patriarch Abram had his first son, Ishmael. Abram only began to have children when he listened to the advice of God. There was here perhaps a hint that young master Henry needed to listen to the sagacious counsel of his 'godfather' Lord Burghley. Shakespeare may perhaps have been drawing attention to this divine intervention by pairing the 86s with 356s. 356 is the value of 'the number eight' in Greek, ή όγδοάς, so two of them make 16. Abram's age appears in Genesis 16,16:

> *16:16* And Abram was fourscore and six years old, when Hagar bare Ishmael to Abram.

While 6 is the number of procreation, it is clear the youth addressed in the sonnet falls short of this achievement. He is in danger of squandering his potential and burning up his 'self-substantial fuel'. Therefore, the value of 1218 in this line could point to Αστηϱ οϱθϱινος – the morning star.[4] This is the brightest and most glorious body in the early morning sky, but soon fades into oblivion when the sun rises. In the language of flowers, the primrose carries the same symbolism. As Perdita puts it in *A Winter's Tale*:

> . . . pale primroses

> That die unmarried, ere they can behold
> Bright Phoebus in his strength

It happens that 'The primrose' has a gematria value of 517, and this is the 'S' gematria total of line 6. This kind of rose might be foreshadowed as the 'only herald of gaudy spring'.

I believe there could be a further 'conceit' baked into the numbers in line 6. Just as the youth falls short of achieving marriage and 'tender heirs', I think the line values could all be intended to come one short of the desiderata. If 105 was 106, it would give the value of the Hebrew word נון – 'Nun', meaning to 'propagate' or 'increase' (as well as 'a fish'). If 517 were 518, it would give the value of 'Queen Isis', who, from an esoteric perspective, symbolises the ideal marriage partner. The reference text, in this case would be Plutarch's *De Iside et Osiride*. If I am correct in this, the notarikon score of 1218 + 1 could provide for Σωθις – Sothis. In section 61 of his account, Plutarch writes:

> Sothis in Egyptian signifies 'pregnancy' (caesis) or 'to be pregnant' (cyein) : therefore in Greek, with a change of accent, the star is called the Dog-star (Cyon), which they regard as the special star of Isis.

The value of 3786 + 1 = 3787 might relate to the classic 'coupling vessel' known as Noah's Ark. The proportions of the ark were set out in Genesis 6, 15, and these were accorded great respect by cabalists and the magi of the Renaissance.

The ark was commonly viewed in the Renaissance as a divinely proportioned container for 'the microcosmic man'. In Agrippa's words, 'God himself taught Noah to build the ark according to the measure of man's body . . . for as the body of man is in length 300 minutes, in breadth 50, in height 30; so, the length of the ark was 300 cubits, the breadth 50, and the height 30'.[5]

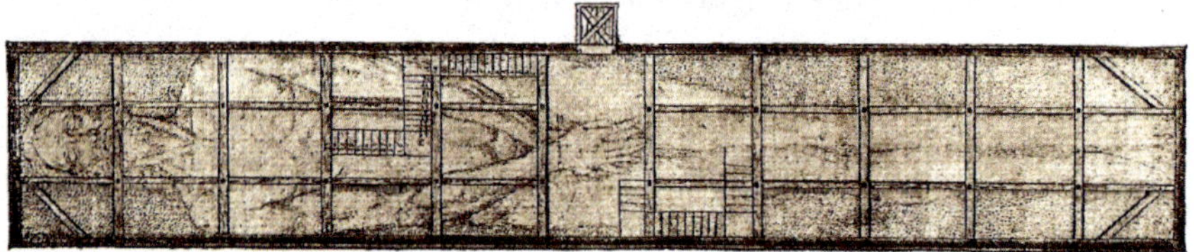

Drawing by Arias Montanus showing Christ's body in the ark, 1593 [6]

Arius Montanus emphasised the coffin-like nature of the ark when he said, 'these are the measurements for a man lying on the ground and dead'.[7] If Christ looks squashed a bit tight in his 'coffin', it may be because the overt description was at one level a euphemism for a smaller microcosm – a certain part of a man. At a deep esoteric level, the Ark had a procreative function, the finer details of which are not taught at Sunday school.

It will be found that an Ark with a perimeter of 3787 will have a length of 1623. It can therefore hold, ראשית האון – 'the first-fruits of his virility'.[8] If that concept is a little stiff to conceive, one could settle for a Latin alternative at the same value, 'veretrum erectum'. This was the favoured circumlocution in Victorian times for references to that unmentionable bounder, Sir John Thomas, the hard-riding member for Shaftesbury.

Whilst the exhortation to marry and procreate is overt, as well as cabalistic, in the first sonnet, there are several more themes almost completely buried beneath the superficial stratum of the poetry. The first of these is a concern never to be forgotten. In other words, the poet seeks to open the doors to eternity. This is expressed through reference to the great heavenly wheel of the Zodiac.

The Zodiac

The importance of this consideration may be indicated because the theme can be detected in the very first line. The four scores of the line sum as 49 + 384 + 928 + 2352 = 3713. A circle of this circumference has a diameter of 1182. This is the value of Ο Ζωδιακος – 'The Zodiac'. Reference in the line to 'fairest creatures' could therefore allude to the original meaning of the term, which derives from the Greek word, ζῴδιον – 'little creature(s)'.

I then put the gematria scores of lines 1 and 2 together: 2352 + 2448 = 4800. This number can denote the perimeter of a Zodiacal square. It does so not merely because the sides each measure 1200, thereby bounding a circle of 1200 diameter, but because the two diagonals form a cross summing to 3394,[9] which is the value of the 12 signs of the Zodiac in Hebrew:

טלה, שור, תאומים, סרטן, אריה, בתולה, מאזנים, אקרב, קשת, גדי, דלי, דגים

44 + 506 + 497 + 319 + 216 + 443 + 148 + 303 + 800 + 17 + 44 + 57 = 3394

The Hebrew words should be read from right to left to give:
Aries, Taurus, Gemini, Cancer, Leo, Virgo, Libra, Scorpio,[10] Sagittarius, Capricorn, Aquarius, Pisces.

I then noticed that the gematria scores of the first and last lines sum as, 2352 + 3198 = 5550. That was interesting, and it became even more compelling when I later discovered that lines 9 and 12 also sum to the same total: 3530 + 2020 = 5550. It is another pattern that doesn't look remotely accidental. Having no better plan, I decided to put them together: 5550 + 5550 = 11100. This is very attractive because it gives the value of the twelve signs of the ancient Greek Zodiac:

Αμμων,[11] Ταυρος, Διδυμοι, Καρκινος, Λεων, Παρθενος, Χηλαι, Σκορπιος, Τοξευτης, Αιγοκερος, Υδροχοος, Ιχθυης

931 + 1071 + 538 + 471 + 885 + 515 + 649 + 750 + 1343 + 1209 + 1514 + 1224 = 11100

Aries, Taurus, Gemini, Cancer, Leo, Virgo, Libra, Scorpio, Sagittarius, Capricorn, Aquarius & Pisces

Having the full circle of the Zodiac indicated from the first to the last line of this sonnet makes a powerful statement. It harmonises the *Sonnets* with 'the turning spheres of heaven' and, by indicating cycles of time at different scales, from the small year of 365 days to the great year of precession, launches them on a course into eternity.

It is almost certainly relevant that the four line numbers where the 11100 total is found sum as 1 + 9 + 12 + 14 = 36. This is divisible by 12, so it might hint at the passage of three years – a theme found in Sonnet 104. However, I believe 36 could have a more eternal message. Philo of Alexandria stated, 'By the use of 36, the creator made the World'.[12] This is connected to it being 6 x 6, which is to say the square of the number of days of Creation. However, it is also well known that the sum of the first 36 numbers is the canonical, and woefully misunderstood, figure of 666. Plato, who attached some importance to numbers, wrote 36 dramatic dialogues before laying down his stylus, and Shake-speare's *First Folio* (1623) matched this with 36 plays. Some things were built to last.

An alternative way of referencing the astrological signs comes courtesy of the book of *Revelation*. In Chapter 21, verses 19 and 20, the foundations of the holy city, New Jerusalem, are garnished with 12 precious stones. In esoteric science, these are understood to represent the twelve signs of the Zodiac.[13]

The gematria value of the first line, 2352, which we have already discussed, may give a subtle hint of this. It would do so because 2352 is exactly a quarter of 9408, which is the value of the sentence in *Revelation* where the first four stones of New Jerusalem are introduced:

> ὁ θεμέλιος ὁ πρῶτος ἴασπις, ὁ δεύτερος σάπφιρος, ὁ τρίτος χαλκηδών, ὁ τέταρτος σμάραγδος
> The first foundation was jasper; the second, sapphire; the third, a chalcedony; the fourth, an emerald;
> *[Rev. 21, 19. See Appendix 3 for breakdown of the gematria count]*

By this means, the first line of the *Sonnets* points to one sign, and presumably the first (Aries), of St John's heavenly Zodiac.

In astrology, the Zodiacal signs are generally categorized as being of three types: cardinal, mutable and fixed. The four gems corresponding to the four Cardinal Signs are:

χαλκηδών, σάρδιον, τοπάζιον, ἀμέθυστος
1513 + 435 + 588 + 1225 = 3761
chalcedon (Capricorn), sardius (Libra), topaz (Cancer), amethyst (Aries)

The Cardinal number 3761 can be found as the gematria score of line 11 (see above). The four Mutable Signs are signified by these stones:

ἴασπις, σμάραγδος, χρυσόλιθος, χρυσόπρασος
501 + 619 + 1689 + 2021 = 4830
jasper (Pisces), emerald (Sagittarius), chrysolite (Virgo), chrysoprasus (Gemini)

The number 4830 can be found by adding the gematria scores of lines 3 and 5: 1771 + 3059 = 4830. The Fixed Signs are:

σάπφέιρος, σαρδόνυξ, βήρυλλος, ὑάκινθος
1166 + 885 + 840 + 760 = 3651
sapphire (Aquarius), sardonyx (Scorpio), beryl (Leo) jacinth (Taurus)

Unfortunately, I cannot find 3651 anywhere. However, I can see 3615 in line 8. Therefore, I wondered if this might be intended to represent the fixed signs as a numerical 'anagram'. If we accept Shakespeare wasn't dyslectic, and had no problem in his ability to concentrate, I wondered if this could be another example of a deliberate 'mistake'. A hint that this might be so comes because the difference between 3651 and 3615 is the number just seen above from the four lines pointing to the Greek Zodiac, 36.

Another 'mistake' appears if we add together the gematria values of all six lines so far unused in the two Zodiacal schemes. These are lines 2, 4, 6, 7, 10 & 13, and their scores sum as:

2448 + 1397 + 3786 + 1657 + 2034 + 2817 = 14139

This is exactly 6 more than the perimeter of a square that can be drawn around the Zodiacal circle of 11100 circumference – ideally, it should have four sides of 3533.24 and hence a perimeter of 14133. 14139 would work if *Pi* is taken at a wonky 3.14, but Shakespeare was better than that: more in the mould of a 'senior wrangler' than a Blazing-Saddles cowboy. There might be a clue in that the 'error' of 6 being accrued as the sum of 6 lines. Thus, I had a suspicion the 'errant' 6 could also be intentional.[14]

A third possible 'mistake' comes because the score of line 9 is 3530. If it had been 3 larger, at 3533, it would have supplied the diameter of the 11100 Zodiacal circle quite accurately. It would also have made the perimeter of a square around the circle 12 larger.

If the three 'mistakes' were actually part of a plan, what could they signify? Well, since the figure of 3615 is 36 too low and the figure of 14139 is 6 too high, the net error would be 36 - 6 = 30 (too low). 30 is very significant in a Zodiacal context because it marks one twelfth of 360; therefore, it signals the number of degrees in each of the 12 signs of the Zodiac.

At this stage, I decided to pursue these clues pointing to 3, 6, 12 and 36 one stage further. They seemed to apply to the Zodiac of the 12 New Jerusalem stones. The total value of the stones is the sum of the three groups:

3761 + 4830 + 6351 = 12242

Initially, I divided 12242 by 6 and found (just over) 2040. At this value appear the words, Σωθικός κύκλος – 'Sothic Cycle'. This seemed promising as an elaboration and development of the astrological theme.

The Sothic Cycle was the 'great year' made up of 1461 solar years, which was used in ancient Egypt and based on the heliacal rising of Sirius – the star of Isis, which the Greeks knew as Σῶθις – 'Sothis'.[15] According to Tacitus, 1461 years also denoted the periodicity with which the Phoenix flies to the altar of the sun at Heliopolis and consumes itself in flames.[16] Coming across this symbolism gave me a jolt when I remembered that Marlowe's *impresa* motto – the inverted-torch allusion of, 'That which nourishes me destroys me' – is paraphrased in line 6, the focal line of the sonnet: 'Feed'st thy lights flame with selfe substantiall fewell.' What might support this conclusion is that the line's gematria score of 3786 accurately counts the letters of, Χϱιστοφεϱ Μαϱλω Φοινικος – 'Christopher Marlowe (of) the Phoenix'.

I next divided 12242 by 12 and found the result was 1020 (and a small fraction). That was also revealing because line 1020 of the *Sonnets*, which is the 12th line in Sonnet 73, is the place where the second and even more obvious paraphrase of Marlowe's motto is found: 'Consum'd with that which it was nurrisht by.' This line, which also contains Phoenix symbolism, will come under the spotlight in the next chapter.

When 12242 is divided by 36, it takes us to 340. Here we find the gematria value of, 'The Firebrand'. Clearly, this gets to the essence of Marlowe's motto.

These 'coincidences' give reason to believe the 'just-missed-targets' of 3651, 14133 and 3533 were indirectly indicated. It also points to a technique of engineering 'deliberate mistakes' that do not reduce overall accuracy (except on the surface level) but add to the information field by creating significant 'mistake factors'. To appreciate strategems of this nature requires a certain subtlety of mind and the capacity to dive beneath the surface of literal meaning. I suspect it is a characteristic of the Rosicrucian way of thinking. I know it is anathema to the mindset of material science.

Gone Fishing

Up to this point, we have identified two major themes in the first sonnet: one urging a young man to reproduce, and a linked concern with sending these lines into eternity by means of the Zodiacal wheel. The paraphrase of Marlowe's impressa motto in line 6 can be related to both through the emblem of the Phoenix.

Now, one more piece of symbolism will be revealed in numbers with a parallel target: a concern with resurrection and regeneration. More specifically, this is a focus on the episode in the final chapter of St John's gospel where the disciples go fishing on the Sea of Galilee and catch 153 great fishes.

Before delving into the fine detail, it should be explained that there are 154 sonnets in Shakespeare's sequence, but there are grounds for believing this is made up of 153 sonnets and a supernumerary 'one'. That was the conclusion of Professor Alistair Fowler, the foremost scholar of structural patterns in Renaissance poetry.[17]

Fowler was initially concerned with explaining the pattern created by the distribution of three sonnets with metrical irregularity. These are sonnets 99 (15 lines), 126 (12 lines) and 145 (tetrameters). He interpreted a quatrain in Sonnet 136 to indicate this sonnet should be excluded from the total:

> In things of great receit with ease we prooue.
> Among a number one is reckon'd none.
> Then in the number let me passe vntold,
> Though in thy stores account I one must be,

If this happens, not only is the new total of 153 a 'triangular number' – the 17th – but when arrayed as such, in the form of a pebble diagram, sonnets 99, 126 and 145 mark out a perfect sequence of three more triangular numbers: the 4th, 7th and 10th.[18] The base of the pebble diagram, being 17 sonnets, also marks out the first distinctive group of 'procreation' sonnets.

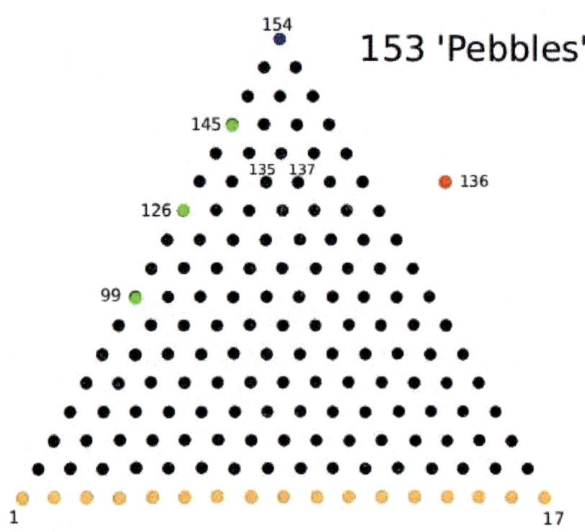

To my mind, Fowler's scheme based on triangular numbers looks correct. However, for anyone unsatisfied with this explanation, there are at least four other ways of arriving at a total of 153 sonnets. For example, only the sonnets 2-154 are numbered; the first has no numeral assigned. Another consideration is that two sonnets receive the same number: both the 116th and the 119th are labelled 119. One could also claim that Sonnet 145 isn't a sonnet because it isn't written in iambic pentameter, and it seems to have been written by a child. Finally, Sonnet 154 is merely a paraphrase of Sonnet 153, or vice versa – arguably, they are one sonnet dressed in different words.

The number 153 has an interesting back-story, and it is worth having a quick dip into it. The appearance that dragged it screaming out of the closet comes in John 21, 11:

> Simon Peter went up, and drew the net to land full of great fishes, an hundred and fifty and three: and for all there were so many, yet was not the net broken.

Along with 666, it is one of just a small handful of explicit references to numerology which otherwise lie hidden in the *New Testament*, and other classical texts.

In the *Old Testament*, 153 makes a covert appearance in Ezekiel 47, 10.

> And it shall come to pass, that the fishers shall stand upon it from Engedi even unto Eneglaim; they shall be a place to spread forth nets; their fish shall be according to their kinds, as the fish of the great sea, exceeding many.

What the eye doesn't see, the mind doesn't stress about! The two places named are written in Hebrew as עין-עגלים (Eneglaim) and עין-גדי (Engedi). The prefix to both names is the word 'Ayin', which means many things – most commonly an 'eye', but in this case a 'fountain' or 'spring'. By gematria, the name 'Eglaim' has a value of 153 and Gedi a value of 17. Together they sum to 170. This points to a concern with 153 being the 17th triangular number and divisible by 17 – all in the context of a pair of eyes and of catching fish in a net. I might add, the word דיג – 'dayeg', meaning 'fishing' or 'fisherman', has a gematria valuc of 17, too.

If primary sources were required, one could travel back to Ancient Egypt. Here, the 153rd chapter of *The Book of Coming Forth by Day,* a.k.a. *The Book of the Dead,* the has two variants. Firstly, there is, 'The Chapter of Coming Forth from the Net', alternatively titled, 'The Chapter of Coming Forth from the Catcher of the Fish'. The vignettes accompanying the second of these shows three dog-headed apes pulling to land a net 'full of great fishes'. In the Saite Recension, the rubric is added that this chapter, when performed on the day of the birth of Osiris, will ensure that the soul of the deceased shall live for evermore, and he shall not die a second time.[19] In context, one should also bear in mind that Osiris was reputedly slain on the 17th day of the month Athyr. It was similar to the way Noah's Ark set sail on the 17th day of the second month (Gen. 7, 11) and grounded on Ararat on the 17th day of the fifth month (Gen. 8, 4).

The fact that 17 is supremely important in relation to the mystical qualities of the number 153 is driven home when we take the time to count John 21, 11 in the original Greek. There are actually two common variants of the text, and both have a claim to authenticity. The gematria value of the *Textus Receptus* version comes in at a round 17,000. However, in the *Nestle-Aland* edition, it totals 17,340 (see Appendix 3). This is a bit more subtle. If divided by 17, we get 1020. This is significant on account of being one twelfth of 12,240 (as seen above). When we recall the 12 stones of New Jerusalem sum to 12,242, it might represent one sign of the Zodiac. So, whichever version of verse 11 you pick, it was divisible by 17, and we may be fairly sure John had an abacus to hand when composing his gospel.

Aside from 153 having an intimate relationship with the number 17, it has some other properties. There's a neat trick where you cube its digits, add them together, say 'Abracadabra'; and lo and behold, you have the number you first thought of: $1^3 + 5^3 + 3^3 =$

153. More seriously for mundane geometrical calculations, 153 provides a useful way to calculate the square root of three rather accurately. In the old days, the rule of thumb approximation was 26 divided by 15. In Hebrew, you could knock this out by dividing 'a pair of eyes' by 'your eye':

> עין + עין (Ayin + Ayin) = 130 + 130 = 260
> עינך (Eynekha) = 150
> 260 ÷ 150 = 1.733333

A much more accurate version comes from dividing 265 by 153:

> 265 ÷ 153 = 1.732026
> √3 = 1.732051

This calculation seems to have carried some freight when it came to resurrection symbolism. In John 20, there's a cryptic exchange between the freshly risen Jesus and Mary Magdalene:

> 20:15 Jesus saith unto her, Woman, why weepest thou? whom seekest thou? She, supposing him to be the gardener, saith unto him, Sir, if thou have borne him hence, tell me where thou hast laid him, and I will take him away.
> 20:16 Jesus saith unto her, Mary. She turned herself, and saith unto him, Rabboni; which is to say, Master.

The word Rabboni was not Greek, which explains why it needed to be glossed as 'Master'. The original was Hebrew, and it looked like this, רב בונה. It means 'Master Builder' and it has a gematria value of 265. The reference was to 'the temple of the body' which Jesus had predicted he would rebuild in three days. In Greek, Mary has a value of 152,[20] which is very close, but not quite good enough. Fortunately, her title, η Μαγδαληνη – 'The Magdalene', hits the nail on the head with a flawless 153.[21]

By this stage, you may be wondering what all this has got to do with catching fish. The answer lies in the sacred geometry of the Vesica Piscis. When two equally-sized circles are overlapped so that they touch each other's centre points, a vesica is formed in the middle. The width and the height of the vesica lie in a square-root-of-three relationship.

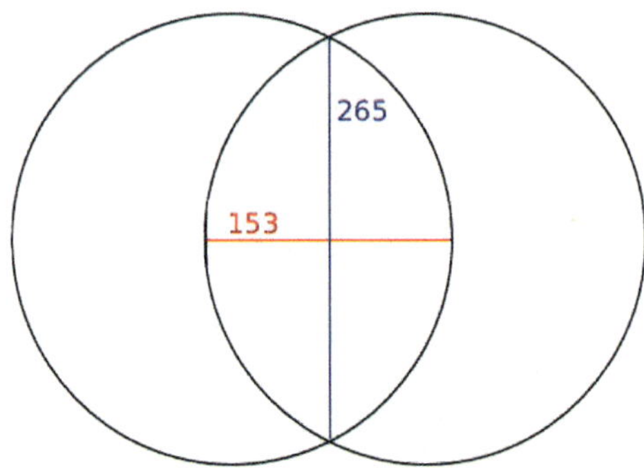

As a literary device, the shape of the vesica lends itself to the symbolism of an eye or a fish:

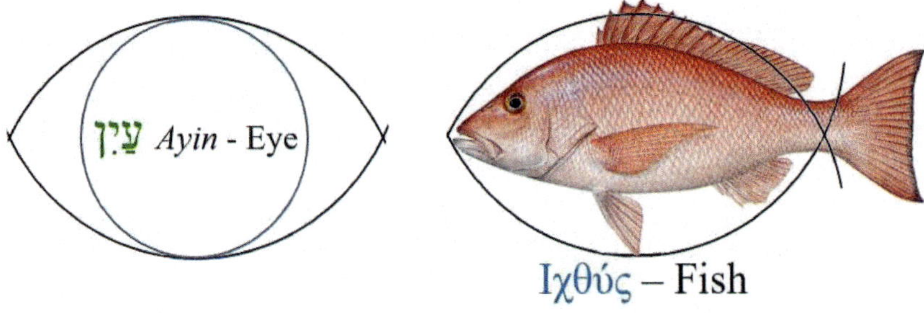

Furthermore, in the context of resurrection and rebirth, which is to say being 'born again', the shape can also represent the sacred yoni.

In St John's story of 153 fish, that number is a hint of what lies beneath the surface. The main esoteric content remains concealed in the language of gematria. Two items in the story are of particular interest. These are, Το δικτυον – 'The net', and Ιχθύες – 'Fishes'. Both are valued at 1224, which is precisely 8 x 153.[22]

If we look again at the line scores for Sonnet 1, we can clearly see both 1224 and 2 x 1224 = 2448.[23] This alerts us to the resurrection symbolism in Chapter 21 of John's gospel.

S-not	S-gem	Line	1	L-not	L-gem
49	384	*1*	FRom fairest creatures we desire increase,	928	2352
86	392	*2*	**That thereby beauties *Rose* might neuer die,**	356	2448
82	341	*3*	**But as the riper should by time decease,**	379	1771
69	345	*4*	**His tender heire might beare his memory:**	186	1397
83	453	*5*	**But thou contracted to thine owne bright eyes,**	362	3059
105	517	*6*	**Feed'st thy lights flame with selfe substantiall fewell,**	1218	3786
52	274	*7*	**Making a famine where aboundance lies,**	958	1657
158	480	*8*	**Thy selfe thy foe,to thy sweet selfe too cruell:**	779	3615
112	458	*9*	**Thou that art now the worlds fresh ornament,**	1297	3530
86	344	*10*	**And only herauld to the gaudy spring,**	356	2034
80	438	*11*	Within thine owne bud buriest thy content,	1157	3761
78	367	*12*	And tender chorle makst wast in niggarding:	1083	2020
102	418	*13*	Pitty the world,or else this glutton be,	1224	2817
116	371	*14*	To eate the worlds due,by the graue and thee.	1319	3198

It is time now to take a closer look at the group of nine lines, from 2 to 10, defined by the paired values of 356 and 86. What is really going on here? Could it be that the aooarent references to Henry Wriothesley were just a blind: a politic measure of plausible deniability? Might those twinned numbers define a container.[24] If so, what secrets might it hold?

The first clue comes from the addition of the two defining numbers: 86 + 356 = 442. This provides the value of, Ο βολος – 'The casting of a net'. Since there are two pairs of these, we can select another word with the same value: Θάλασσα, which means 'sea'. The combination of these two items looks promising.

Now, if we take the focal line at the centre of the pattern, line 6, and add its number to the notarikon score, we find 6 + 1218 = 1224. The fishes are starting to line up.

When analysing the gematria scores of lines 1 and 2, we saw they sum to 4800, and that was interpreted in terms of the 12 signs of the Hebrew Zodiac. It happens that this number also arises in our 'container'. It comes as the sum of the notarikon scores from lines 4 to 9:

186 + 362 + 1218 + 958 + 779 + 1297 = 4800.

There is a good chance the double reference comes about because 4800 also supplies the exact value of Jesus' instruction to the disciples in John 21, 6:

> Βάλετε εἰς τὰ δεξιὰ μέρη τοῦ πλοίου τὸ δίκτυον, καὶ εὑρήσετε
> – 'Cast your nets on the right side of the ship and ye shall find'.
> [*All long quotations in Greek are counted in Appendix 3*]

Furthermore, 4800 makes a perfect alignment with the distance of 200 cubits mentioned just two verses later:

> 'And the other disciples came in a little ship; (for they were not far from land, but as it were two hundred cubits,) dragging the net with fishes.'

It does this because a Biblical cubit was comprised of 24 'digits', and thus, 24 x 200 = 4800 digits. St John's twinned allusion to this number indicates it was important to him. It may represent his invocation of the Hebrew Zodiac. If so, one can imagine a great net cast 360 degrees around the Earth in the form of longitude and latitude lines projecting out to the surrounding heavens.

One detail that can be highlighted is that the nets were cast to the right side of the boat, not the left. In this, there is a parallel with the youth who announces the resurrection to Mary Magdalene (in Mark 16, 5): he was sitting on the right side of the 'empty tomb' – in the same way that Jesus sits at the right hand of the Father. In Greek, the word δεξιός means 'on the right side', and it has a gematria value of 349. We can find this number in the first letters of the nine lines forming the 'container'.

> T + B + H + B + F + M + T + T + A
> 100 + 2 + 8 + 2 + 6 + 30 + 100 + 100 + 1 = 349

The final letters of the 9 lines (e, e, y, s, l, s, l, t, g) sum to 737. This can point to the word η σκαφη, which can mean a boat, a vessel or any sort of container. Putting together the first and last letters of the 9 lines, we find: 349 + 737 = 1086. That made me jump because 1086 is the value of 'Marlowe', and the lines centre on line 6, which is a paraphrase of his *impresa* motto. However, in a fishing context, the more obvious word valued at 1086, is 'water'. Of course, with Shake-speare, it is possible that more than one meaning was intended.

The notarikon values of the lines defined by the two 356 values sum as:

356 + 379 + 186 + 362 + 1218 + 958 + 779 + 1297 + **356** = 5891

Considering this might represent a container on a fishing trip, I tried it out as the circumference of a vesica piscis. This can be calculated as one third of the combined circumferences of the two circles forming it. Its width is the radius of (one of) these circles. For 5891, the width comes out at just over 1406. I then made an eye by drawing an inscribed circle having 1406 as its diameter. It has a circumference of 4418.

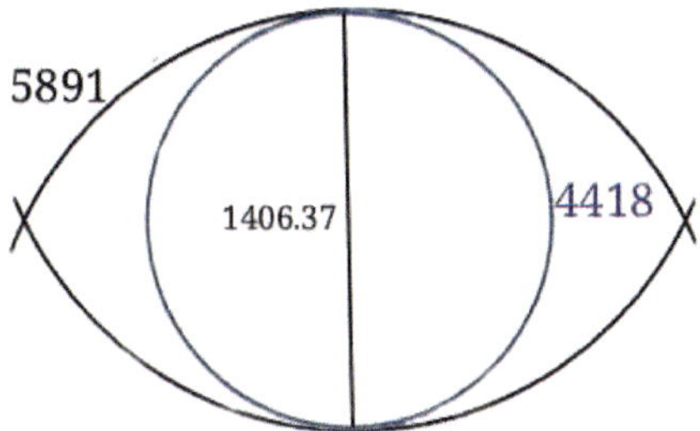

I was pleased to find 4418 has the value of Ιχθύες – 'Fishes': it has this when the letters are counted by their letter-names.[25] It is quite a catch – and as such gives good support to the fishing trip theme interpreted in this group of lines.

ΙΧΘΥΕΣ: Ιώτα + Χι + Θητα + Υψιλον + Επψιλον + Σιγμα
1111 + 610 + 318 + 1260 + 865 + 254 = 4418

I now decided to examine what might be in the apple of the eye. Initially, I drew a hexagram. The sides of the hexagram are found by dividing the diameter by 1.1547 (two thirds of √3). This comes out at 1218, which is the value of line 6, in the centre of the group. It offers another indicator we are on the right track.

However, neither the hexagram nor the hexagons it defines appear to contain a numerical message.

The geometric form that does appear to advance the message is a pentagram. The side length of such a pentagram is found by dividing the circle's diameter by 1.051462 (Appendix 2).

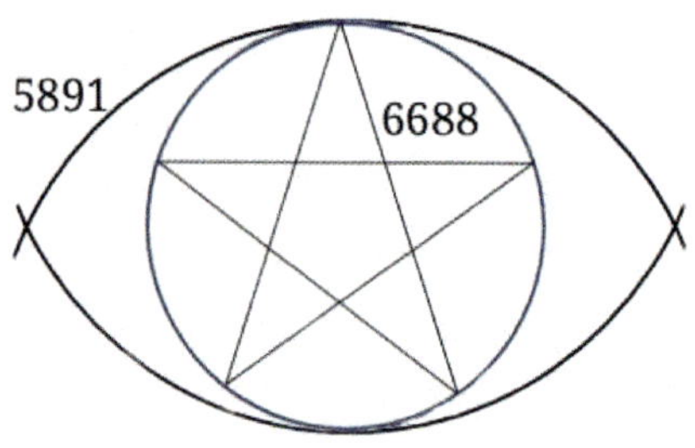

I found the total length of the pentagram comes out at 6688. This is extremely auspicious because it counts a longer version of the previous quotation from John 21,6:

> ὁ δὲ εἶπεν αὐτοῖς, βάλετε εἰς τὰ δεξιὰ μέρη τοῦ πλοίου τὸ δίκτυον, καὶ εὑρήσετε. ἔβαλον οὖν.
> And he said unto them, Cast your nets on the right side of the ship and ye shall find; they cast therefore.

This is very good. However, it turns out there is more to the total of 6688 than simply a longer quotation. That is because 6688 marks the perimeter of a rectangle enclosing a vesica piscis with a width of 1224 and a diagonal of 2448:

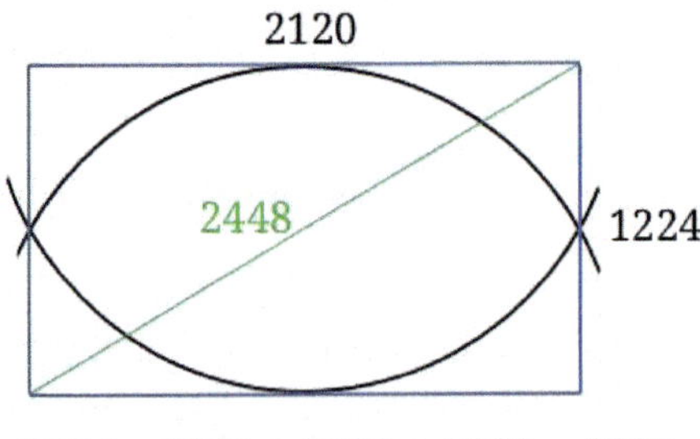

1224 + 1224 + 2120 + 2120 = 6688

This rectangle captures the essence of the covert symbolism in the fishing trip in John 21. One wonders if John had the dimensions of this rectangle in mind when he put together the words of his sixth verse? From the point of view of Shake-speare, the configuration is also of interest because 2120 is the gematria value of the author's designation, 'OUR EVER-LIVING POET', in the *Sonnets'* dedication:

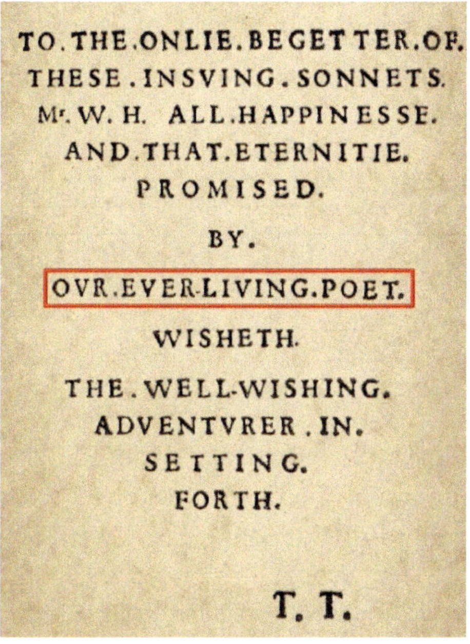

TO.THE.ONLIE.BEGETTER.OF.
THESE.INSVING.SONNETS.
Mr. W. H. ALL.HAPPINESSE.
AND.THAT.ETERNITIE.
PROMISED.

BY.

OVR.EVER-LIVING.POET.

WISHETH.

THE.WELL-WISHING.
ADVENTVRER.IN.
SETTING.
FORTH.

T. T.

O	U	R	E	V	E	R	L	I	V	I	N	G	P	O	E	T	
50	200	80	5	700	5	80	20	9	700	9	40	7	60	50	5	100	**2120**

And now comes the part that may point to the person who is resurrected. If we go back to the pentagram in the vesica's eye, we can find the pentagon drawn around its vertices (points) by dividing its length by *Phi* (the Golden Section) – 1.618.

$$6688 \div 1.618 = 4133$$

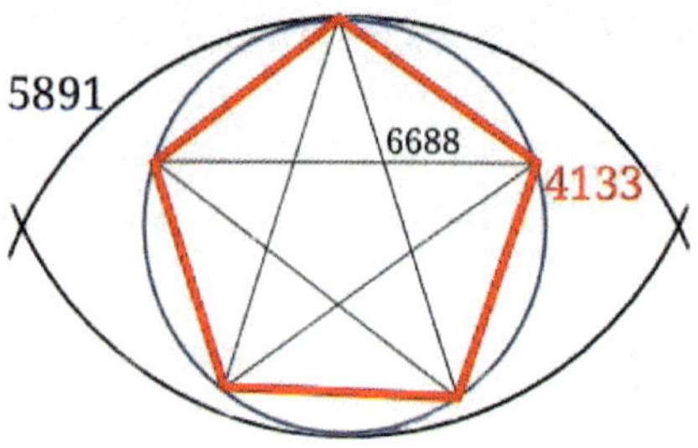

4133 can be interpreted to support of the candidacy of Christopher Marlowe because it counts the message, 'Our Ever-Living Poet, Christopher Marlowe' – through a combination of both the 'L' and 'S' codes together:

	O	U	R	E	V	E	R	L	I	V	I	N	G	P	O	E	T	
L	50	200	80	5	700	5	80	20	9	700	9	40	7	60	50	5	100	**2120**
S	14	20	17	5	20	5	17	11	9	20	9	13	7	15	14	5	19	**220**

	C	h	r	i	s	t	o	p	h	e	r	M	a	r	l	o	w	e	
L	3	8	80	9	90	100	50	60	8	5	80	30	1	80	20	50	900	5	**1579**
S	3	8	17	9	18	19	14	15	8	5	17	12	1	17	11	14	21	5	**214**
																			4133

This interpretation is further advanceded by the dimensions of the small pentagon at the heart of the pentagram. Its perimeter can be found by dividing the pentagram by *Phi* cubed – 4.236.

$$6688 \div 4.236 = 1579$$

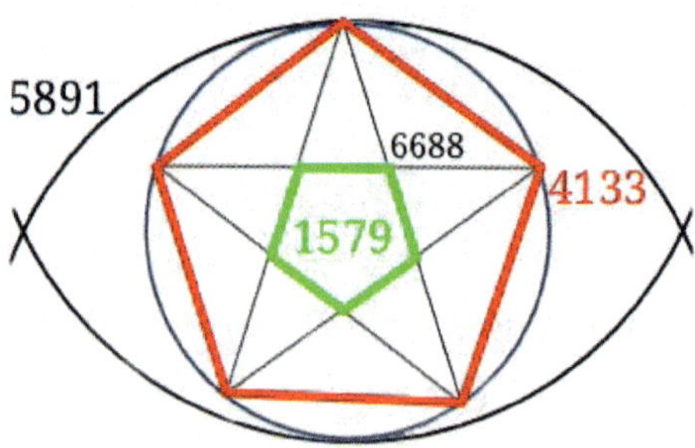

We already know that 1579 is the value of, 'Christopher Marlowe'. Thus, the two pentagons in the eye can be construed to signal the resurrection of an 'ever-living poet Christopher Marlowe'. While the sceptic will turn away in disgust and say this is *leger-de-main* and proves absolutely nothing, an open-minded investigator may find some degree of curiosity pricked. Of course, the sceptic is perfectly correct that the numerical alignment doesn't prove anything. All that can be claimed is that its presence appears concordant with the kind of message an ever-living Christopher Marlowe might have wished to leave behind.

There is one other geometric form that fits within the pupil of this eye and provides a few more grains of evidence in Marlowe's favour. This is the square whose diagonal is equal to the vesica's width (and the circle's diameter). It has four sides of 994.5 and a perimeter of 3978. The latter is the value of a couple of expressions in Greek that might be relevant. The first is, Χριστοφερ Μαρλω διφυης – 'Christopher Marlowe twice-born'. The word 'diphues' was an epithet of the god Dionysus and signified his 'double nature'.[26] Dionysus was first born to his mother Semele, and when she got blasted by a divine thunderbolt, he was born again from the 'thigh' – a delicate euphemism for the scrotum – of Zeus. He also visited the underworld later in life and managed to resurrect his mother. On account of that exploit, he was sometimes given the additional title τρίγονος – 'thrice born'.

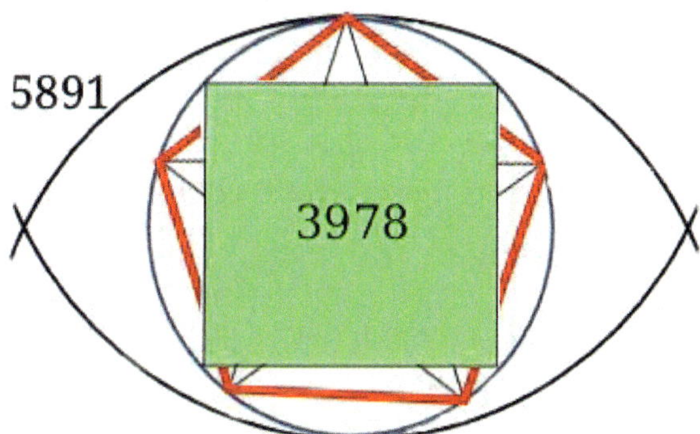

Another word connected to the theme and having the same value as 'diphues' is, ο επενδυτης – 'the over-garment'. Initially, it seems out of place – until one realises it is modestly covering up the exposed body of the pentagram. In John 21, 7, it was exactly this word that became translated into English as 'fisher's coat'. It was this garment Simon Peter put on to cover his nakedness before leaping into the sea to do battle with the net of 153 fishes:

> Therefore that disciple whom Jesus loved saith unto Peter, It is the Lord. Now when Simon Peter heard that it was the Lord, he girt his fisher's coat unto him, (for he was naked,) and did cast himself into the sea.

This is a curious passage. For sheer incomprehensibility it almost rivals the episode in Mark 14, 51-52 when Jesus was arrested in the Mount of Olives. In that story, all the disciples fled after a short skirmish with men sent by the chief priests and elders. The only one remaining with Jesus was 'a certain young man, having a linen cloth cast about his naked body'. When the arresting party made a grab for him, 'he left the linen cloth, and fled from them naked'. The tableau clearly left a strong impression on Mark. The interesting point here is that a linen cloth in Greek is η σινδών, and it has gematria value of 1122, just the same as ο επενδυτης and διφυης. One doesn't need to be Sherlock Holmes to realise there were ἐντὸς σινδόνος – 'esoteric mysteries', or 'things behind the veil' going on here and associated with that particular number. Some form of initiatory 'baptism', or rebirthing procedure, seems a likely possibility.

So far, all the heavy lifting in the 9-line group has been done by its notarikon values. It would be surprising if the gematria scores of the group didn't also contain some sort of message. I think they do. The 9 values sum as:

2448 + 1771 + 1397 + 3059 + 3786 + 1657 + 3615 + 3530 + 2034 = 23297

When I found this, I could initially make no sense of it at all. However, after a while, I did notice it is just shy of a rather obvious target: 23409, which is 153^2. If the author was any old cobbler, it would be possible to fudge it and say $\sqrt{23297} = 152.6$, which rounds up to 153 – *ergo* the hunch is proved, sort of. Alternatively, one could surmise that since the *Sonnets* were, 'buylded far from accident', it would be more appropriate to assume a more surgical reason for the divergence.

The precise difference between 23409 and 23297 is 112. What I noticed, after a certain amount of head-scratching, is that 112 is smaller than 153 by a ratio of 0.73203 – which looks an awful lot like the square root of three (give or take the odd 1). It occurred to me, therefore, I just needed to add 112 to 153 to get 265, and thus, the dimensions of our original fish. The neatest way of representing this geometrically is to split the 112 into two components of 56 and put them either side of the 153-sided square:

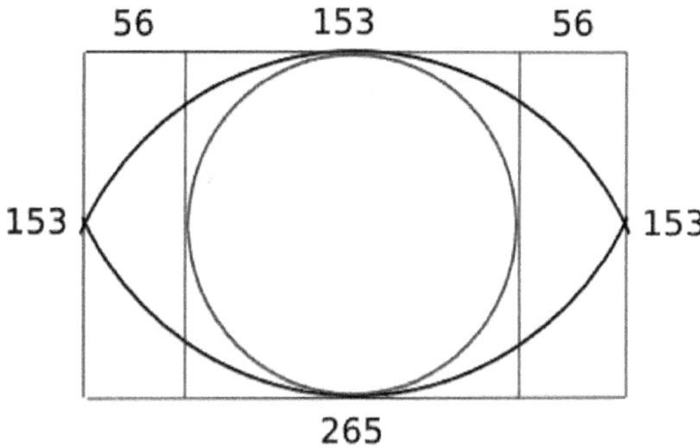

This format takes account of the √3 vesica proportions and retains a central figure of 153 squared. The begging question is, what might have possessed Shake-speare to put the square and the rectangle over the fish?

One reason could be that St John beat him to it by fifteen hundred years, or maybe it was some unknown Egyptian priest three thousand years before. The 153 square has a delightfully mystical property in that its area is equal to the sum of the first 17 cubes:

$1^3 + 2^3 + 3^3 + 4^3 + 5^3 + 6^3 + 7^3 + 8^3 + 9^3 + 10^3 + 11^3 + 12^3 + 13^3 + 14^3 + 15^3 + 16^3 + 17^3 = \mathbf{23,409}$ $\quad 153 \times 153 = \mathbf{23,409}$

That's rather impressive. For another thing, John must have figured out that 153^2 is 17 x 1377; and 1377 is the value of '153 fishes' written in Greek: ιχθύες ρνγ – 'fishes 153' (1224 + 153). The square is obviously much ado about 17.

But what was the attraction for our poet? How might it become personal? Firstly, we need to look at the two side panels – the rectangles measuring 56 by 153. They each have a perimeter of 418 (which is also the addition of 153 and 265). There may be some significance in 418 being the gematria value of Παλλας Αθηνη – the 'spear-shaking goddess' Pallas Athene. However, this doesn't take any account of the doubling of the value. A more pleasing solution comes from 418 + 418 = 836. This is the value of Διθυραμβος – 'Dithyramb'. This was the song sung to mourn the death and celebrate the resurrection of Dionysus. Literally, *Di-thyr-ambos* means 'two-door(s)-both', and it gave rise to his epiphet of, 'child of the double door'. It means he was twice born: – born once, died and born again. On the diagram, the two side panels, either side of the central square, take the form of two doors. Visually, it is a good match.

A second feature is provided by the area of each rectangle. They both measure 56 x 153 = 8568 square units. This is exactly three times 2856, the gematria value of Χριστοφερ Μαρλω – 'Christopher Marlowe'.

Ch	*r*	*i*	*s*	*t*	*o*	*ph*	*e*	*r*	*M*	*a*	*r*	*l*	*owe*	
Χ	**ρ**	**ι**	**σ**	**τ**	**ο**	**φ**	**ε**	**ρ**	**Μ**	**α**	**ρ**	**λ**	**ω**	
600	100	10	200	300	70	500	5	100	40	1	100	30	800	**2856**

Thus, each side can represent an equilateral triangle embodying his name. If one side points up and the other points down, the pair of them can be merged to form a hexagram – two triangles on two doors united in one person, dead and alive.

As an added bonus, the circle that can be drawn around the six points of the resulting star has a circumference of 3298. A careful study reveals the number 3298 can be found in just one place in the *Sonnets*. It is the gematria value of line 1579: in other words, the line with the value of, 'Christopher Marlowe'. That looks like an interesting coincidence. Line 1579 will be explored in depth in

Chapter 8.

We have already seen the central square, with four sides of 153 has an area with mystical properties associated with resurrection. The area of a 153-sided square becomes of personal significance when the number of lines from which it was derived is added to it: 23409 + 9 = 23418. This is eighteen times 1301, the value of Κιτ Μαρλω – 'Kit Marlowe', and six times 3903, the total of Marlowe's portrait inscription. The nine-line group is centred on line 6, where Marlowe's motto is paraphrased. It can be represented visually as a large hexagram:

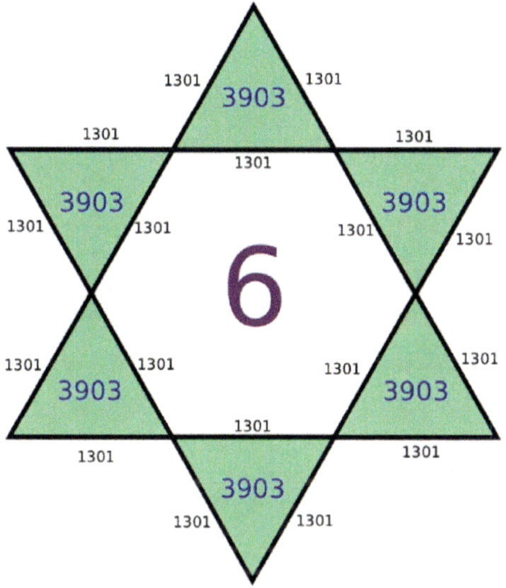

If Kit Marlowe were seeking to initiate his resurrection, I think the symbolism in this hexagram would be picture-perfect.

The perimeter of the square might be significant, too. At 4 x 153, it comes to 612 in total. This is the value of the word Πυρκαια, which means, 'a funeral pyre'. It seems apt for a group focussed on line 6, which is all about fire and has the gematria value of, 'Christopher Marlowe (of) the Phoenix'.

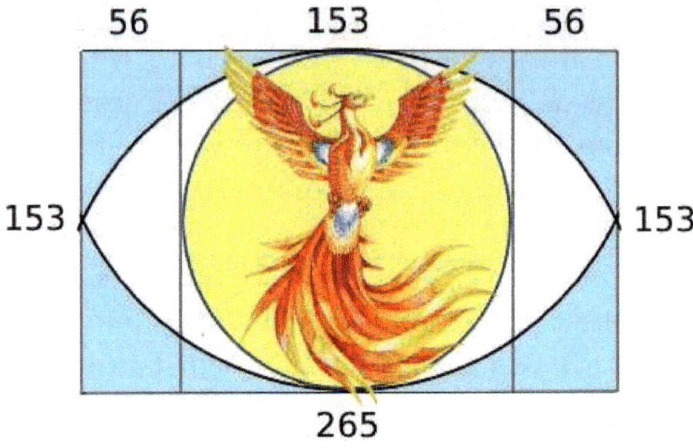

Nothing has been proved yet, but if the *Sonnets* were written by an 'ever-living Christopher Marlowe', we are beginning to see evidence fully aligned with that position. On the other hand, if they were written by the low-profile actor from Stratford-upon-Avon, it has to be wondered why the theme of resurrection would be such a high priority for him.

The burning question now is whether of not the Marlowe symbolism extends to the second place where his motto is paraphrased. That's where we shall go next.

Chapter 5 Notes

---

[1] Agrippa's code was almost certainly that used by the Rosicrucians. In *The History of Freemasonry* (1881, p. 350), Albert Mackey writes, "Agrippa's *Three Book of Occult Philosophy* . . . may be considered as the text book of the old Rosicrucian philosophy." He also describes the 28th Degree of the Scottish Rite – Knight of the Sun – which is entirely devoted to an exposition of numerical Cabala, as being, "a mere condensation of Rosicrucian doctrines." (p. 353).

[2] A perfect number is one that is the sum of all of its divisors except itself.

[3] See Butler, *Number Symbolism*, p.22-25 & 60, and Fowler, *Spenser and the Numbers of Time*, p.48-50.

[4] It would be tedious if I were to demonstrate the gematria count of every word and phrase mentioned henceforward. However, I invite you to take nothing on trust and see if you can catch me out with a mistake by counting some words and phrases independently.

[5] Agrippa. *Three Books of Occult Philosophy*. Book II, xxvii.

[6] Benedictus Arias Montanus. *Antiquitatum Judaicorum* libri IX, (1593), Plate L.

[7] Montanus, op. cit., p.76.

[8] A description of Jacob's firstborn son Reuben, in *Genesis* 49,3.

[9] To find one diagonal, you multiply the side length by √2.

[10] The modern Hebrew spelling of Scorpio has *Ayin* as the first letter (AaQRB), but in classical times an *Aleph* could be used instead (AQRB).

[11] The word Κριός is often cited for Aries, but the numbers say otherwise.

[12] C.D. Yonge (translator), *The Complete Works Of Philo – Complete and Unabridged*. Hendrickson Publishers, 1969. Part III, section 49. 1125-6.

[13] If the sixth gemstone is spelled as σάρδιος rather than σάρδιον, the full text of these two verses has a gematria total of 24024 – a figure of astrological significance. The former spelling is found in the *Textus Receptus* versions, but not others, such as the Nestle-Aland, *Novum Testamentum Graece*. Most modern editors are sadly unaware of the numerological underpinnings of these sacred texts.

[14] A third possible 'mistake' comes because the score of line 9 is 3530. If it had been 3 larger, at 3533, it would have supplied the diameter of the 11100 Zodiacal circle accurately. The square drawn around the circle would also have had a perimeter 4 x 3 = 12 greater.

[15] When discussing line 6 above, we noticed its 'L' notarikon score plus one gave 1219, the value of Σωθις – Sothis.

[16] *Annals* (VI, 29).

[17] Fowler, *Triumphal Forms*, p. 184.

[18] It is unlikely this architectural feature was dropped in at random. I believe the scheme would also have taken in sonnet 154. This is irregular, too, because it simply paraphrases sonnet 153. If so, the irregular sonnets now mark out the 1st, 4th, 7th and 10th triangular numbers. If we sum these, we get 22, and the 22nd triangular number is 253, which is 1(00) more than 153. 253 is a complete

number because it counts the gematria values of the 22 letters of the Hebrew alphabet (by the Hebrew 'S' code).

[19] E.A. Wallis Budge (trans.), *The Book of the Dead*, Arkana Penguin, 1989 pp.510-517.

[20] Actually, in this verse the name is spelled Μαριαμ – 'Mariam', with a value of 192. Elsewhere John uses Μαρία – 152.

[21] Presumably, Jesus was confident in his building skills when he predicted he would 'rear up' in three days a temple that took 46 years to build (John 20, 2). In Greek, the designation Ραββουνι and Mark's spelling of the name Μαρίᾳ τῇ Μαγδαληνῇ (Mary Magdalene) both have the same value – 635. The latter would be 605 but for the presence of three iota subscripts – on the final elements of each word).

[22] For those interested to explore the symbolism further, I would recommend starting with, John Michell, *The Dimensions of Paradise*, Ch. 5.

[23] We can also understand the number 17 is subtly indicated by the line numbers where these two occur. 1224 appears doubled in line 2 and once in line 13: 2 + 2 + 13 = 17.

[24] 86 does give the value of a Hebrew word, כוס – Kos, which means a 'vessel' or 'cup'.

[25] This technique is variously referred to as 'milliu', 'filling' or 'plenitude'.

[26] The designation is found in the *Orphic Hymn 30 to Dionysos*, which known and published in the sixteeth century. Rather appealingly, the value of 'διφυης' is served up in the form of double digits – 1122. It might not be a coincidence.

6
Marlowe's Motto Revisited

We have just seen Marlowe's motto, 'Quod Me Nutrit, Me Destruit', paraphrased in line 6. A second and even closer re-wording occurs in the 1020th line, which is the 12th in Sonnet 73. Whilst it has always been assumed this sonnet was penned, like all the others, by the bald-headed townsman of Stratford-upon-Avon, in the alternative scenario that Marlowe wrote it, one would expect to find evidence of his calling-card here. Once again, no direct proof can be expected from gematria. Instead, we will simply be on the lookout for structured patterns pointing in that direction.

73

THat time of yeeare thou maist in me behold,
When yellow leaues, or none, or few doe hang
Vpon thofe boughes which fhake againft the could,
Bare rn'wd quiers,where late the fweet birds fang.
In me thou feeft the twi-light of fuch day,
As after Sun-fet fadeth in the Weft,
Which by and by blacke night doth take away,
Deaths fecond felfe that feals vp all in reft.
In me thou feeft the glowing of fuch fire,
That on the afhes of his youth doth lye,
As the death bed,whereon it muft expire,
Confum'd with that which it was nurrifht by.
This thou perceu'ft,which makes thy loue more ftrong,
To loue that well,which thou muft leaue ere long.

The location in this line is connected to line 6 and the

resurrection symbolism discovered in the group of 9 lines around it in Sonnet 1 in several ways. Firstly 1020 is 153 x 6.66666 – an infinity of 6's. Then it is 1/17th of 17340, the gematria value of John 21, 11 – the verse introducing 153 fish. It is also 1/12th of 12240, which indicates the number of 'fishes' or 'the net' (x 10).

For the erudite cabalist, 1020 comes with the gematria values of two fell opposites. The first is Ο πυρρος, which means 'the red-head' or 'the inflammable' and was connoted with πυρσός, meaning 'firebrand'. It's nemesis at 1020 is λουτρον, meaning a bath – the water in which the flames of a torch may be extinguished. However, the correspondence I like best comes in Latin: avis ardens – 'the burning bird'. These could be no more than a trio of coincidences, but, if so, they seem fitting.

Mind the Gap!

We should be aware that the gap separating the two variants of the motto in lines 6 and 1020 is 1014. In context, this number is also drawn to attention because 1014 is the gematria value of the significant initial phrase in line 6, 'Feed'st thy lights flame'.

F	e	e	d	s	t	t	h	y	l	i	g	h	t	s	f	l	a	m	e	
6	5	5	4	90	100	100	8	400	20	9	7	8	100	90	6	20	1	30	5	**1014**

I believe the reason for such a loaded sign – or 'sphragis' (σφράγις – gematria value 1014) – giving this figure is because 1014 is a distinctive measure that points to the height of an isosceles triangle with two sides of 1205 and one of 1301. That is, two 'Kit Marlowe's and one 'Κιτ Μαρλω'. Remember that all the inscriptions on Marlowe's *impresa* motto added to 3 times 1301 (3903) and hence an equilateral triangle – the alchemical symbol of fire. This triangle can carry the same symbolism.

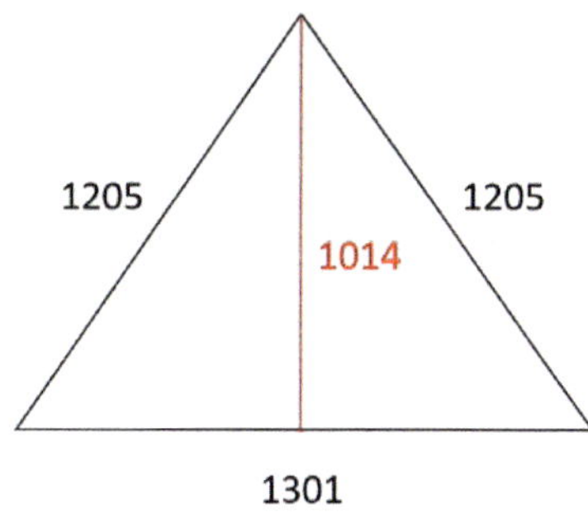

There may be second reason for the modified sides, and, if so, this would lie in the triangle's perimeter of 3711. This is a measure of Marlowe's motto in combination with the original from which it was derived. When both are counted by the four possible codes, they sum to exactly 3711:

'S'n	'S'g		'L'n	'L'g	
57	296	Quod me nutrit me destruit	174	1511 =	2038
46	242	Qui me alit me extinguit	136	1249 =	1673
					3711

Line 2014 itself has a double valuation on account of the hyphen in 'Sun-set'. This gives it two distinct sets of values which may be put together. In this case, the line number can form part of the calculation, too:

75	320	*1014*	As after Sun-set fadeth in the West,	1107	2189
93	320	*1014*	As after Sun-set fadeth in the West,	1197	2189

75 + 320 + 1014 + 1107 + 2189 = 4813
93 + 320 + 1014 + 1197 + 2189 = 4705
9518

9518 seems like a gloriously obscure number. In fact it is so off-beat I could find no rhyme nor reason about it, at least not on an initial inspection. However, when I added its divisors, I found they came to 14280:

1	9518
2	4759
	14280

As six times 2856, 14280 measures the two opposed equilateral triangles making a hexagram fitting the name Χριστοφερ Μαρλω – 'Christopher Marlowe'. In the previous chapter we found this geometric figure in the 'double doors' on either side of the 153-265 vesica. They aptly symbolise the nourishing and quenching of Marlowe's flame – the rising and the setting of his sun.

The Vesica Returns

If the regular gematria values of 'Quod me nutrit me destruit' and 'Qui me alit ne extinguit' are added together, they make: 1511 + 1249 = 2760. This is the gematria total of the previous line, number 1013, 'In me thou seest the twi-light of such day'. The word 'twi-light' could be an allusion to the twinned mottos because the prefix 'twi' means both 'double' and 'half', while the dimming light signifies the quenching of the Sun's flames.

	73	**'L'n**	**'L'g**
1009	THat time of yeeare thou maist in me behold,	821	1666
1010	When yellow leaues,or none,or few doe hange	1478	4595
1011	Vpon those boughes which shake against the could,	1396	2645
1012	Bare rn'wd quiers,where late the sweet birds sang.	1354	4226
1013	In me thou seest the twi-light of such day,	593/573	2760
1014	As after Sun-set fadeth in the West,	1197/1107	2189
1015	Which by and by blacke night doth take away,	1052	3562
1016	Deaths second selfe that seals vp all in rest.	664	1566
1017	In me thou seest the glowing of such fire,	482	2335
1018	That on the ashes of his youth doth lye,	733	2114
1019	As the death bed,whereon it must expire,	1051	2409
1020	Consum'd with that which it was nurrisht by.	2854	4680
1021	This thou perceu'st,which makes thy loue more strong,	1430	4487
1022	To loue that well,which thou must leaue ere long.	2195	4723

Line 1013 is also important because it marks the start of a structural group of 9 lines. This is centred on line 1017, which has the same initial four words, 'In me thou seest'. Line 1021 finishes the group: its opening three words carry the same meaning, 'This thou perceu'st'. One reason for having a group containing the *impresa* motto (paraphrased) centred on line 1017 is that the Latin name for a motto, verbum – 'the word', has this value. Line 1017 itself has a gematria value of 2335, which could give, verba mea – 'my words', plus, 'Quod me nutrit me destruit' (824 + 1511 = 2335). The line number where the motto is placed, 1020, has the value of, meis verbis – 'in my words'.

I believe the key to the group resides in the combined line numbers. If all 9 are summed, we find:

1013 + 1014 + 1015 + 1016 + 1017 + 1018 + 1019 + 1020 + 1021 = 9153

The trivial reason why this should be significant is that 9.153 is 9 x 153 = 1377, and hence, ιχθύες ϱνγ – 'fishes 153'.

A more important clue comes from 1017, the central line number, being 9 times 113. From this it follows that since 9153 is 9 times 1017, it will be also be divisible by 113 – exactly 9 x 9 times. I happened to know a classical approximation of Pi can be found in the fraction 355/113 (3.1415929). Therefore, I thought I would try 9153 as the diameter of a circle. When multiplied by this fraction, it produces a circumference of exactly 28,755. This delivers another extraordinary coincidence because it measures precisely, in square units, the area of the 153:265 vesica piscis – the one contained in the rectangle with double-doors on either side:

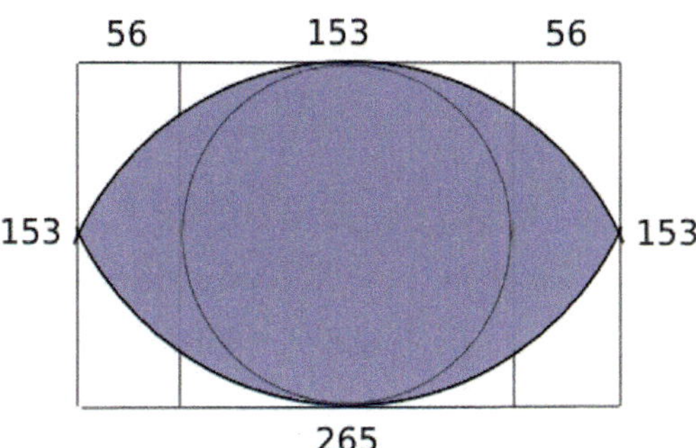

The area is calculated by squaring the width and multiplying by a fiddly fraction: 153 x 153 x 1.22837. The precise formula can be found in Appendix 3. The vesica area matches the circle circumference to an accuracy level of 0.9999976.

A most noteworthy feature of the vesica is that its area breaks down as 81 x 355. It can thereby serve to unite 'Marlowe' – valued at 81 by the 'S' code – and 'Shakespeare' – which is 355 by the 'L' code.

M	a	r	l	o	w	e	
12	1	17	11	14	21	5	**81**

S	h	a	k	e	s	p	e	a	r	e	
90	8	1	10	5	90	60	5	1	80	5	**355**

If correct, it suggests the two were one. Or, as the author of that mysterious poem, *'The Phoenix and the Turtle'* puts it, 'Single nature's double name'.

Evidence this is more than a fantastic fluke comes when one adds the first and last letters of the 9 lines:

I, A, W, D, I, T, A, C, T: 9 + 1 + 900 + 4 + 9 + 100 + 1 + 3 + 100 = 1127
y, t, y, t, e, e, e, y, g: 400 + 100 + 400 + 100 + 5 + 5 + 5 + 400 + 7 = 1422
2549

2549 provides for the conjoined names of 'Kit Marlowe' and 'William Shakespeare': 1205 + 1344 = 2549:

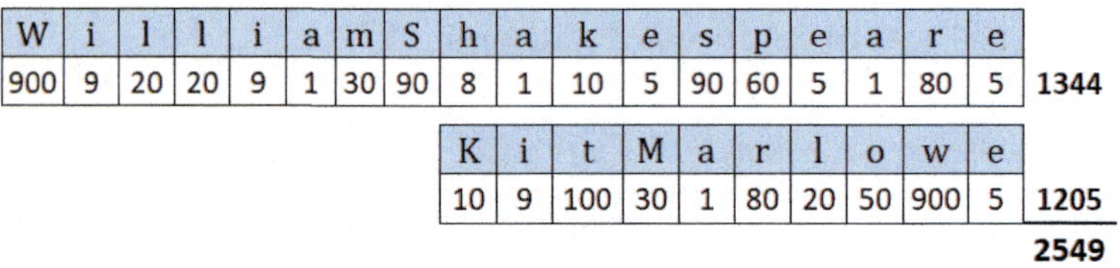

W	i	l	l	i	a	m	S	h	a	k	e	s	p	e	a	r	e	
900	9	20	20	9	1	30	90	8	1	10	5	90	60	5	1	80	5	**1344**

K	i	t	M	a	r	l	o	w	e	
10	9	100	30	1	80	20	50	900	5	**1205**
										2549

Those resistant to the idea the total 2549 should be broken down in this way might ask why he didn't make it completely obvious by having the first and last letters sum neatly to 1205 and 1344? The reason surely lies in his artistry: our ever-living poet would never create anything literal and blunt if a more subtle and deeply-layered alternative could be dreamed up. To confute the genius behind Hamlet and Macbeth with the bluster of Sir Toby Belch or Bottom the Weaver would be naive.

The rationale for the selection of the two numbers lies in their product. When multiplied together, 1127 and 1422 make 1,602,594. On its own, this gives the area of a circle with a circumference of 4488. Initially, I liked that this was equated with a claim in Paul's *First Epistle to the Corinthians*: ὡς σοφὸς ἀρχιτέκτων θεμέλιον ἔθηκα – 'As a wise master-builder, I have laid the foundation'.[1] To my mind, it describes the creator aptly. Within this circle may be inscribed an equilateral triangle with three sides of 1237 and thus a perimeter of 3711. As seen above, 3711 counts the combined mottos, 'Quod me nutrit me destruit' and 'Qui me alit me extinguit'. Herein lies the first justification.

The triangle can also be converted to a hexagram by doubling its value: 2 x 3711 – 7422. As such, it can be seen to fill the circle with the alchemical symbols of fire and water, united and harmonised, or burning and quenching. An indication that this may have been intentional comes from the fact that πυρ και ύδωρ – 'fire and water' has the close value of 7424 when the words are counted by 'plenitude' – i.e. the names of the letters:

Πι	**Ὑψιλον**	**Ρω**	**Κάππα**	**Ἀλφα**	**Ιῶτα**	**Ὑψιλον**	**Δέλτα**	**Ωμέγα**	**Ρω**	
90	1260	900	182	532	1111	1260	340	849	900	**7424**

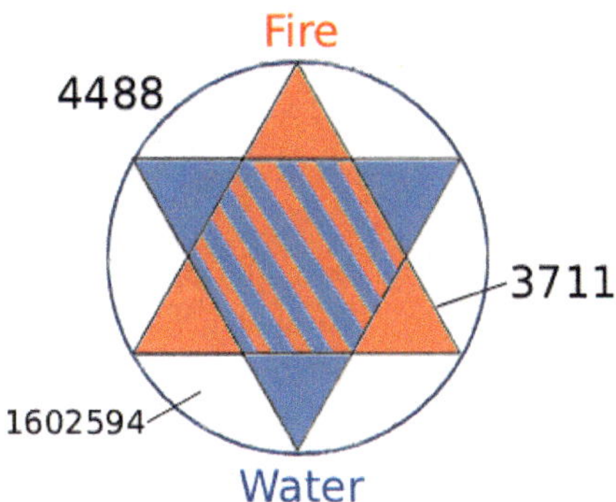

I was curious to see if there might be any deeper significance in 2549 being made from components of 1127 and 1422. If the author really was 'a wise master-builder', I felt sure he would have wanted to give us evidence thereof. So, I decided to compare their product to that of the target figures, 1205 and 1344:

1205 x 1344 = 1619520
1127 x 1422 = 1602594
16926

The difference between the two is precisely 16926. There is no way that five-digit figure can have arisen here by chance. The name, Κιτ Μαϱλω – 'Kit Marlowe' has a value of 1301. If you square it, the result is 1692601. Thus, the squaring of Kit Marlowe's name confirms the division of 2549 into components of 1205 and 1344.

It doesn't end there. The real stroke of genius arrives via the three critical lines, 1013, 1017 and 1021. All it takes is a little more 'squaring'. In esoteric philosophy, 'squaring' means 'making true and correct'. The correlate is that a carpenter's try-square symbolises the touchstone of that which is True.

Here, the matter for squaring resides in the three parallel expressions, 'In me thou seest', 'In me thou seest', & 'This thou perceu'st'. Their combined gematria value is: 732 + 732 + 1608 = 3072. It will be found that a square with this perimeter has diagonals of 1086 – 'Marlowe'.[2]

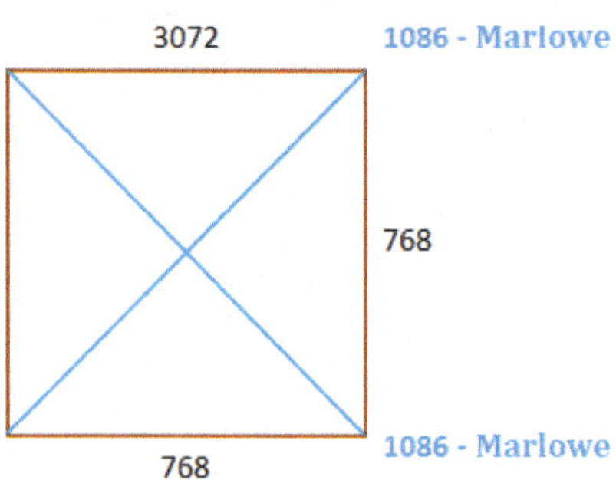

What is particularly significant about the this square is that the two diagonals sum as 1086 + 1086 = 2172. Here is another 'squaring' number: this time for someone called, 'Kit Marlowe'.

The most artful way to 'square' a name is to set its two elements at right-angles to each other and thereby make a right-angled triangle. In the hypotenuse and the perimeter you will have two personal ciphers. A second way of doing this is by making the longer element of a name the hypotenuse and its shorter partner one of the perpendiculars. Here are the two triangles for the name 'Kit Marlowe':

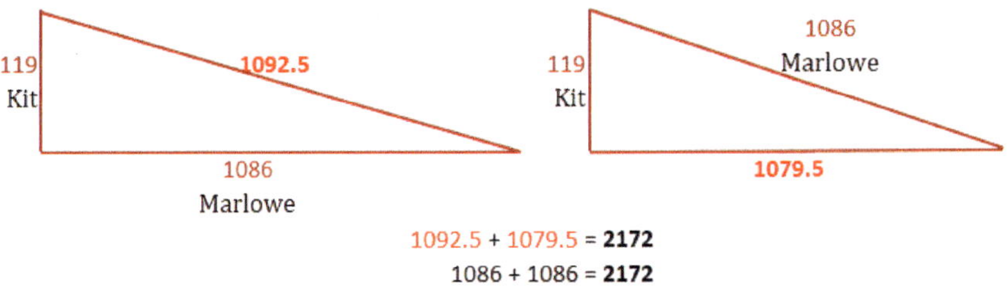

In parallel fashion, we see the two components of the name 'Christopher Marlowe' are 493 and 1086. If these are 'squared' to form a rectangle, the area of the rectangle will be 535398. This is the same as the area of a square with sides of 731.7. When rounded to the nearest whole number (732), this, the value of, 'In me thou seest'.

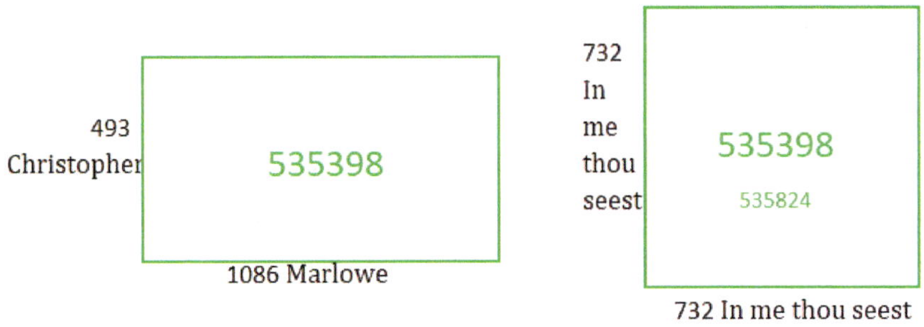

So, by simply putting together three phrases with values of 732, 732 and 1608, the three names, 'Marlowe', 'Kit Marlowe' and 'Christopher Marlowe' can be *squared*. It is very neat.

The three line numbers from whence the three phrases come now provide a way of checking our right-angles are perfectly true.

First we need to very precisely calculate the diagonal of the 'Christopher Marlowe' rectangle. Cranking Pythagoras' Theorem up to ten digits, we find it comes out at 1192.662987:

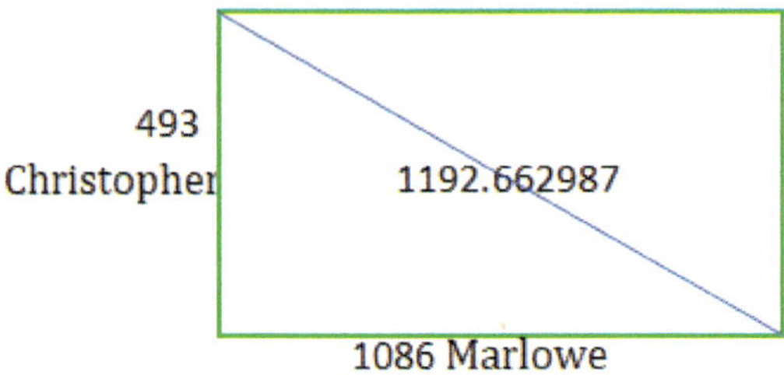

Now, any child, since the death of Thales in 545 B.C.E., will tell you the three corners of a right-angled triangle lie on the circumference of a circle whose diameter is its hypotenuse. If they are really on the ball, they will also tell you the same is true for the diagonals of a rectangle formed from the same perpendiculars. The figure below shows the result of circumscribing the rectangle of Marlowe's name:

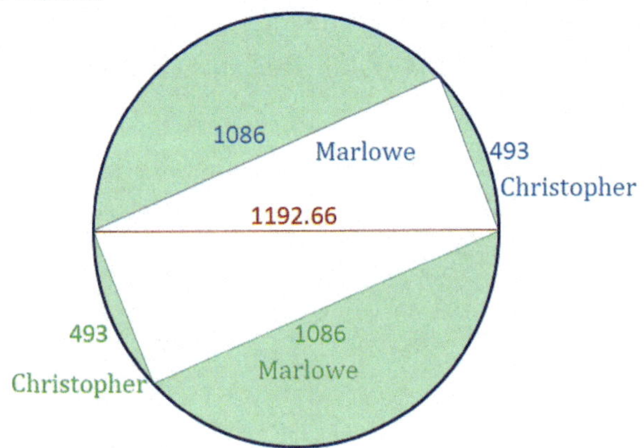

On the diagram, the green shaded area is the part we are interested in. This can be calculated by taking the area of the rectangle from the area of the circle:

Circle:	$(1192.662987 \div 2)^2 \times \pi = 1117185.6905$
Rectangle:	$493 \times 1086 = 535398$

Difference: 1117185.6905 – 535398 = 581787.6905

This is the same area as that generated by a 'squaring' of the three critical lines numbers.

1013 + 1017 + 1021 = 3051

It will be found that a square with a perimeter of 3051 has sides of 762.75 and an area of 581787.5625. The two areas are identical to six digits – a one in a million possibility. The difference between the two areas is a measly 0.128. It computes to a very respectable margin of 0.99999978 accuracy.

The economy with which this extremely precise formulation has been orchestrated is stunning. Simply by placing the values 732, 732 & 1608 on lines 1013, 1017 and 1021, the names 'Marlowe', 'Kit Marlowe' and 'Christopher Marlowe' are perfectly *squared*. The odds of such a concatenation of coincidences appearing at such a significant location are far slimmer than one in a million. Although not conclusive, this is the first small nugget of evidence of the hard variety.

The three lines may indicate another puzzle, although one of a more oblique and playful character. Their notarikon totals, sum as:

593 + 482 + 1430 = 2505

2505 provides the value of three loaded words from the most famous verse in the *Book of Revelation*, Αριθμος ανθρωπου εστιν – 'It is the number of a man'. This naturally leads to the questions, 'What number? 'What man?'

Astute readers will have spotted that the first notarikon value of 593 (line 1013) has come by counting the 't' and 'l' in 'twi-light' separately. If it is taken as one word not two, the 'l' can be discounted, and so the line value goes down to 573, and hence the total reduces to 2485. We can then add the two alternatives to give: 2485 + 2505 = 4990. This proves to be the number of a man called, Χριστοφερ Μαρλω – 'Christopher Marlowe'. It does so because

4990 breaks down to 2856 – the value of that name – by multiplying its component digits: (2 x 856) + (28 x 56) + (285 x 6) = 4990.

A puzzle of a slightly more straightforward nature arises if we put together the notarikon scores for all nine lines in the group:

593 + 1197 + 1052 + 664 + 482 + 733 + 1051 + 2854 + 1430 = 10056

This is also the number of a man's name, albeit one coming in a short phrase. It counts the words, Το ονομα μου Κιτ Μαϱλω – 'My name is Kit Marlowe'. It does so when its constituent letters are counted by their names – i.e. by the technique of 'filling':

Ταυ	Όμικρον	Όμικρον	Νυ	Όμικρον	Μυ	Αλφα	Μυ	Όμικρον	Ύψιλον
701	360	360	450	360	440	532	440	360	1260

Κάππα	Ιώτα	Ταυ	Μυ	Αλφα	Ρω	Λάμβδα	Ωμέγα	
182	1111	701	440	532	900	78	849	**10056**

It should be stressed these latter two examples are no more than playful puzzles with scant independent weight as evidence. Their significance lies in the way they contribute to an overall picture for the 9-line group. They play a supporting role to the more substantial evidence provided by the various ways the poet's name is *squared* at this location.

The Motto Line

When totted up, the letter values of the paraphrased motto come out as follows:

Sn	Sg	Line	73	Ln	Lg
109	451	*1020*	Consum'd with that which it was nurrisht by.	2854	4680

On first looking setting eyes on these numbers, they didn't appear promising. I felt frustrated that I could find no quick solution. However, when I thought about it, it seemed the obscurity may have been deliberate because, for anyone aware of Marlowe's motto, this line would have drawn more attention than most others. And at the time of publication people were far more attuned to numerological clues than we are today. Thus, it would have been a dangerous place to drop simplistic references.

I started to think about the problem from the creator's angle. If I had been Marlowe, how would I have proved it was my motto in this line? It occurred to me, a good way to prove it would be once again to use the 'touchstone' of a right-angled triangle. To obtain two suitable perpendiculars, an obvious solution is to use the 'S' and 'L' code gematria values. This gives perpendiculars of 296 and 1511 respectively.

	Q	u	o	d	M	e	N	u	t	r	i	t	M	e	D	e	s	t	r	u	i	t	
L	70	200	50	4	30	5	40	200	100	80	9	100	30	5	4	5	90	100	80	200	9	100	**1511**
S	16	20	14	4	12	5	13	20	19	17	9	19	12	5	4	5	18	19	17	20	9	19	**296**

By means of these side lengths, we arrive at a right-triangle with a hypotenuse of $\sqrt{(1511^2 + 296^2)}$ = 1539.7198. I wondered if there was any way line 1020 might be persuaded to spit out this number.

I took the line's main gematria figure of 4680, and tried it as the perimeter of a square. This has four sides of 1170. There was an indication that it could be the way to go because the sum of the aliquot parts (the factors minus the number itself) of 4680 is 11700.[3] The area of a square with a perimeter of 4680 and sides of 1170 is 1368900. I now decided to look for another shape with the same area. The first form that came to mind was an equilateral triangle. It is the simplest polygon as well as being the symbol of fire or water (depending on orientation). Such a triangle with an area of 1368900 has sides of (fractionally over) 1778. This calculation looked suitable because 1778 gives us το πυϱ ασβεστον – 'The unquenchable fire'. What else would the ever-living poet want to illuminate his motto?

It was when I measured the height of the triangle, I had my Eureka moment. It comes out at 1539.8066. This matches the motto hypotenuse to within a degree of 0.99994% accuracy. While there are not quite as many nines as we have seen previously, I think there are sufficient to demonstrate a linkage between the motto and its *Sonnets* variant.

The number 3906, which was the 'super-grand-total' of Marlowe's portrait inscription – the motto, the other words, his age, the year and the three missing letters – can also be found at line 1020. It derives from the super-grand-total of all four line counts plus the line number:

109 + 451 + 2854 + 4680 + 1020 = 9114

If 9114 measures the perimeter of an ark – as the container of a man's body – its length will be 3906: (9114 ÷ 14) x 6 = 3906. We recall that 3906 is also the value of Χϱιστοφεϱ Μαϱλω Πυϱσος – 'Christopher Marlowe Firebrand'.

Summary

We began this chapter looking for evidence of Marlowe's calling-card in association with the second iteration of his motto in the *Sonnets*. I think we have found it. There is a good case to be made that Marlowe wrote Sonnet 73 and incorporated information about himself in it. The thesis is still far from proved, but we are moving forward in the accumulation of an increasingly credible body of circumstantial evidence.

We will next look at Sonnet 76, where Shake-speare teases his readers with a riddle about his hidden name. Could there be any signs of Marlowe's name concealed there?

Chapter 6 Notes

---

[1] 1 Cor. 3, 10. See Appendix 3.
[2] The area of the 3072 perimeter square is equal to that of an equilateral triangle with sides of 1167. 1167 is the sum of 81 and 1086, which are the 'S' and 'L' values of 'Marlowe'.
[3] The aliquot parts of 4680 are: 1, 2, 3, 4, 5, 6, 8, 9, 10, 12, 13, 15, 18, 20, 24, 26, 30, 36, 39, 40, 45, 52, 60, 65, 72, 78, 90, 104, 117, 120, 130, 156, 180, 195, 234, 260, 312, 360, 390, 468, 520, 585, 780, 936, 1170, 1560, 2340.

7
Every Word Almost Tells My Name

76

VVHy is my verſe ſo barren of new pride?
So far from variation or quicke change?
Why with the time do I not glance aſide
To new found methods,and to compounds ſtrange?
Why write I ſtill all one,euer the ſame,
And keepe inuention in a noted weed,
That euery word doth almoſt fel my name,
Shewing their birth, and where they did proceed?
O know ſweet loue I alwaies write of you,
And you and loue are ſtill my argument:
So all my beſt is dreſſing old words new,
Spending againe what is already ſpent.
For as the Sun is daily new and old,
So is my loue ſtill telling what is told.

Sonnet 76 contains a riddle about the author's name; and the final line hints it might require a numerical solution. In the seventh line, he writes that every word almost tells his name – except there is a curious typo, and 'tell' (or possibly 'spell') has been replaced by 'fel'. Why would William Shakespeare, the wool-trader's son from a market town in Warwickshire who made the big-time on the London stage, want to tease his readers about the heavily disguised nature of his name? It defies sense. In addition to this, the word 'fel' is so far removed from 'tell' or 'spell' it cannot be anything other than a deliberate 'weed'. No printer could screw up that badly and escape a beating.

If the error happened 'accidentally-on-purpose', the most likely meaning for the word 'fel' is actually a sheepskin or a fleece. In which case, it suggests the author's name was 'dressed' in something. To the classically-trained mind, it recalls the story of Odysseus who fooled the Cyclops by adopting the pseudonym 'Nobody' and escaping from his cave hidden underneath the 'fell' of a large ram.

The location of this riddle about his name is hardly likely to be random. For one thing, it comes in Sonnet 76, and the number here has the value of, 'Name'. The line is the 1057th in the sequence, and according to this value, it aligns with the goddess, 'Pallas Minerva'. As a spear-shaker, Pallas stands very well for the author. She was especially suitable in this case as she also carried the aegis, which offered protection in the form of a shield. The word aegis implies both a shield and a goat's hide, and so this is another item that qualifies as a 'fell'. Thus, the printer's 'typo' in this sonnet conjures up a magical hide to conceal ('hide') the author's true name.

Sn	**Sg**	**Line**		**Ln**	**Lg**
81	381	*1057*	That euery word doth almost fel my name,	1086	3423

Looking at the numbers, the notarikon value of this line jumps out because 1086 is the value of 'Marlowe'. The same is true by the S-code because 81 is the value of 'Marlowe' in that code, too. Peering a little deeper, the number 1467 can be found twice. Firstly, it comes through the addition of 1086 and 381. Secondly, the main gematria total is 3423, and this provides the perimeter of an 'ark' (6:1 rectangle) with a length of 1467. This number *almost* tells the poet's name because it indicates a famous allusion to Marlowe.

Prefixed to the first edition of his poem *Hero and Leander* in 1598 was a dedicatory letter from the publisher Edward Blount, to Marlowe's patron, Sir Thomas Walsingham. The letter, which is replete with ambiguities about the poet's current state of being/not-being, refers to Marlowe as, 'The unhappily deceased author'. That expression has a gematria value of 1467. It seems fitting to find the unhappy 'corpse' enclosed in the coffin-like proportions of an ark.

Another piece of the puzzle arises when the two gematria values are combined: 381 + 3423 = 3804. This comprises the sum of 1579, 1205 and 1020, which represent, 'Christopher Marlowe', 'Kit Marlowe' and the signature-line where his *impresa* motto is paraphrased.[1] A visual way of representing the breakdown is via the geometry of a right-angled triangle:

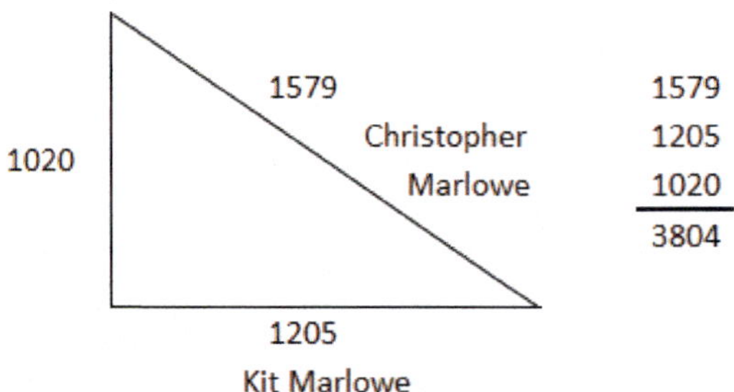

Incidentally, this triangle suggests another reason why he would have wanted to place his (paraphrased) motto at line 1020: it *proves* his ownership of it.

An important thing about the gematria value of 3423 is that it depends on the 'v' in the second word, 'euery'. If it is counted as it is printed, 'u', the figure is reduced by 500 to 2923. It would thereby indicate a perfect blend of, 'Christopher Marlowe' and his covering 'fel', the wool-dealer's son, 'William Shakespeare' – 1579 + 1344 = 2923.

There is also a small riddle in the line above, 'And keepe inuention in a noted weed,'. The curious expression, 'a noted weed', which implies a 'necessary disguise',[2] has gematria values of 1114 by the L-code and 91 by the S-code. Adding these two numbers produces 1205, and hence, 'Kit Marlowe'.

A cryptographic technique mentioned earlier, and demonstrated in the dedication to the *Sonnets*, is gridding. When a text is laid out as in grid formation, artful patterns can be engineered, and subsequently detected. These would otherwise remain invisible to the reader.

When the letters of Sonnet 76 are arrayed as a 14-row grid,

one can pick out the letters of the name 'Marlowe' in a symmetrical formation that looks somewhat like an eye. This is fitting because it points to line 1057, which has both its notarikon scores equated with 'Marlowe'. The eye points towards the critical word, 'fel'.

1051	VV H y i s m y v e r s e s o b a r r e n o f n e w p r i d e
1052	S o f a r f r o m v a r i a t i o n o r q u i c k e c h a n g e
1053	W h y w i t h t h e t i m e d o I n o t g l a n c e a s i d e
1054	T o n e w f o u n d m e t h o d s a n d t o c o m p o u n d s s
1055	W h y w r i t e I s t i l l a l l o n e e u e r t h e s a m e
1056	A n d k e e p e i n u e n t i o n i n a n o t e d w e e d
1057	T h a t e u e r y w o r d d o t h a l m o s t f e l m y n a m e
1058	S h e w i n g t h e i r b i r t h a n d w h e r e t h e y d i d
1059	O k n o w s w e e t l o u e I a l w a i e s w r i t e o f y o u
1060	A n d y o u a n d l o u e a r e s t i l l m y a r g u m e n t
1061	S o a l l m y b e s t i s d r e s s i n g o l d w o r d s n e w
1062	S p e n d i n g a g a i n e w h a t i s a l r e a d y s p e n t
1063	F o r a s t h e S u n i s d a i l y n e w a n d o l d
1064	S o i s m y l o u e s t i l l t e l l i n g w h a t i s t o l d

The three letters 's', 'y' and 'd' cutting across the middle of the 'Marlowe' eye have a combined gematria value of 494. This can count the expression, 'mine eye', which seems an appropriate description of the shape. 494 is just one more than the value of 'Christopher', and when added to the 1086 of the 'Marlowe' letters, makes 1580. This almost tells his name, 'Christopher Marlowe' – 1579.

One noteworthy feature of a grid is that it offers a new way of assigning numeric values to letters. It does this on account of their relative locations, as counted in rows and columns. Each letter will have two of these depending on whether rows or columns are counted first. For example, the letter 'f' beginning the word 'far' in the second line could either be 23 (2-3) if rows were counted first, or 32 (3-2) if columns were counted first.

A particularly strategic letter is the 'y' in the pupil of the Marlowe 'eye'. Its location is 2310 or 1023. I couldn't find much use for the former, but the latter picks out the value of the initials, 'W.S & C.M.' It aligns well with the theme of disguise. The combined value of the two coordinates is 3333. Initially, I tried to make sense of this as, 971 + 1391 + 971: Μαρλω Χρι<u>στ</u>οφερ[3] Μαρλω – 'Marlowe

Christopher Marlowe'. I reasoned the unusual repetition of Μαρλω might somehow reflect the two sides of the 'Marlowe eye'. But, I could find no obvious reason for the doubled surname, so it felt rather forced. Then, with a little lateral thinking, I found a more pleasing solution: 3 x 3 x 3 x 3 = 81; and 81 is the value of 'Marlowe' by the 'S' code. I like that: it's playful, it's creative and it fits the context perfectly.

The grid location of 'fel' ought to be part of the plan, too. The 'f' is located at 7-24 or 24-7. The sum of 724 and 247 is 971. That's handy – it's the value of Μαρλω once again. The third letter 'l', should be special because the eye points it out. It is located at 726 or 267 and so produces a location total of 993. At this value, is found, Λογος τελειος – 'Logos teleios', which means the 'perfect word'.[4] It seems that the author was very happy with the 'typo' that has generated well-meaning emendations from learned editors of the poem for over four centuries. Ignorance is bliss.

As a whole word, 'fel' has a coordinate value of (724 + 247) + (725 + 257) + (726 + 267) = 2946. I believe this may be intended to represent the addition of 1367 + 1579, the two axes defining an equilateral triangle with sides of 1579.

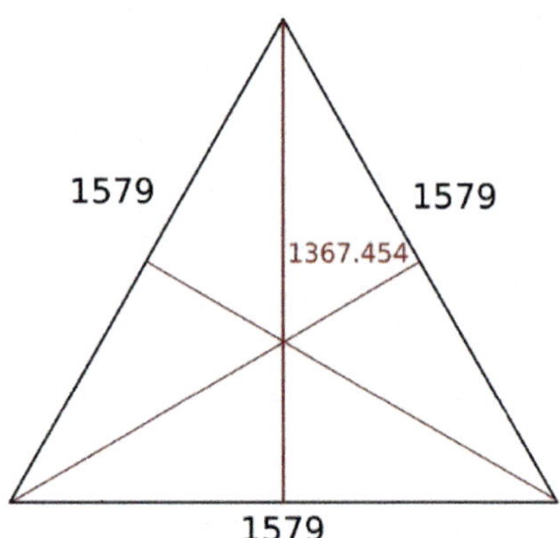

Aside from the side lengths each telling the name 'Christopher Marlowe', I believe this figure may have been chosen on account of its three internal axes: 3 x 1367.454 = 4102.364. This is a unique number which 'fells' the name Κιτ Μαρλω – 'Kit Marlowe' into its two components. It does so when it forms the perimeter of the square within a 'Κιτ Μαϱλω-sided square' cutting it according to Κιτ and Μαϱλω:

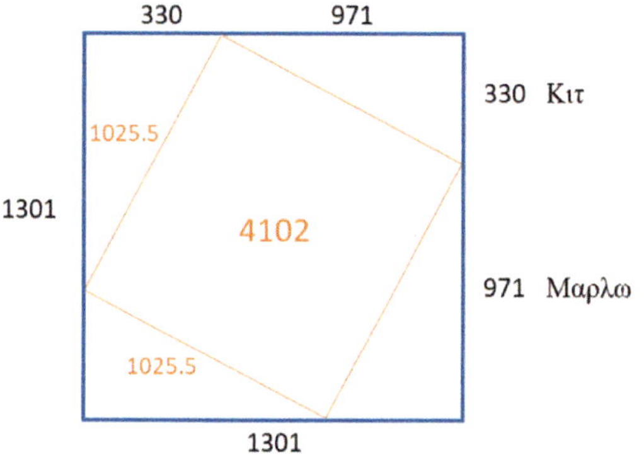

The perimeter of the square is 4102.218, so it comes to within 0.999955 of the target figure, which is quite accurate.

Sonnet 76 is made up from 448 characters. The divisibility of this number means it can be configured in several different regular, rectangular grids. These no longer abide by the 14-line sonnet structure: the letters are simply filled in from the top until the rectangle is completed.

If you make a grid with 28 columns and 16 rows, you find all the letters making the name 'Kit Marlow' in a block in the centre.

W	H	y	i	s	m	y	v	e	r	s	e	s	o	b	a	r	r	e	n	o	f	n	e	w	p	r	i
d	e	S	o	f	a	r	f	r	o	m	v	a	r	i	a	t	i	o	n	o	r	q	u	i	c	k	e
c	h	a	n	g	e	W	h	y	w	i	t	h	t	h	e	t	i	m	e	d	o	I	n	o	t	g	l
a	n	c	e	a	s	i	d	e	T	o	n	e	w	f	o	u	n	d	m	e	t	h	o	d	s	a	n
d	t	o	c	o	m	p	o	u	n	d	s	s	t	r	a	n	g	e	W	h	y	w	r	i	t	e	I
s	t	i	l	l	a	l	l	o	n	e	e	u	e	r	t	h	e	s	a	m	e	A	n	d	k	e	e
p	e	i	n	u	e	n	t	i	o	n	i	n	a	n	o	t	e	d	w	e	e	d	T	h	a	t	e
u	e	r	y	w	o	r	d	d	o	t	h	a	l	m	o	s	t	f	e	l	m	y	n	a	m	e	S
h	e	w	i	n	g	t	h	e	i	r	b	i	r	t	h	a	n	d	w	h	e	r	e	t	h	e	y
d	i	d	p	r	o	c	e	e	d	O	k	n	o	w	s	w	e	e	t	l	o	u	e	I	a	l	w
a	i	e	s	w	r	i	t	e	o	f	y	o	u	A	n	d	y	o	u	a	n	d	l	o	u	e	a
r	e	s	t	i	l	l	m	y	a	r	g	u	m	e	n	t	S	o	a	l	l	m	y	b	e	s	t
i	s	d	r	e	s	s	i	n	g	o	l	d	w	o	r	d	s	n	e	w	S	p	e	n	d	i	n
g	a	g	a	i	n	e	w	h	a	t	i	s	a	l	r	e	a	d	y	s	p	e	n	t	F	o	r
a	s	t	h	e	S	u	n	i	s	d	a	i	l	y	n	e	w	a	n	d	o	l	d	S	o	i	s
m	y	l	o	u	e	s	t	i	l	l	t	e	l	l	i	n	g	w	h	a	t	i	s	t	o	l	d

The location coordinates of the letters give some indication that they were deliberately placed:

1012	**K**	1210
913	**I**	139
915	**T**	159
815	**M**	158
813	**A**	138
914	**R**	149
814	**L**	148
1014	**O**	1410
1015	**W**	1510
8225		5021

Firstly, it can be seen that the right-hand total of 5021 is a perfect mirror of 1205 – 'Kit Marlowe'. Then, 8225 constitutes the perimeter and diagonals of a square with sides of 1205. It should be noted the accuracy here is somewhat wanting: with a 8225 total, the square would have sides of 1204.523, but rounding takes it up to 1205.

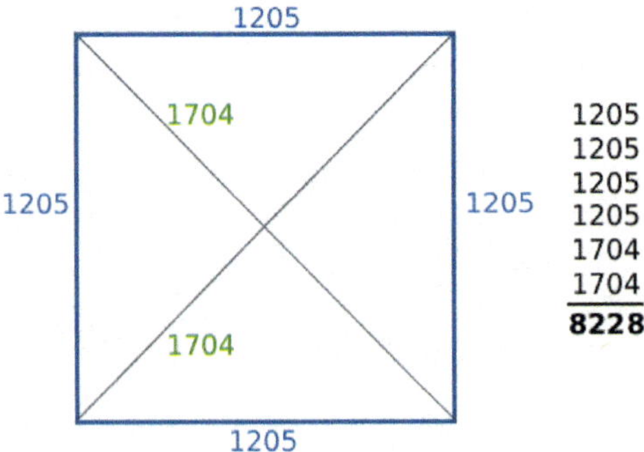

Normal service returns, however, when the letter coordinates of 'MARLO' are added in the left-hand column. Their sum of 815 + 813 + 914 + 814 + 1014 = 4370 supplies the perimeter of the square placed within a 1205 sided square such the its corners intersect the sides by 119 and 1086 – 'Kit' and 'Marlowe'. The degree of accuracy here returns to a very healthy 0.9999997.

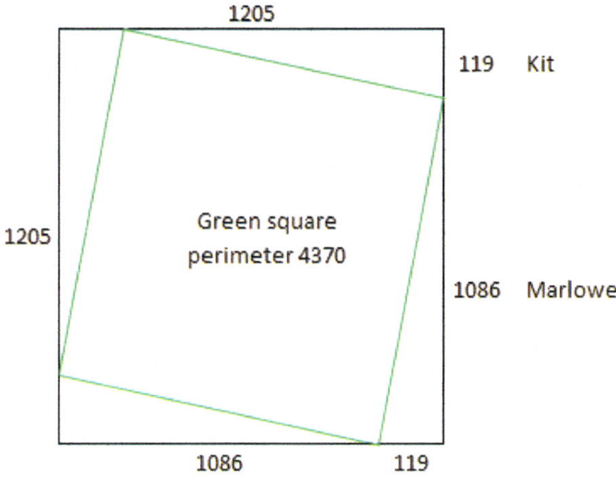

If both sets of coordinates are added for 'MARLO', they sum as 4370 + 2003 = 6373. This uses the identical geometric figure to split a 1793-sided square into two components of 214 and 1579. These are the 'S' and 'L' values of 'Christopher Marlowe'. The accuracy here is 0.99988.

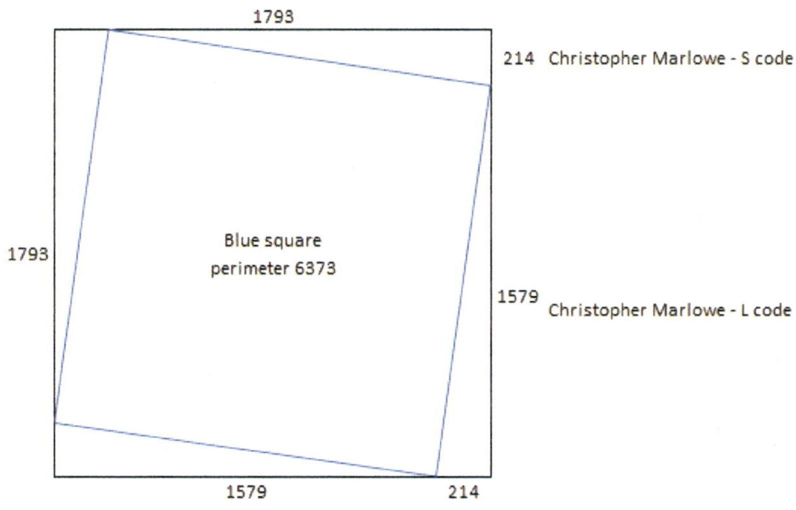

It is reassuring that a consistent geometric pattern is used to validate the breakdown of the author's name. The only problem I have is understanding how it is possible to engineer a plan of this complexity in the first place.

An entirely different indicator that the word 'fel' was deliberately curated derives from its position within the entire sonnet sequence. My word-processor tells me there are 17648 words in the *Sonnets* (assuming hyphenated words are counted single), and 'fel' is the 8632nd of these. This means there are 8631 words before 'fel', and it comes as the 9017th word from the end. The first figure, 8631, measures the perimeter of an ark with a length of 3699: (8631 ÷ 14) x 6 = 3699. This is a perfect fit for the unhappily 'deceased' corpse of, 'Our ever-living poet, Christopher Marlowe' (2120 + 1579). On the other side, 9017 provides for the symbol of a resurrected man called 'Marlowe' coming in the form of a 1086-sided pentagram combined with the circle which circumscribes it: (5 x 1086) + 3587 = 9017. Once armed with the correct key, every word tells his name. And every picture tells his story.

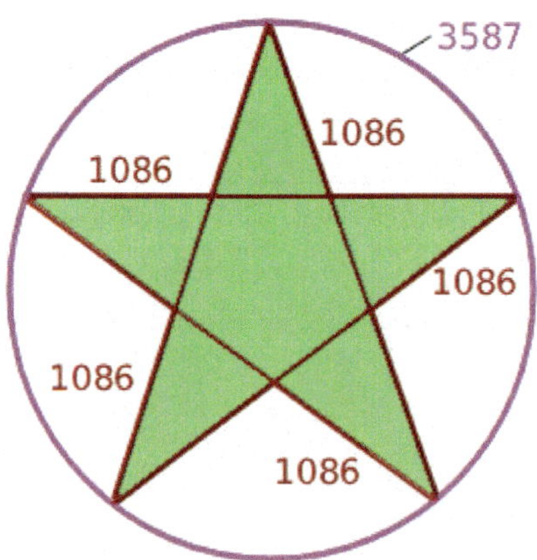

The significant thing about 8632 itself is that the sum of its divisors is 17640 [5] – which just falls 8 short of the *Sonnets'* total of 17648. However, when we read, 'That euery word doth almost fel my name', we 'tell' (count) 8 words. If we add these 8 to the figure of 17640, it completes the total. The positioning of 'fel' is as precise as its spelling. There are no typos in *Shake-speares Sonnets*.

Chapter 7 Notes

---

[1] The latter might even be hinted at through an anagram of 'fel' and 'name': 'enflame'.
[2] The O.E.D. cites 'needed' as an Old English version of 'noted'. 'Weeds' were the costumes or disguises that people, such as actors, wore.
[3] Here I have counted the digraph στ as *digamma* (6) rather than *sigma-tau* (500).
[4] The two Greek words, Λογος τελειος, have a special signification in esoteric circles because they constitute the title of the crucial final section of the *Corpus Hermeticum*: the Asclepius.
[5] 1 + 2 + 4 + 8 + 13 + 26 + 52 + 83 + 104 + 166 + 332 + 664 + 1079 + 2158 + 4316 + 8632 = 17640

8
The Marlowe Lines

To this point, an indirect case has been advanced for Marlowe's authorship of the *Sonnets* based on gematria. It has been targeted on three locations of high strategic significance: the first sonnet, Sonnet 73, where Marlowe's motto appears paraphrased, and Sonnet 76, where the author makes a riddle out of his name. While gematria is a subjective science, if someone other than Marlowe wrote the *Sonnets*, it should not have been possible to build such a tight and coherent case for his authorship from those verses.

Some critics might imagine that with a little ingenuity one could use gematria to conjure up any kind of convincing evidence in any part of any poem. I believe that would be to greatly underestimate the difficulty of finding systematic and meaningful patterns in random lines of verse. Other critics might claim that I have cherry-picked three locations which by some weird quirk of stochasticity have lent themselves to an interpretation in Marlowe's favour. I don't believe entropy can ever be so saturated with information, and especially not in those locations where one would expect Marlowe to place his name were he the author.

If the thesis is correct and Marlowe did write the *Sonnets*, there are some other places where he must have left his calling card. These places cannot be cherry-picked because they are the lines that match the gematria value of his name. These are non-negotiable. If the wool-dealer's son from Stratford-upon-Avon wrote everything from his own mind and about entirely unrelated concerns, it is going to be an uphill battle trying to build a case for Marlowe, based on gematria, in those lines. It should be as difficult as doing so from phrases plucked at random from *Das Kapital* or *The Bhagavad Gita*. In which case, the cold, hard laws of probability inform us any traces of Marlowe's name detected there would be isolated, marginal and ludicrously contrived. On the other hand, if the thesis of Marlowe's authorship is correct, the kind of encoded signatures that he would have left must be consistent, direct and unambiguously present. What is more, since we are talking about no lesser writer than Shakepeare, there should be the hallmarks of genius in their construction. Would a fair-minded reader be able to tell the two alternatives apart? I think they would.

In my view, there are five locations that cannot be avoided if we are going to subject the hypothesis to a critical test of credibility. The places that must be examined are the lines:

119 (7th line in Sonnet 9) – 'Kit'
493 (3rd line in Sonnet 36) – 'Christopher'
1086 (8th line in Sonnet 78) – 'Marlowe'
1205 (1st line in Sonnet 87) – 'Kit Marlowe'
1579 (10th line in Sonnet 113) – 'Christopher Marlowe'

As we examine them, it will be seen these lines all appear inconspicuous on the surface – they arouse no suspicion in the reader; and, even when even when subjected to an initial count of their letter-values, they appear innocuous and unremarkable. However, each of them has been engineered in a way that requires a specific key to unlock its message. Once the correct key has been identified, the mechanism can be turned not once but several times to reveal the complete solution. This is true artistry and craftsmanship. We should expect nothing less from William Shakespeare.

119 – Kit

119 is not just the value of 'Kit'; it also counts the value of 'Kit Marlowe' by the S-code. The strained wording and wacky

spelling found in this line suggest that something remarkable might be happening beneath the hood.

Sn	Sg	Line	Ln	Lg
105	395	*119* **When euery priuat widdow well may keepe,**	2805	6421

The profusion of 'w's, 'v's and 'y's serve to give the line an unusually high gematria total.[1] 6421 may have been selected as a symbol of resurrection and eternal life because it is the precise value of a relevant passage from *Revelation:* την πολιν την αγιαν ιερουσαλημ καινην καταβαινουσαν απο του θεου εκ του ουρανου – 'the holy city, new Jerusalem, coming down from God out of heaven,' (*Rev.* 21, 2 – see Appendix 3).

6421 is the primary key in this line. The way it is applied is remarkable. What is required is to take each of the other totals for the line from it, individually. Take 2805 from 6421 and 3616 remains. This supplies an equilateral triangle with sides of 1205.3, emblematic of, 'Kit Marlowe'. Take 105 from 6421, and 6316 remains. This provides a square with sides of 1579, and hence 'Christopher Marlowe'. Take 395 from 6421 and 6026 is left. This is sufficient for a pentagon with sides of 1205.2, and hence 'Kit Marlowe', once again. Thus, by subtraction from the largest figure, the other three totals individually supply the first three regular polygons, all with sides measuring his name.

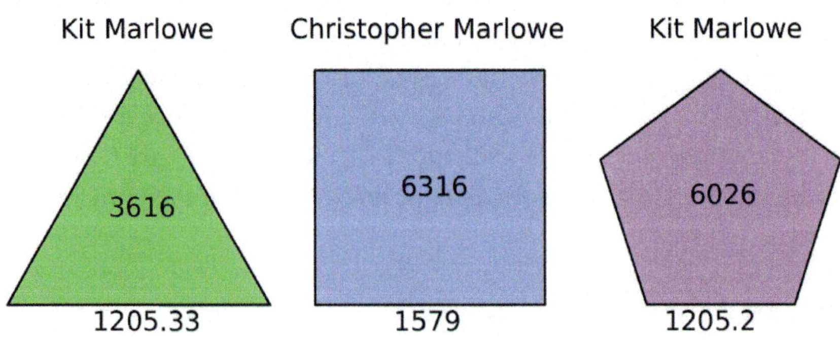

The 3-4-5 sequence of polygons leads back to Pythagoras' famous right-angled triangle. In section 56 of *De Iside et Osiride*, Plutarch explained the Egyptian connection:

> This triangle has its upright of three units, its base of four, and its hypotenuse of five, whose power is equal to that of the other two sides. The upright, therefore, may be likened to the male, the base to the female, and the hypotenuse to the child of both, and so Osiris may be regarded as the origin, Isis as the recipient, and Horus as perfected result.

There can be little doubt that Shakespeare knew his Plutarch nor that Horus prefigures the resurrection of slain Osiris.

We can now add the three name values: 1205.33 + 1579 + 1205.2 = 3989.53. This rounds up to 3990, which is the gematria value of Οσιϱις – 'Osiris', when counted by the letter-names:

Ὀμικρον	Σίγμα	Ιώτα	Ρω	Ιώτα	Σίγμα	
360	254	1111	900	1111	254	**3990**

Note, that if the triangle and pentagon had sides of exactly 1205, the total would have been one short, at 3989. Thus the author was more meticulous than one otherwise might have supposed.

Next, after a polite round of applause, comes an encore because one can also take 395 from 2805 to give 2410, which is exactly twice 1205 – 'Kit Marlowe'. Therefore, if the line number itself is included, his name is numbered x1, x2, x3, x4 and x5. That's 10 'Kit Marlowes', 4 'Christopher Marlowes' and a spare 'Kit' thrown in for good measure. It is even possible that the 14 'Marlowes' represent the 14 parts that Osiris' body was cut into when he was murdered by his brother Set, and that his 'widdow' Isis needed to reassemble. Whatever the rationale, it's a jaw-dropping piece of literary engineering. One can only marvel at the technical skill involved in its creation.

It perhaps comes as a relief to know the bard didn't have a weird thing about 'priuat widdows', or that he couldn't spill to sieve his lice. He was actually razor-sharp at selecting and lettering his words. As his friend Thomas Nashe observed, 'His pen was sharp-pointed like a poniard; no leaf he wrote on but was like a burning-glass to set on fire all his readers'.[2]

493 – Christopher

The numbers in this line have consequences no less mind-boggling than those in line 119. However, aside from the presence of 'Christopher', God knows what the special mysteries of 493 entail. It may, or may not, be related to the words, ο θεος οιδεν – 'God knows' (or 'God knoweth'), from *2 Corinthians*, 12, 2, which have a value of 493. The passage that it comes from is highly mysterious, but it addresses the theme of resurrection, or at least traffic with the living-dead, and is somehow linked to the number 14. Furthermore, the wording may suitable for a person whose name is 'in Christ', but which may no longer be uttered lawfully:

> 12:2 I knewe a man in Christ aboue fouretеene yeeres agoe, whether in the body, I cannot tell, or whether out of the body, I cannot tell, **God knoweth**: such a one, caught vp to the third heauen.
> 12:3 And I knew such a man (whether in the body, or out of the body, I cannot tell, **God knoweth**.)
> 12:4 How that he was caught vp into Paradise, and heard vnspeakeable wordes, which it is not lawfull for a man to vtter.

This passage leads us towards the most famous description of resurrection in the *New Testament*, which comes in, *1 Corinthians*, chapter 15. Here St Paul distinguishes between the natural body and the spiritual body and their correlates, the natural man and the heavenly man. A twofold division is also found in Sonnet 36:

491 LEt me confesse that we two must be twaine,
492 Although our vndeuided loues are one:
493 So shall those blots that do with me remaine,
494 Without thy helpe , by me be borne alone.
495 In our two loues there is but one respect,

496 Though in our liues a seperable spight,

If 493 is doubled to make 986, we have the value of ἐπουράνιος – 'heavenly', which is the adjective used for St. Paul's 'second man' (verse 48). And then, if we count the value of the phrase, 'those blots that do with me remaine,' it comes to 2000. This is the value of ψυχικός – the word Paul uses for 'natural' (verse 44). In this way, Marlowe could be writing about his confusing condition of being both alive and dead at the same time.

130 410 *493* **So shall those blots that do with me remaine,** 1396 2279

In this line, it is the line-number itself that is the algorithmic key; and here, it must be added to each total. If 493 is added to the lower figure of 130, it produces 623. In this lies the perimeter of a square that fits in a 214-sided square such that its corners intersect the sides by 133 and 81 – these are the values of, 'Christopher' and 'Marlowe' by the S-code:

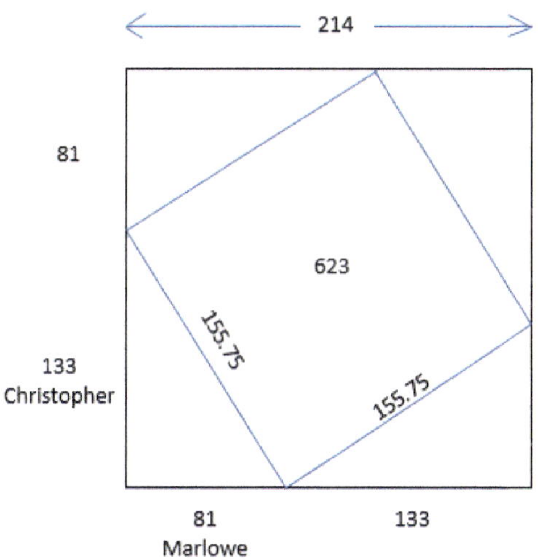

When 493 is added to the gematria total of 2279, it rises to 2772. This supplies the perimeter of the right-angled triangle with perpendicular sides of 493 and 1086 – 'Christopher' and 'Marlowe'. His name is tried, square and true.

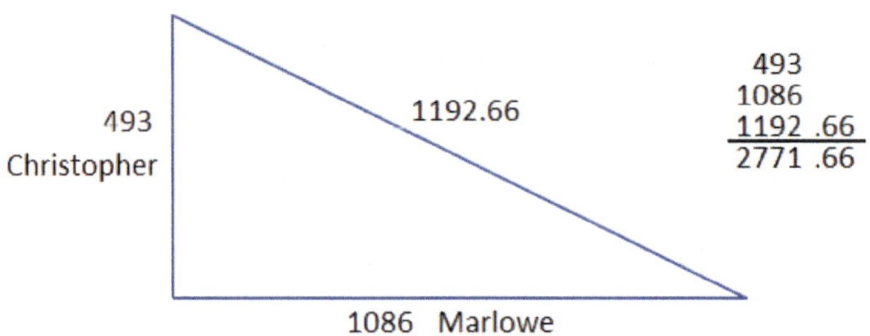

Then, when 493 is added to the four counts for the line, the sum is 130 + 410 + 1396 + 2279 + 493 = 4708. This number rather ingeniously unites the lower and the higher values (S and L) of the name 'Christopher Marlowe': 214 x (1 + 5 + 7 + 9) = 4708. Are these the first man (earthy) and the second man (heavenly)?

A curious duplication also emerges. It can be seen, for example, the number 1396 occurs in two contexts: firstly as an original artefact (L-code notarikon) and secondly because if 493 is added to both 410 and 1396, it makes 1396 x 2. By this means we arrive at 1396 x 3 = 4188. Here we have a number that is not personal but which points to a specific type of cipher. The value of, Ιησους Χριστος – 'Jesus Christ', who is the prototype of all resurrected men, is 2368. This number can be ciphered: (2 x 368) + (23 x 68) + (236 x 8) = 4188.

Returning to the line, the number 1526 also emerges by two means: firstly, through being the sum of 130 and 1396 and secondly as (130 + 493) + (410 + 493) = 1526. Clearly, this double symmetry echoes the twofold theme of the sonnet.

It happens that a right-angled triangle with perpendicular sides of 1396 and 1526 has a perimeter of 4990. We have seen this before: it's a cipher for 2856 – Χριστοφερ Μαρλω – 'Christopher Marlowe', because (2 x 856) + (28 x 56) + (285 x 6) = 4990.

The fact that 1396 and 1526 both appear twice actually suggests a doubling of the 4990-triangle (or a rectangle made from two such triangles), and by this means a new total appears of 9980. If this length is configured to make the circumference of a circle, the diameter will be 3177. 3177 is an identical cipher for 1579 – 'Christopher Marlowe' – because (1 x 579) + (15 x 78) + (157 x 9) =

3177.

It can also be noticed that if 1396 and 1526 are added, they make 2922. If then a 'mishap' were to occur to the 9, and it got printed as a 6 (such as befell Sonnet 116 – mislabelled as 119), the number would be 2622, which is the same cipher for 2362 - Χριστοφερ Μαρλω – ('Christopher Marlowe' with the *stau* digraph counted as *digamma*) because, (2 x 362) + (23 x 62) + (236 x 2) = 2622. Is such playfulness allowed? God knows!

1086 – Marlowe

This comes as the eighth line of Sonnet 78.

32 240 *1086* **And giuen grace a double Maiestie.** 50 2024

(N.B. the first 'i' in 'Maiestie' is a 'j')

Here the gematria total 2024 is the critical number. Just like the figure of 6421 chosen for line 119, it has the theme of eternity because it gives the value of the same passage from *Revelation*, albeit in shortened form: την πολιν την αγιαν ιερουσαλημ καινην – 'the holy city, new Jerusalem' (*Rev.* 21, 2). Having this scriptural link with a line numbered 1086 may also be related to the fact that *Revelation* 22, 1, (the 'river of water of life'), has a complete value of 10859 – approximating to 10860 (see Appendix 3). The theme of water which brings the dead back to life is particularly apposite at this location because 'water' also shares a value of 1086 in English gematria.

The algorithm in this line comes in two parts. Initially, it is given by the word 'double'. Maybe this is because 1086 is double 543, and at this value are the words, אהיה אשר אהיה – 'I am that I am' (*Exodus* 3:14), which must be the starting point of all naming references in Western culture – as well as being intrinsically double in nature. The second strand of the algorithm is pentagonal geometry with its governing ratio of *Phi*. I don't know why this should be so, but a playful possibility comes from the fact that when multiplied by 1.618, 1086 gives 1757 and when divided by 1.618, it gives 671. The sum of these <u>two</u> is 2428, which is the value of the blunt message, '**Marlowe wrote this**'. While the difference between the two takes us back to where we started – 1086 - **Marlowe**.

Overall, the key requires adding 2024 to each of the other numbers and then doubling the sum – in order to create a structure with pentagonal geometry:

(2024 + 32) x 2 = 4112 (2024 + 240) x 2 = 4528 (2024 + 50) x 2 = 4148

4112 supplies a pentagram whose interior pentagon has a perimeter of 971, hence Μαϱλω – 'Marlowe'. 4528 gives a pentagram surrounded by a pentagon of 2799 perimeter – Μαϱλω – as counted by the 'names' of its letters ('filling'). 4148 measures the exterior perimeter of a pentagram with sides of 1086 – 'Marlowe'.

4112 ÷ 4.236 = 971 (4.236 is *Phi* cubed)
4528 ÷ 1.618 = 2799
4148 = 5430 – (5430 ÷ 4.236) 5430 = 1086 x 5

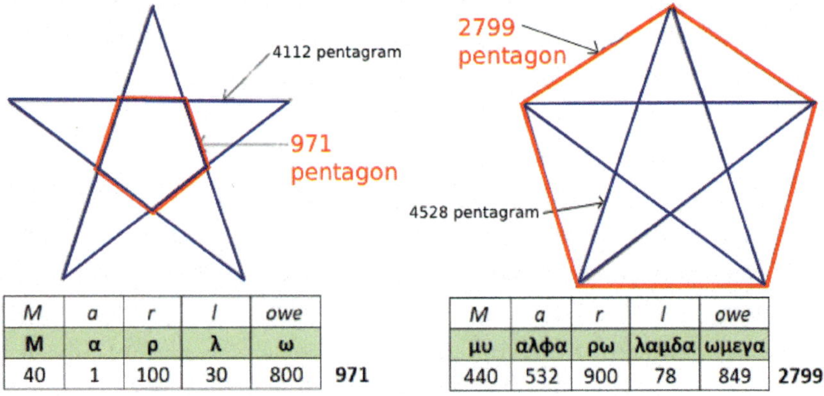

M	a	r	l	owe	
Μ	**α**	**ρ**	**λ**	**ω**	
40	1	100	30	800	**971**

M	a	r	l	owe	
μυ	**αλφα**	**ρω**	**λαμδα**	**ωμεγα**	
440	532	900	78	849	**2799**

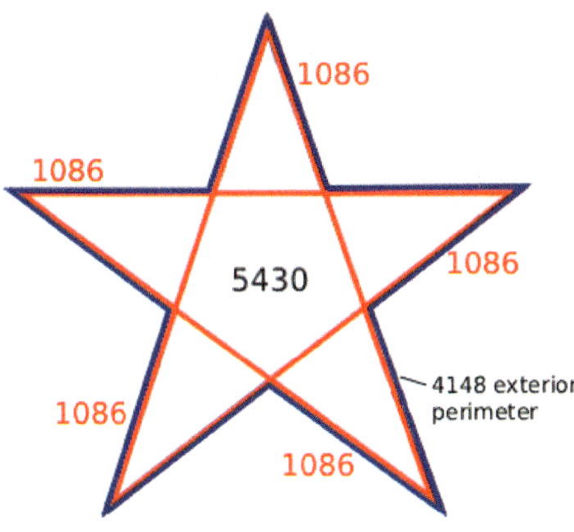

These patterns are too consistent to have arisen by chance, and all point back to different versions of the name given by the line number. They also employ the three main dimensions of a regular five-sided polygon. The consistent application of an algorithm generating such a well-targeted result cannot be the product of chance.

The pentagram also provides a rationale for the 'four-code-total' of 32 + 240 + 50 + 2024 = 2346. This is because a circle of this circumference can be drawn around a pentagram with a total length of 3551 – and the difference between the two figures is 1205 - 'Kit Marlowe'.

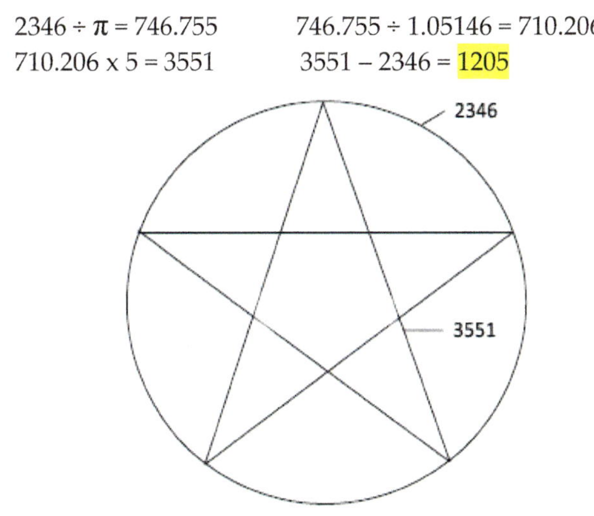

The algorithm in this line was fiendish to crack, but the end result is an unambiguous endorsement of Marlowe's genius.

1205 – Kit Marlowe

Line 1205, signifying the value of 'Kit Marlowe', comes as the first line of Sonnet 87:

82 461 *1205* **FArewell thou art too deare for my possessing,** 307 2968

A familiar resurrection theme can be found from the two final words 'my possessing', which have a gematria value of 961. This is takes us to, Η καινη Ιερουσαλημ – 'The New Jerusalem'.[3] Aside from the connection with the dead returning to life, the preoccupation with the heavenly city may come from the theme of 'naming' associated with it: 'I will write vpon him the Name of my God, and the name of the citie of my God, which is the newe Jerusalem, which commeth downe out of heauen from my God, and I will write vpon him my newe Name' (*Revelation* 3, 12).[4]

The symbolism here is no less complex than in line 1086, and it took me a long time to work out its operation. Essentially, the gematria value of 2968 is used in combination with other values to create vesicae piscis figures to form, 'The Eyes of Horus'. The reason for choosing a geometric figure with proportions of the square root of three in this line may be because 1205 multiplied by $\sqrt{3}$ is 2087. This provides for the resurrection cry, οι νεκροι εγερθησονται αφθαρτοι – 'The dead shall be raised incorruptible' (*1 Corinthians* 15, 52).

Adding 2968 to the line number 1205 makes 4173. This measures the combined circumferences of the two circles making a vesica in whose 'eye' sits a 1579 (total length) pentagram – 'Christopher Marlowe'. If a 1579 hexagram is required by the same geometry, the two generative circles should havecircumferences totalling 3818. This number is provided by adding 2968 to the other three line totals: 2968 + 82 + 461 + 307 = 3818.

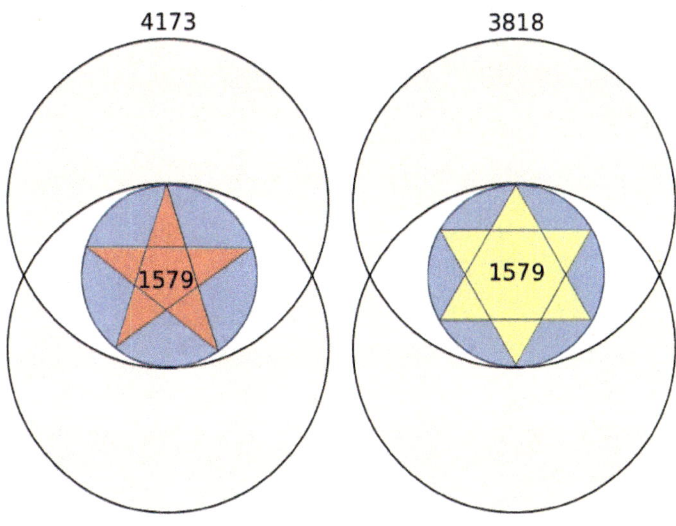

4173 ÷ 3 = 1391 (ves. perimeter) 1391 ÷ 4.18879 = 332.0768 (ves. width)
5 x (332.0768 ÷ 1.051462) = 1579.1194
3818 ÷ 3 = 1272.6666 1272.6666 ÷ 4.18879 = 303.8268
6 x (303.8268 ÷ 1.1547) = 1578.7311

The eyes reveal the value of the name 'Christopher Marlowe' by means of pentagonal and hexagonal symmetry. That these symbolise the two Eyes of Horus – the sun and the moon – is possibly indicated when the key number 2968 is extended through the sum of its divisors to 6480.

2968	1484	742	424	371	212	106	53	6480
1	2	4	7	8	14	28	56	

This can be considered as 3240 x 2. At 3240, can be found, Το Ωψ Ωρου – The Eye of Horus.[5] Obviously, the doubling allows for the two eyes. It can further be seen that 2968 minus the notarikon figure of 307 gives 2661, where an alternative formulation, Το ομμα του Ωρου – 'The eye(s) of Horus', can be found. This reading is further supported because when all four line scores are added to the line number, they make 82 + 461 + 307 + 2968 + 1205 = 5023. This can unite Χρι<u>στ</u>οφερ Μαρλω (2362) with Το ομμα του Ωρου: 2362 + 2661 = 5023.

In addition, the two numbers 3818 and 4173 have a very unusual property in common: both have factors which sum to 6048:

1	3818
2	1909
23	166
46	83
6048	

1	4173
3	1391
13	321
39	107
6048	

If these two 6048s are taken for a pair of circles which overlap to make a vesica, the 'eye' they form holds a hexagram with a total extent of 5001.6583.

(6048 + 6048) ÷ 3 = 4032 vesica perimeter
4032 ÷ 4.18879 = 962.5691 vesica width
6 x (962.5691 ÷ 1.1547) = 5001.6583 hexagram

This number perfectly measures the combined pentagram and hexagram inside 1579-circumference circles:

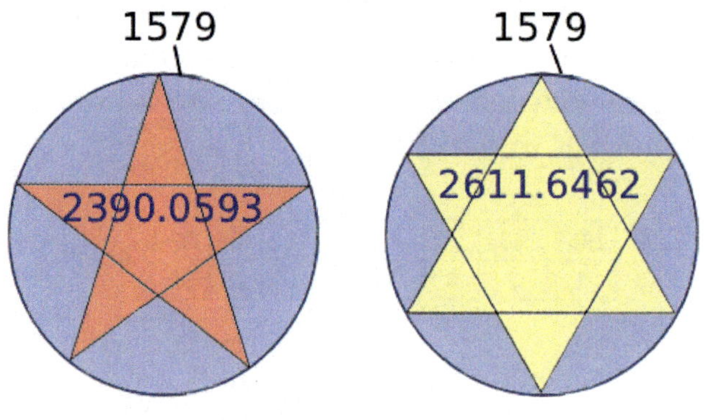

1579 ÷ π = 502.6113
5 x (502.6113 ÷ 1.051462) = 2390.0593
6 x (502.6113 ÷ 1.1547) = 2611.6462
2390.0593 + 2611.6462 = 5001.7055

This is the exact inverse of the two Horus eyes above, where 1579 measured the pentagram and hexagram. It demonstrates the unique properties of the two numbers 3818 and 4173 in relation to Christopher Marlowe's number 1579. The accuracy level is very high, too, at 0.99999. Artefacts like this do not arise by chance.

As a final flourish, 3818 can also be taken to signify both the opening of an eye and the resurrection of the dead: εὗρον δὲ τὸν λίθον ἀποκεκυλισμένον ἀπὸ τοῦ μνημείου – 'And they found the stone rolled away from the sepulchre' (Luke 24, 2).

1579 – Christopher Marlowe

There should be a lot going on here . . . and there is. 1579 comes as the tenth line of Sonnet 113. This sonnet is one of huge strategic significance in the overall scheme because it is placed in the upper centre of the *Sonnets'* 153 triangle. The first quatrain quite plainly describes the Eye of Horus:

> SInce I left you, mine eye is in my minde,
> And that which gouernes me to goe about,
> Doth part his function, and is partly blind,
> Seemes seeing, but effectually is out:

The partially blind eye was the Moon, which waxes and wanes over the course of a lunar month. Therefore, the placement of the sonnet gives us the symbolism of the 'Eye in the Triangle'.

This is the poet's eye looking out from the heart of his *Sonnets* monument. Through the number 153, it portends resurrection. Here, the Egyptian symbolism of Osiris coming forth as his son Horus becomes the template for the resurrection of Christopher Marlowe, the 'murdered' poet.

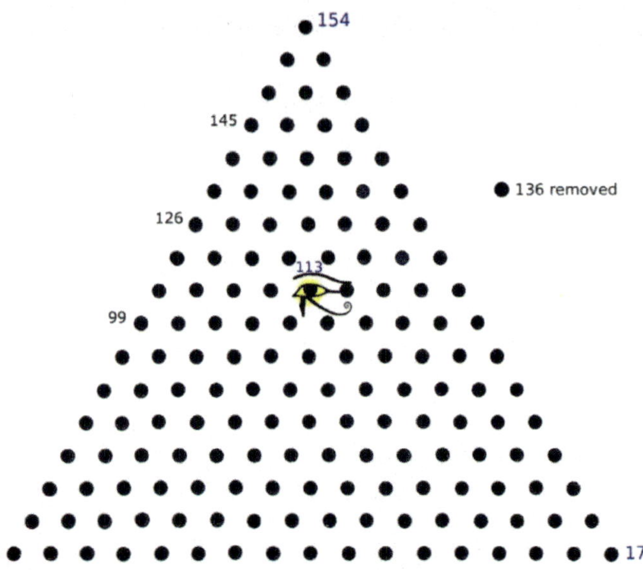

Not only is the sonnet containing line 1579 positioned as the Eye of Horus, but the line itself is singled out as a focal point. Close scrutiny reveals that line 1579 is the centrepoint of a 17-line group marked by two lines which begin with the words 'And that'. What is more, they both have identical gematria values of 2759:

113	*1570*	SInce I left you,mine eye is in my minde,	2097
	1571	**And that** which gouernes me to goe about,	**2759**
	1572	Doth part his function,and is partly blind,	1838
	1573	Seemes seeing,but effectually is out:	1898
	1574	For it no forme deliuers to the heart	1876
	1575	Of bird,of flowre,or shape which it doth lack,	2795
	1576	Of his quick obiects hath the minde no part,	1954
	1577	Nor his owne vision houlds what it doth catch:	3937
	1578	For if it see the rud'st or gentlest sight,	1658
	1579	The most sweet-fauor or deformedst creature,	3298
	1580	The mountaine,or the sea,the day, or night:	1739
	1581	The Croe,or Doue,it shapes them to your feature.	2923
	1582	Incapable of more repleat,with you,	2300
	1583	My most true minde thus maketh mine vntrue.	2434
114	*1584*	OR whether doth my minde being crown'd with you	4723
	1585	Drinke vp the monarks plague this flattery ?	2034
	1586	Or whether shall I say mine eie saith true,	2571
	1587	**And that** your loue taught it this *Alcumie*?	**2759**
	1588	To make of monsters,and things indigest,	1300

This grouping will be examined shortly. One other hint that 1579 could be special is that it marks the first of three lines starting with the letter 'T'. The 'Triple Tau' is an important symbol in Freemasonry, especially in the Royal Arch Degree. On the 'Companion's Jewel' of this degree there is a motto subscribed to the Triple Tau emblem, 'Theca ubi res pretiosa deponitur': this means, 'The place where the precious thing is hidden'. This aptly describes the line bearing the number of Christopher Marlowe's name.

Line 1579 Counted

76	443	*1579*	**The most sweet-fauor or deformedst creature,**	283	3298
70			*(these values counted without the hyphen)*	277	

The first thing one notices here is the presence of the two numbers 443 and 283. By English gematria these serve up an auspicious conjunction of, 'The Sun' and 'The Moon', respectively. Here are the two eyes of Horus. According to Plutarch, these bodies also represent Osiris and Isis respectively.[6]

The dualism is further reflected in the two phrases, 'The most sweet-fauor' and 'deformedst creature'. The left eye (the Moon) was gouged out by the rival god Set in a fight, but when it was later restored by Isis, it was only partially healed. Those two expressions in the line have gematria values of 2320 and 848 (not including the word 'or'). If used as the perpendiculars of a right-angled triangle, the two generate a hypotenuse of 2470. This combines the counter-balanced opposites of Ισις – 'Isis' (420) and Τυφων – 'Typhon' (2050), which represent. 'Knowledge' and 'Ignorance'. Typhon was the Greek name for Set – the adversary who slew Osiris and blinded Horus.

Put together, 2320 and 848 sum to 3168, which is highly significant as the traditional perimeter of the cosmic temple. It has also been described as, 'The paramount number of the ancient canon'.[7] In esoteric Christianity, it marks the place where Lord Jesus Christ (3168 in Greek) was crucified in the centre of the universe, at a spot marked by a 'cross of the elements': υἱὸς θεοῦ, πυρ, υδωρ, αηρ, γη – 'Son of God, fire, water, air, earth' (3168).

The four totals combined are 76 + 443 + 283 + 3298 = 4100. This is a number with solar significance because it gives the value of the cardinal markers of the year (in Latin): Aequinoctium Vernum, Solstitium, Aequinoctium Auctumnale, Bruma – 'Spring equinox, Summer solstice, Autumn equinox, Winter solstice'. This is another cross marking out line 1579 as the centre, or omphalos, of the *Sonnets*.

If the hyphen does not split 'sweet-fauor' in two, the four totals sum: 70 + 443 + 277 + 3298 = 4088. This leads to one of the best-known quotations from the New Testament: Και γνωσεσθε την αληθειαν και η Αληθεια ελευθερωσει υμας - 'And ye shall know the truth and the truth shall make you free.' (John 8, 32). Christopher Marlowe can only be free when the truth about him and his disguise as Shakespeare is known.

The significance of the gematria total 3298 relates to the Greek form of his name, Χριστοφερ Μαρλω, valued at 2856. 3298 is connected to it by a √3 relationship. For example, an equilateral triangle with three sides of 3298 will have a height of 2856. A variation of the latter is what is hinted at by the line values. If the notarikon figure of 70 is added to the actual line number 1579, it produces 1649, which is exactly half of 3298, or 2856 divided by the square root of 3.

These numbers supply the ingredients of a right-angled triangle with relative proportions of 1, 2 and the square root of 3, and internal angles of 30, 60 and 90 degrees.

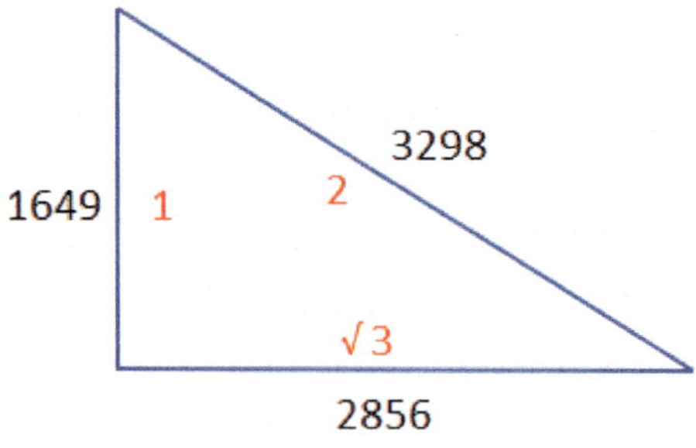

The circle that can be drawn around the apices of this triangle has a diameter of 3298. What is relevant about encircling the right-triangle is that it necessarily implies a mirrored triangle of the same dimensions – or a rectangle with sides of 1649 and 2856 and which has a 3298 diagonal. The perimeter of this rectangle is 9010. 9010 is also the value of the Χριστοφερ Μαρλω, but this time when the name is counted by 'filling' – counting the names of each of its Greek letters.

Ch	*r*	*i*	*s*	*t*	*o*	*ph*	*e*	*r*	*M*	*a*	*r*	*l*	*owe*	
χι	**ρω**	**ιωτα**	**σιγμα**	**ταυ**	**ομικρον**	**φι**	**εψιλον**	**ρω**	**μυ**	**αλφα**	**ρω**	**λαμδα**	**ωμεγα**	
610	900	1111	254	701	360	510	865	900	440	532	900	78	849	9010

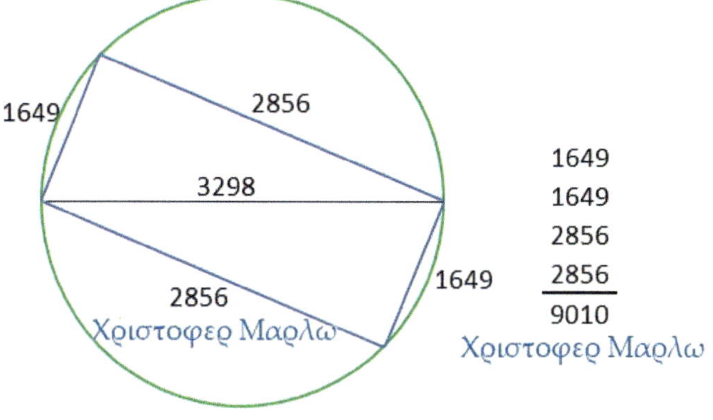

The fact 3298 helps to reveal an integral relationship between 2856 and 9010 can be expressed in another way. This occurs when a right-angled triangle is constructed with perpendicular sides of 2856 and 9010 and a hypotenuse of 9452. The interesting thing about this triangle is that it is entirely made up of units of 2856 and 3298: the upright is 2856, the horizontal is 3298 + 2856 + 2856 = 9010; the hypotenuse is 2856 + 3298 + 3298 = 9452.

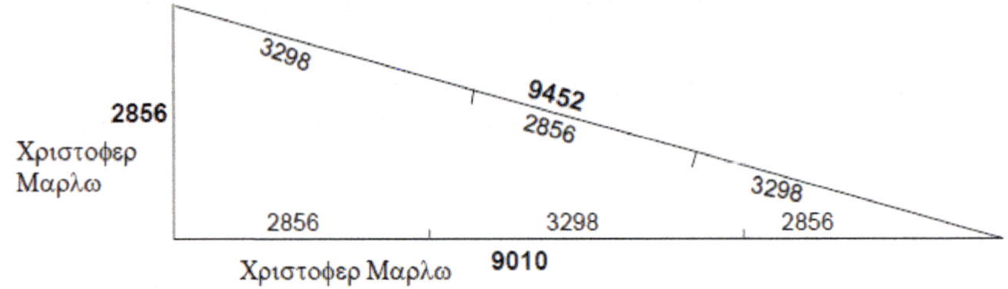

Another unusual property can be seen if 9010 is taken and folded into an isosceles triangle with a base of 3298 and two sides of 2856. The height of this triangle is 2332. If this line is folded around into a square, the area of the square will be equal to that of a 3 - 4 - 5 triangle with a perimeter of 2856 (714 + 952 + 1190).

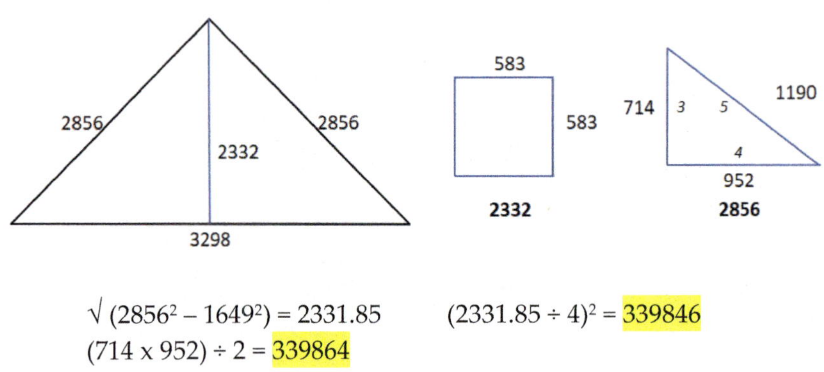

$\sqrt{(2856^2 - 1649^2)} = 2331.85$ $(2331.85 \div 4)^2 = 339846$

$(714 \times 952) \div 2 = 339864$

There is something even more extraordinary afoot here because 3298 also connects with the alternate numeration of Marlowe's name in Greek when the στ ligature (*stau*) is counted as *digamma* rather than *sigma* + *tau*. It will be recalled that this reduces the value of his name to 2362. When this version is counted by 'filling', the larger total sums to 8154.

Ch	*r*	*i*	*st*	*o*	*ph*	*e*	*r*	*M*	*a*	*r*	*l*	*owe*	
Χ	**ρ**	**ι**	**στ**	**ο**	**φ**	**ε**	**ρ**	**Μ**	**α**	**ρ**	**λ**	**ω**	
600	100	10	6	70	500	5	100	40	1	100	30	800	**2362**

Ch	*r*	*i*	*st*	*o*	*ph*	*e*	*r*	*M*	*a*	*r*	*l*	*owe*	
χι	**ρω**	**ιωτα**	**διγαμμα**	**ομικρον**	**φι**	**εψιλον**	**ρω**	**μυ**	**αλφα**	**ρω**	**λαμδα**	**ωμεγα**	
610	900	1111	99	360	510	865	900	440	532	900	78	849	**8154**

If 2362, 8154 and 3298 are added, the total becomes 13,814. This measures the outer perimeter of a vesica piscis with a width of 3298: it therefore holds a 2856-sided hexagram within its inscribed circle – like another Eye of Horus radiating the name Χριστοφερ Μαρλω.

13814 ÷ 4.18879 = 3297.85   3297.85 ÷ 1.1547 = 2856.02

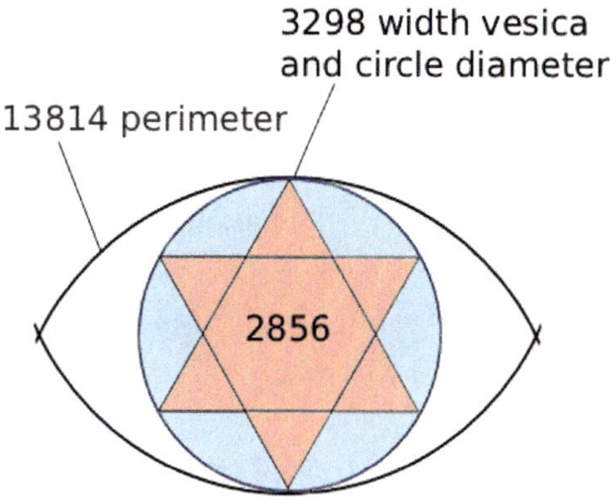

This 'eye' also holds the 9010-perimeter rectangle with sides of 2856 and 2856 divided by √3.

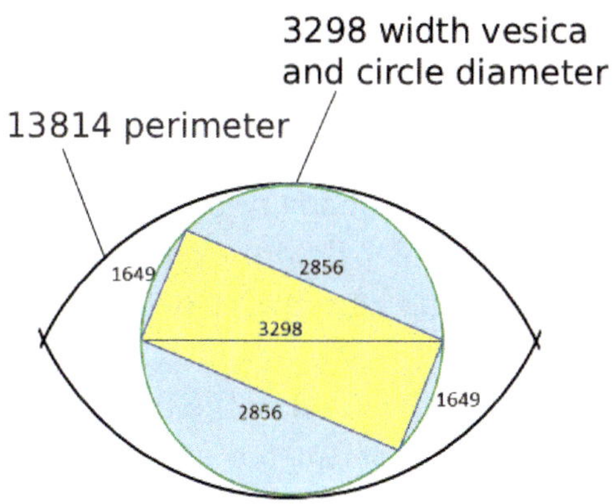

Thus, 3298 has the property of harmonising the normal and 'filling' values of both Χριστοφερ Μαρλω and Χρι**στ**οφερ Μαρλω at the same time – that's four different name values. It is an extraordinarily powerful number for someone called 'Christopher Marlowe', especially in a sonnet whose theme is the Eye of Horus.

The properties of the 3298-diameter circle are not even exhausted yet because its area is equal to that of a square with sides of 2923. This, as the sum of 1344 and 1579, unites 'William Shakespeare' with 'Christopher Marlowe'. Squaring the circle with his alter-ego might just have been on the poet's mind.

$\pi \times (3298 \div 2)^2 = 8{,}542{,}622$ $\qquad \sqrt{8{,}542{,}622} = 2922.78$

Additionally, if the line number, 1579, is taken from the lower of the two four-code-totals gives: 4088 -1579 = 2509. This can be considered as uniting, 'Will Shakespeare' with 'Kit Marlowe': 1304 + 1205 = 2509.

There is support for such a 'double-act' interpretation in line 1581, the third TTT line of the group:

134 462 *1581* **The Croe, or Doue, it shapes them to your feature.** 862 2923

It can be seen that the main gematria value is 2923 – the same number joining 'William Shakespeare' and 'Christopher Marlowe'. Here, the black and white birds may aptly symbolise two opposite sides of the same coin.

"And that" – The 17 Line Group Around 1579

Earlier mention was made of the 17-line group around line 1579. What might be its role? Before examining the whole group, we need to understand the significance of the two bounding figures of 2759.

If the pair are understood as the two diagonals of a square, the square will have a perimeter of 7803. This matches the perimeter of the initial triangle seen above for 2856 and 3298.

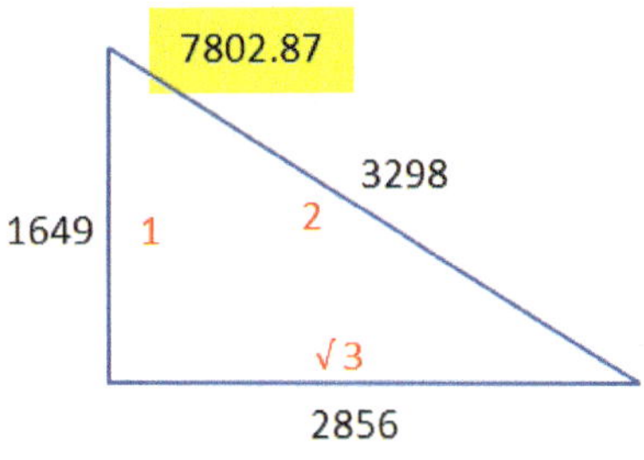

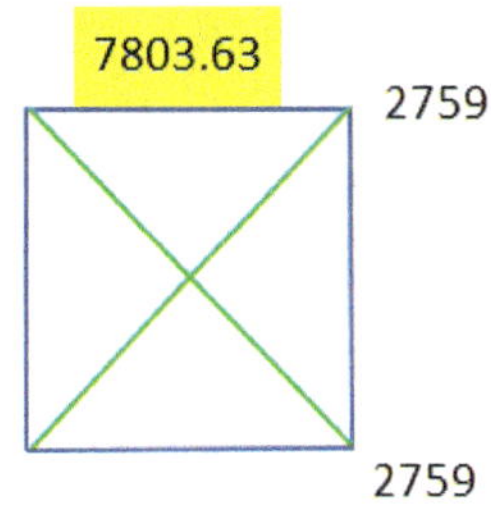

Finding this match ties the pair to line 1579 quite nicely, but I wondered if it might lead somewhere deeper. So I took the perimeter of the square and reconfigured it as the perimeter of a circle. I found this circle has a diameter of 2483.9727. That was revealing because the average value of 1579 x √2 and 1579 x √3 is 2483.9757. It is an extremely accurate match. Here, we should bear in mind the figures of √2 and √3 have a *squaring* function as they measure the diagonals of the 1579 square and the 1579 cube.

A bonus feature of the 2759 pair is that when combined, they make the 5518 perimeter of a square with an area of 1,903,020. Since this can be broken down as 1579 x 1205.2, it presents, 'Christopher Marlowe' times 'Kit Marlowe'. So, the two figures of 2759 are fitting boundary markers for the group around line 1579.

87	345	*1571*	And that which gouernes me to goe about,	1146	2759
60	399	*1572*	Doth part his function,and is partly blind,	150	1838
66	351	*1573*	Seemes seeing,but effectually is out:	246	1898
84	350	*1574*	For it no forme deliuers to the heart	273	1876
113	371	*1575*	Of bird,of flowre,or shape which it doth lack,	1181	2795
119	373	*1576*	Of his quick obiects hath the minde no part,	416	1954
100	446	*1577*	Nor his owne vision houlds what it doth catch:	1722	3937
117	407	*1578*	For if it see the rud'st or gentlest sight,	441	1658
70/76	443	*1579*	The most sweet-fauor or deformedst creature,	277/283	3298
132	372	*1580*	The mountaine,or the sea,the day, or night:	564	1739
134	462	*1581*	The Croe,or Doue,it shapes them to your feature.	862	2923
96	315	*1582*	Incapable of more repleat,with you,	1469	2300
118	455	*1583*	My most true minde thus maketh mine vntrue.	550	2434
112	459	*1584*	OR whether doth my minde being crown'd with you	2319	4723
95	424	*1585*	Drinke vp the monarks plague this flattery ?	500	2034
134	388	*1586*	Or whether shall I say mine eie saith true,	1364	2571
102	406	*1587*	And that your loue taught it this Alcumie?	731	2759
1739 /1745	**6766**			**14211 /14217**	**43496**

1739 + 6766 + 14211 + 43496 = 66212

1745 + 6766 + 14217 + 43496 = 66224

Now, if we look at the totals of the 17-line group, we find 66212 and 66224 (according to hyphenation). It will be seen they have an average value of 66218. This is just 2 more than 24 times 2759, so it is a good indication that we are still on track. The figure of 24 echoes the end digits of the two totals – 12 and 24 – and thereby suggests the hours in a day. These are presided over by the sun and moon, which is to say the Eyes of Horus.

Adding the totals 66,212 and 66,224 produces 132,436. Since this is divisible by 113 (which is also the sonnet number), I first decided to test it as the diameter of a circle using the fraction 355/113. This generates a circumference of 416,060. If this is placed in a square with sides of 132,436, the difference between the perimeter of the square and the circumference of the circle is: 529,744 – 416,060 = 113,684. This is extremely close to 72 x 1579 (113,688). My best explanation for the factor of 72 belongs to the legend of the calendar from ancient Egypt. It was said the Thoth took 1/72nd of the moon's light from the 360 days of official calendar and used it to add 5 extra days, thereby bringing it up to 365. In which case, the 132,436 total ties 1579 to the Sun and the Moon as the arbiters of time: the Eyes of Horus.

A more precise calculation comes from dividing 132,436 by 113 to get 1172. A rectangle of that area, with sides of 113 and 1172, has a diagonal of 1177.435. If this rectangle is taken for the object of an eye, the circle that may be drawn around it, as a pupil, has a circumference of 3699, and it rests in a vesica with a perimeter of 4932.

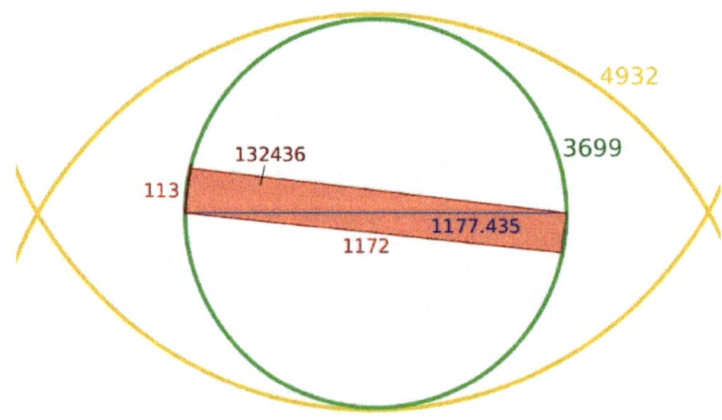

$\sqrt{(113^2 + 1172^2)} = 1177.435$ $\qquad$ $1177.435 \times \pi = 3699.021$

$1177.435 \times 4.18879 = 4932.028$

Putting these two figures together gives us 3699 + 4932 = 8631. This number we have seen before. In Sonnet 76, 8631 was the word-count before the deliberate typo 'fel' in the riddle about his name. We saw it measures the perimeter of an ark (a 6:1 rectangle) with a length of 3699. By this means, it is a perfect fit for, 'Our ever-living poet, Christopher Marlowe'.

Summary

The case for Marlowe's authorship would have collapsed if the five locations corresponding to the value of his name were random lines of text. They would have enabled only foolish or highly contrived solutions. That is clearly not the case. On the contrary, these lines have been engineered with great skill to generate geometric messages highly relevant to the identification of Christopher Marlowe. To find such artefacts in one such strategic line would be persuasive, to find them in all five is conclusive. Having said that, the best evidence is yet to come.

Chapter 8 Notes

---

[1] It is the 3rd highest out of 2155 lines in the *Sonnets*. The only lines with more are 217 with 7382, and 100 with 7045.
[2] Thomas Nashe. *The Unfortunate Traveller*, 35.
[3] This base form of the name is not quoted verbatim from any New Testament source.
[4] The name that God used in Exodus 3,14 was, 'I am that I am'. We saw when discussing line 1086 the value of the expression in Hebrew is 543. That number can be found here by adding 82 and 461. In sonnet 121, the author actually writes, 'I am that I am', so the concept can't have been unacceptable to him.
[5] The Greek/Egyptian importance of this number is emphasised by the fact that it simultaneously provides, Ωσιρις, Ισις and Ωρυς – 'Osiris', 'Isis' and 'Horus': 1320 + 420 + 1500 = 3240.
[6] See Plutarch, *De Iside et Osiride*, Section 52.
[7] John Michell, *The Dimensions of Paradise*, 10.

9
Kit's Cryptogram – Part 1

To this point, a case has been built for Marlowe's authorship of the *Sonnets* that is too strong to be discounted. The identifying symbolism is coherent and completely plausible. The underlying numerical patterns fit together with the words they represent in a series of mathematical 'coincidences' of inordinate improbability. Common sense tells us it would be impossible for them to exist in such a structured form beneath the surface of *Shakespeares Sonnets* unless placed there by design. However, common sense cuts no ice with those who have careers, investments, status and a beloved icon to lose. The defenders of orthodoxy will dig their heals in and fall back on the the failsafe of a loathing for mathematics: no amount of jiggery-pokery with numbers can ever be permitted to displace them or their jealously-guarded Bard.

Unfortunately for the faithful, there is a problem, and it's a big one. There lies in the *Sonnets* an authentic ciphered message. It resides inside a larger cryptogram, and it says in plain English exactly who wrote them. Spoiler alert: it is not the grain-dealer.

I found this definitive piece of evidence when I returned to the only sure and irrefutable cryptographic solution that had previously been unearthed in the *Sonnets*. John Rollett's discovery of the name 'Henry Wriothesley' came about when he put the letters of the dedication into two regular rectilinear grids. Inspired by Rollett's success, I conceived the idea to construct a far more ambitious grid. I decided to make it from the first letter of every line in the *Sonnets*.

There are 154 sonnets and 14 lines in each, [1] so I made the grid with 14 columns and 154 rows. What did this reveal? I was looking for the name 'Marlowe', but what initially caught my eye on were two instances of the name KIT. They were both formed from adjacent letters arranged in straight lines. On the image below these can be traced from the 'K's in rows 105 and 132. Given the distribution and frequency range of letters in the grid, finding two such KIT acrostics is hardly surprising. However, a closer inspection revealed that a great deal more was happening at both locations.

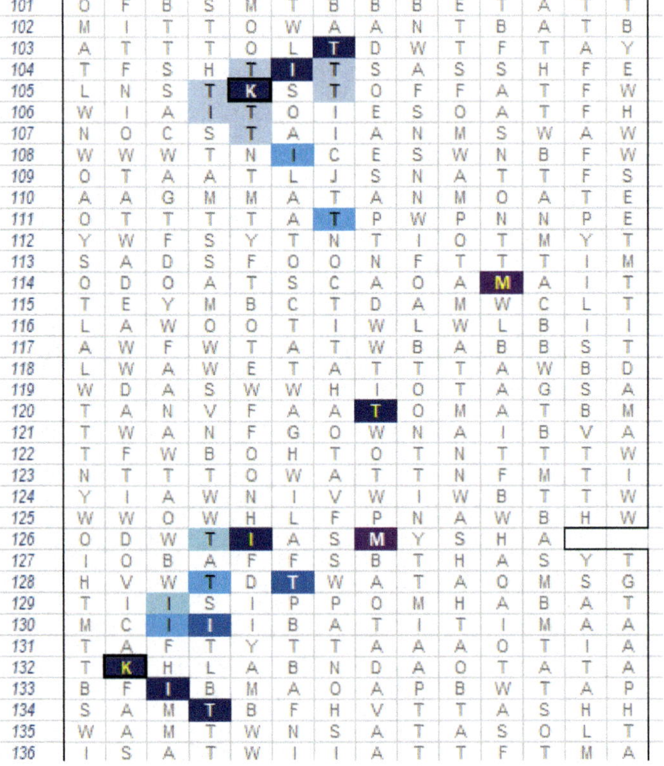

101	O	F	B	S	M	T	B	B	B	E	T	A	T	T
102	M	I	T	T	O	W	A	A	N	T	B	A	T	B
103	A	T	T	T	O	L	T	D	W	T	F	T	A	Y
104	T	F	S	H	T	I	T	S	A	S	S	H	F	E
105	L	N	S	T	K	S	T	O	F	F	A	T	F	W
106	W	I	A	I	T	O	I	E	S	O	A	T	F	H
107	N	O	C	S	T	A	I	A	N	M	S	W	A	W
108	W	W	W	T	N	I	C	E	S	W	N	B	F	W
109	O	T	A	A	T	L	J	S	N	A	T	T	F	S
110	A	A	G	M	M	A	T	A	N	M	O	A	T	E
111	O	T	T	T	T	A	T	P	W	P	N	N	P	E
112	Y	W	F	S	Y	T	N	T	I	O	T	M	Y	T
113	S	A	D	S	F	O	O	N	F	T	T	T	I	M
114	O	D	O	A	T	S	C	A	O	A	M	A	I	T
115	T	E	Y	M	B	C	T	D	A	M	W	C	L	T
116	L	A	W	O	O	T	I	W	L	W	L	B	I	I
117	A	W	F	W	T	A	T	W	B	A	B	B	S	T
118	L	W	A	W	E	T	A	T	T	T	A	W	B	D
119	W	D	A	S	W	W	H	I	O	T	A	G	S	A
120	T	A	N	V	F	A	A	T	O	M	A	T	B	M
121	T	W	A	N	F	G	O	W	N	A	I	B	V	A
122	T	F	W	B	O	H	T	O	T	N	T	T	T	W
123	N	T	T	T	O	W	A	T	T	N	F	M	T	I
124	Y	I	A	W	N	I	V	W	I	W	B	T	T	W
125	W	W	O	W	H	L	F	P	N	A	W	B	H	W
126	O	D	W	T	I	A	S	M	Y	S	H	A		
127	I	O	B	A	F	F	S	B	T	H	A	S	Y	T
128	H	V	W	T	D	T	W	A	T	A	O	M	S	G
129	T	I	I	S	I	P	P	O	M	H	A	B	A	T
130	M	C	I	I	I	B	A	T	I	T	I	M	A	A
131	T	A	F	T	Y	T	T	A	A	A	O	T	I	A
132	T	K	H	L	A	B	N	D	A	O	T	A	T	A
133	B	F	I	B	M	A	O	A	P	B	W	T	A	P
134	S	A	M	T	B	F	H	V	T	T	A	S	H	H
135	W	A	M	T	W	N	S	A	T	A	S	O	L	T
136	I	S	A	T	W	I	I	A	T	T	F	T	M	A

I found that the K in row 105 produced no less than six more KITs written in adjacent squares, albeit in dogleg configurations around it. I also found another straight-line KIT with a letter-spacing interval of three squares down and one to the right. Then, when I looked at the K in row 132, I found four more straight-line KITs composed with regular letter spacing. That is thirteen instances of the name KIT generated from two of the six K letters in the grid. The anomaly is further compounded by the fact that two of the straight-line KITs starting from row 132 were actually KITMs. Naturally, I wondered if the rest of the poet's name could be found.

One KITM had a letter-spacing of two letters across and two up, while the other went three across and six up. The latter seemed to me to be particularly significant because it was directly superimposed on a shorter KIT line (with a spacing of one across and two up). However, from this point neither KITM generates a straight or symmetrical continuation with the same letter spacing. This was disappointing, for it spoiled the hope of finding a conventional acrostic. However, it is not the end of the matter.

While the longer KITM cannot be continued with an interval of three across and six up, it can be continued with an interval of three across and seven up. If this is done, another four-letter section – MARL – is picked out. This gives a minimal spelling of the poet's name, written on two conjoined straight-lines of similarly spaced letters, emerging from a significantly anomalous node of KITs and superimposed on one of them.

The rule that generated the first two sections is based on a vertically rising zigzag with even letter-spacing on each section and the last letter of one section constituting the first letter of the next section. If this rule is followed, the letters KIT MARLOWE WROTE THI can be discovered from an eight-sectioned, ascending zigzag. There is even an S to finish off the message – **Kit Marlowe wrote this** – by making a vertical rise of one square from the final section. This move seems to be justified on account of the final section being formed in adjacent squares. There are also aesthetic grounds for considering it to show that the message has 'tailed off' at this point.

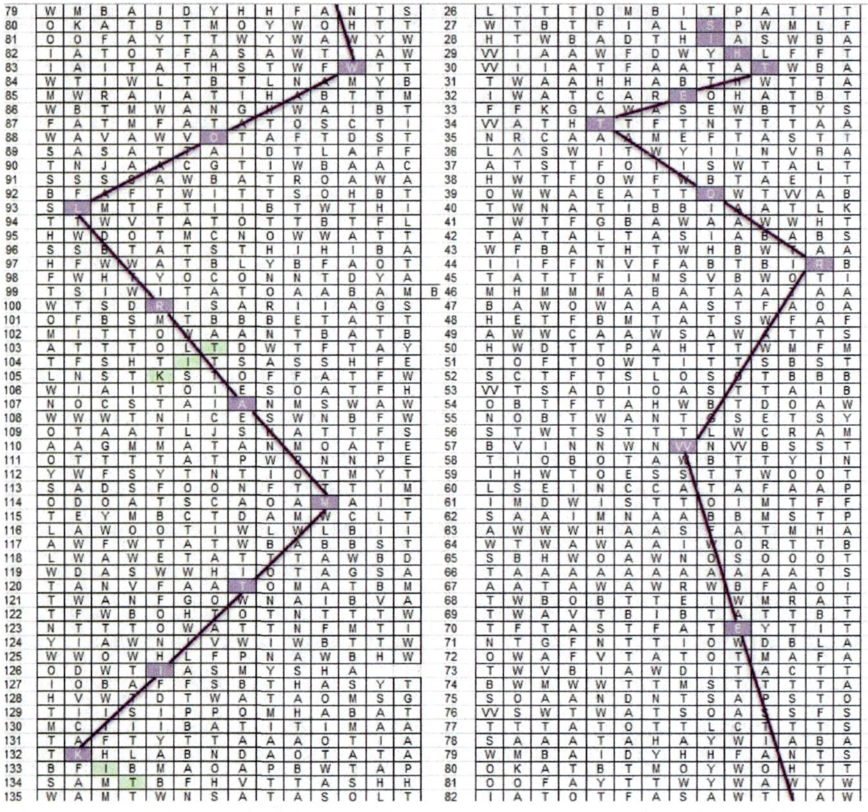

79	W	M	B	A	I	D	Y	H	H	F	A	N	T	S	26	L	T	T	T	D	M	B	I	T	P	A	T	T	T
80	O	K	A	T	B	T	M	O	Y	W	O	H	T	T	27	W	T	B	T	F	I	A	L	S	P	W	M	L	F
81	O	O	F	A	Y	T	T	W	Y	W	A	W	Y	W	28	H	T	W	B	A	D	T	H	I	A	S	W	B	A
82	I	A	T	O	T	F	A	S	A	W	T	I	A	W	29	VV	I	A	A	W	F	D	W	Y	H	L	F	F	T
83	I	A	I	T	A	T	H	S	T	W	F	W	T	T	30	VV	I	I	A	T	F	A	A	T	A	T	W	B	A
84	W	T	I	W	L	T	B	T	L	N	A	M	Y	B	31	T	W	A	A	H	H	A	B	T	H	W	T	T	A
85	M	W	R	A	I	A	T	I	H	A	B	T	T	M	32	I	W	A	T	C	A	R	E	O	H	A	T	B	T
86	W	B	T	M	W	A	N	G	H	W	A	I	B	T	33	F	F	K	G	A	W	A	S	E	W	B	T	Y	S
87	F	A	T	M	F	A	T	A	T	O	S	C	T	I	34	VV	A	T	H	T	T	F	T	N	T	T	T	A	A
88	W	A	V	A	W	V	O	T	A	F	T	D	S	T	35	N	R	C	A	A	A	M	E	F	T	A	S	T	T
89	S	A	S	A	T	T	A	I	D	T	L	A	F	F	36	L	A	S	W	I	T	W	Y	I	I	N	V	R	A
90	T	N	J	A	A	C	G	T	I	W	B	A	A	C	37	A	T	S	T	F	O	T	I	S	W	T	A	L	T
91	S	S	S	S	A	W	B	A	T	R	O	A	W	A	38	H	W	T	F	O	W	F	W	B	T	A	E	I	T
92	B	F	A	F	T	W	I	T	T	S	O	H	B	T	39	O	W	W	A	E	A	T	T	O	W	T	VV	A	B
93	S	L	M	T	F	T	I	I	B	T	W	T	H	I	40	T	W	N	A	T	I	B	B	I	A	A	T	L	K
94	T	T	W	V	T	A	T	O	T	T	B	T	F	L	41	T	W	T	F	G	B	A	W	A	A	W	W	H	T
95	H	W	D	O	T	M	C	N	O	W	W	A	T	T	42	T	A	T	A	L	T	A	S	I	A	B	A	B	S
96	S	S	B	T	A	T	S	T	H	I	H	I	B	A	43	W	F	B	A	T	H	T	W	H	B	W	T	A	A
97	H	F	W	W	A	T	B	L	Y	B	F	A	O	T	44	I	I	F	F	N	V	F	A	B	T	B	I	R	B
98	F	W	H	T	Y	O	C	O	N	N	T	D	Y	A	45	T	A	T	T	F	I	M	S	V	B	W	O	T	I
99	T	S	I	W	I	T	A	T	O	A	A	B	A	M	B 46	M	H	M	M	M	A	B	A	T	A	A	[illegible]	A	A
100	W	T	S	D	R	I	S	A	R	I	I	A	G	S	47	B	A	W	O	W	A	A	A	S	T	F	A	O	A
101	O	F	B	S	M	T	B	B	B	E	T	A	T	T	48	H	E	T	F	B	M	T	A	T	S	W	F	A	F
102	M	I	T	T	O	W	A	A	N	T	B	A	T	B	49	A	W	W	C	A	A	W	S	A	W	A	T	T	S
103	A	T	T	T	O	L	T	D	W	T	F	T	A	Y	50	H	W	D	T	T	P	A	H	T	T	W	M	F	M
104	T	F	S	H	T	I	T	S	A	S	S	H	F	E	51	T	O	F	T	O	W	T	I	T	T	S	B	S	T
105	L	N	S	T	K	S	T	O	F	F	A	T	F	W	52	S	C	T	F	T	S	L	O	S	S	T	B	B	B
106	W	I	A	I	T	O	I	E	S	O	A	T	F	H	53	VV	T	S	A	D	I	O	A	S	T	T	A	I	B
107	N	O	C	S	T	A	I	A	N	M	S	W	A	W	54	O	B	T	F	T	A	H	W	B	T	D	O	A	W
108	W	W	W	T	N	I	C	E	S	W	N	B	F	W	55	N	O	B	T	W	A	N	T	S	S	E	T	S	Y
109	O	T	A	A	T	L	J	S	H	A	T	T	F	S	56	S	T	W	T	S	T	T	T	L	W	C	R	A	M
110	A	A	G	M	M	A	T	A	N	M	O	A	T	E	57	B	V	I	N	N	W	N	VV	N	VV	B	S	S	T
111	O	T	T	T	T	A	T	P	W	R	N	N	P	E	58	T	I	O	B	O	T	A	W	B	T	T	Y	I	N
112	Y	W	F	S	Y	T	N	T	I	O	T	M	Y	T	59	I	H	W	T	O	E	S	S	T	T	W	O	O	T
113	S	A	D	S	F	O	O	N	F	T	T	T	I	M	60	L	S	E	I	N	C	C	A	T	A	F	A	A	P
114	O	D	O	A	T	S	C	A	O	A	M	A	I	T	61	I	M	D	W	I	S	T	T	O	I	M	T	F	F
115	T	E	Y	M	B	C	T	D	A	M	W	C	L	T	62	S	A	A	I	M	N	A	A	B	B	M	S	T	P
116	L	A	W	O	O	T	I	W	L	W	L	B	I	I	63	A	W	W	W	H	A	A	S	F	A	T	M	H	A
117	A	W	F	W	T	A	T	W	B	A	B	B	S	T	64	W	T	W	A	W	A	A	I	W	O	R	T	T	B
118	L	W	A	W	E	T	A	T	T	T	A	W	B	D	65	S	B	H	W	O	A	W	N	O	S	O	O	O	T
119	W	D	A	S	W	W	H	I	O	T	A	G	S	A	66	T	A	A	A	A	A	A	A	A	A	A	A	T	S
120	T	A	N	V	F	A	A	T	O	M	A	T	B	M	67	A	A	T	A	W	A	W	R	W	B	F	A	O	I
121	T	W	A	N	F	G	O	W	N	A	I	B	V	A	68	T	W	B	O	B	T	T	E	I	W	M	R	A	T
122	T	F	W	B	O	H	T	O	T	N	T	T	T	W	69	T	W	A	V	T	B	I	B	T	A	T	T	B	T
123	N	T	T	T	O	W	A	T	T	N	F	M	T	I	70	T	F	T	A	S	T	F	A	T	E	Y	T	I	T
124	Y	I	A	W	N	I	V	W	I	W	B	T	T	W	71	N	T	G	F	N	T	T	I	O	W	D	B	L	A
125	W	W	O	W	H	L	F	P	N	A	W	B	H	W	72	O	W	A	F	V	T	A	T	O	T	M	A	F	A
126	O	D	W	T	I	A	S	M	Y	S	H	A			73	T	W	V	B	I	A	W	D	I	T	A	C	T	T
127	I	O	B	A	F	F	S	B	T	H	A	S	Y	T	74	B	W	M	W	W	T	T	M	S	T	T	T	T	A
128	H	V	W	T	D	T	W	A	T	A	O	M	S	G	75	S	O	A	A	N	D	N	T	S	A	P	S	T	O
129	T	I	I	S	I	P	P	O	M	H	A	B	A	T	76	VV	S	W	T	W	A	T	S	O	A	S	S	F	S
130	M	C	I	I	I	B	A	T	I	T	I	M	A	A	77	T	T	T	A	T	O	T	T	L	C	T	T	T	S
131	T	A	F	T	Y	T	T	A	A	A	O	T	I	A	78	S	A	A	A	T	A	H	A	Y	W	I	A	B	A
132	T	K	H	L	A	B	N	D	A	O	T	A	T	A	79	W	M	B	A	I	D	Y	H	H	F	A	N	T	S
133	B	F	I	B	M	A	O	A	P	B	W	T	A	P	80	O	K	A	T	B	T	M	O	Y	W	O	H	T	T
134	S	A	M	T	B	F	H	V	T	T	A	S	H	H	81	O	O	F	A	Y	T	T	W	Y	W	A	W	Y	W
135	W	A	M	T	W	N	S	A	T	A	S	O	L	T	82	I	A	T	O	T	F	A	S	A	W	T	I	A	W

What to Make of it?

The existence of such an acrostic message built into the heart of *Shakespeare's Sonnets* is initially stunning. It comes in the form of a perfectly composed and correctly spelled sentence. Taken at face value, it is an ideal and unanswerable claim to authorship by Kit Marlowe. The starting point and the termination are clearly signalled. Furthermore, the two longest sections containing the most distinctive element of the message – the author's name – come at the beginning. It is this which prompts the investigator to tease out the rest of the message.

However, those readers with a background knowledge of cryptography will already be feeling uneasy about this solution. They will point out the irregularity between different line sections is a disqualifying feature because it allows for the construction of numerous, substantially different messages. These well-informed people should be congratulated because they are perfectly correct. The acrostic method is predicated on the principle that the letters of a message must be selected by an invariable rule. Thus, they will reason that in having a measure of irregularity, the message cannot be valid. In other words, it is no more than the cryptographer's equivalent of fool's gold.

At this point, we need to pause and take a deep breath. It is a general truth in cryptography, as with any other professional field, that a little knowledge can be a dangerous thing. Whilst it is a commonplace that fool's gold is named for its propensity to dupe greedy and gullible prospectors, it is less well known that pure gold is often found in association with pyrites. Therefore, the real fool may sometimes be the person with just enough expertise to chuckle knowingly when they come across gleaming specks of iron sulphide and walk on by – glowing a nimbus of smug self-satisfaction. Little will they be aware, they may be sauntering away from the mother of all mother-lodes.

When the stakes are high, the security of secret communications is paramount and simplistic assumptions a pitfall. Many an unfortunate Elizabethan had cause to rue the mechanical simplicity of his codes and ciphers while being hung, unmanned, disembowelled and quartered, or slowly broiled alive at the stake. Having worked undercover himself, Christopher Marlowe would have known all about that. Sophistication is very much your friend when life-endangering messages need to be concealed in plain sight. For this reason, the smarter and longer-lived specimen of secret agent made sure to keep his privities to himself by means not just of double but, sometimes, triple encryption.

With this principle in mind, I started to wonder if the irregular appearance of the message could be its strength, rather than its weakness. Might the zig-zag form have actually been drafted with care in order to encode a higher level of syntropy than four blunt words churned out by an unthinking automaton? If this message had been designed by the author of the very precise algorithms we have already seen in the *Sonnets*, would one not expect something ambitious in terms of construction, beauty and relevance? How might the author have set about to achieve such a result?

Enter the Language of Numbers

We recall from the examination of Sonnet 76 that the letters in a grid have location values according to their coordinates. In this case, it is not necessary to rely on the plotting of rows and columns because each letter has a unique locus: the line number from whence it originates. In many ways, this is a superior system because each letter has only one location value.

Following this system, we can see the first letter of the message has a value of 1835 because the 'K' of 'KIT' is the first letter of the 1835th line in the sequence – this being the second line of Sonnet 132. The full set of letter locations runs as follows:

K	1835	W	792
I	1756	R	615
T	1675	O	541
		T	467
M	1594	E	442
A	1493		
R	1392	T	417
L	1290	H	402
O	1225	I	387
W	1160	S	373
E	976		

We can now start looking for evidence that these numbers are not random. We need answers to some questions. Are there any patterns? If so, can they be understood to support the veracity of the message? How convincingly do they do this? What level of statistical (im)probability is involved? Does this come anywhere near William and Elizebeth Friedman's target of one in a thousand million?

A. Beginning, Middle and End

1. Central Point

In Renaissance poetry, the central point was regarded as 'sovereign', and in terms of number symbolism it had the highest significance. With nineteen letters, the central point of this message comes with the E at 976. For Christopher Marlowe, this number was indeed significant because it constitutes the Golden Section (or 'Divine Proportion') division of his name:

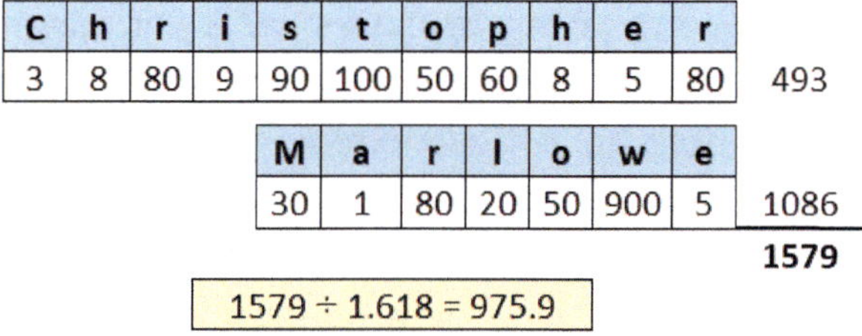

C	h	r	i	s	t	o	p	h	e	r	
3	8	80	9	90	100	50	60	8	5	80	493

M	a	r	l	o	w	e	
30	1	80	20	50	900	5	1086
							1579

1579 ÷ 1.618 = 975.9

2. Starting Point

The second most strategically important part of the message is the first letter, which appears at 1835. What can be noticed about the first and central letters is that they delimit the name '**K**IT MARLOWE'. The sum of the two numbers is 1835 + 976 = 2811. This has relevance because it measures the perimeter of an 'ark' (a 6 x 1 rectangle) with a length of 1205. Therefore, this container is tailor-made for the body of, 'Kit Marlowe':

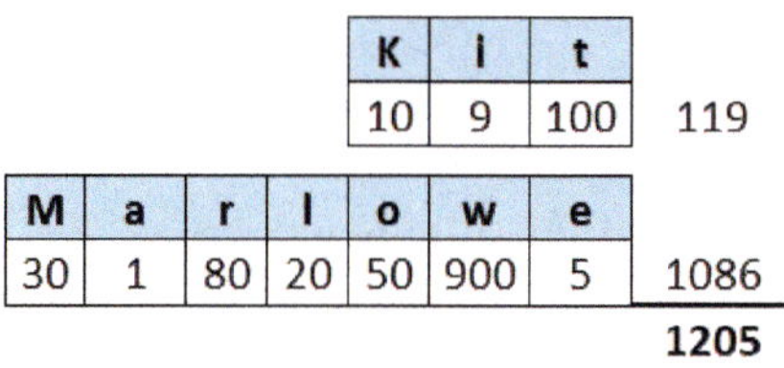

K	i	t	
10	9	100	119

M	a	r	l	o	w	e	
30	1	80	20	50	900	5	1086
							1205

Occurring out of the blue, the number 2811 would have little interpretive significance, but the contextual and topological features of its two components give it evidential weight.

3. End Point

The final letter of the message, the S of THIS, appears at square 373. This number is directly related to both 976 and 1579 by means of the Golden Section and the pentagonal geometry which governs it.

A five-pointed star, or pentagram, with a total length of 1579 (each side measuring 315.8) may be drawn within a pentagon whose perimeter is 1579 divide by the Golden Ratio (1.618) – 976 . The smaller pentagon which it encloses has a perimeter of 373. So the centre-point and the endpoint of the message, at 976 and 373, neatly define a pentagram of 1579 extent – a geometric symbol for the man 'Christopher Marlowe'.

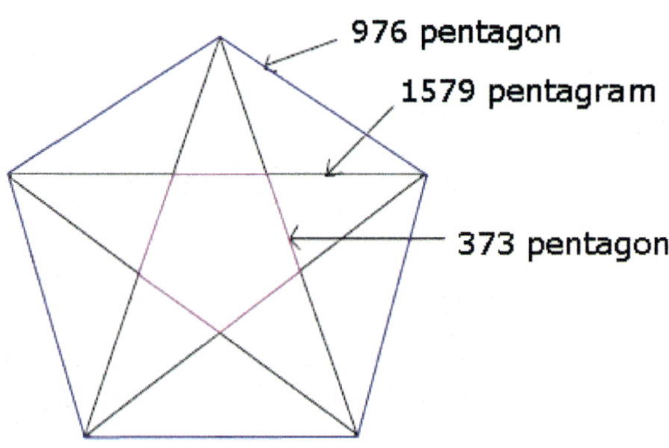

$$1579 \div 1.618 = 975.9$$
$$1579 \div 4.236 = 372.8$$

There may be symbolic importance in the fact that the message starts with a coffin-like container (the ark) and leads on to vibrant star (pentagram) at the end. It suggests a motif of *resurrection* that is both suitable for the resurrected poet and, potentially, for a Freemason. In the climax of the ritual to 'make' a

Master Mason, the candidate is raised from the dead – literally raised out of a coffin – and then given the 'five points of fellowship'.

4. The Final Word - 1579

In case there were any doubt about 976 and 373 pointing to the value of 'Christopher Marlowe' – 1579 – this number also makes an independent and unambiguous appearance in the message. The final word – THIS – is distinctive from the others because the letters of which it is comprised all lie adjacent to one another. The significance is proved because the sum of the letter values is exaqctly 1579.

373 + 387 + 402 + 417 = **1579**

It should also be noticed the numbers have the virtue of breaking down into 1206 and 373, which are the external and internal perimeters of the 1579 pentagram.

At this point, we are prompted to wonder if the 1579 value of THIS might be taken to imply a sub-message of, **'Kit Marlowe wrote *Christopher Marlowe*'**? If so, it raises the possibility that the full form of his name might provide a cryptographic key to the message's tertiary level of encryption – the way the acrostic line has been distorted.

5. Marlowe - 1086

Before moving on, there is one other small item worth noting. The 'M' forming the first letter of 'MARLOWE' comes in line 1594. This number suggests 1086, the gematria value of that name, by means of a simple cipher we have seen before. It forms the sum of its digit products: (1 x 086) + (10 x 86) + (108 x 6) = 1594.

Part A Summary

Of the four words in the message, the first two are actually 'Kit Marlowe' and the last counts the name Christopher Marlowe by gematria.[2] In addition, the positions of the first, central and final letters provide both the perimeter of an 'ark' for Kit Marlowe and define all the dimensions of a 1579 pentagram. The 'sovereign' central figure of 976, which unites both geometric forms, represents the poet's name divided by the Golden Section.

These numbers are not emerging in a haphazard form: they derive from the most strategic elements of the message. They are starting to make the kind of meaningful patterns that would be expected from a cleverly-designed cryptogram. If all these positive results are just flukes thrown up at random, it is extremely unlikely such 'luck' can extend any further.

B. The 'Christopher Marlowe' Cryptogram

While the start, centre and terminal points of the message can be interpreted in Marlowe's favour, what about its most striking feature: the seemingly drunken zigzag. Could there be something grander afoot? Dare one hope for an over-arching design?

Part 1

The fact that there are four words in the message is mirrored in the fact that there are just four letters in the centre of the sections comprised of four letters. These lie on the initial two lines (as can be seen below). The letters, here shown in red, K**IT** M**AR**LOWE WROTE THIS, are located in squares 1756, 1675, 1493 & 1392. The sum of these four is 6316. This is 1579 multiplied by four.

Considering their almost square arrangement in the grid, 6316 can be represented as a square whose sides each assay the name, 'Christopher Marlowe'.

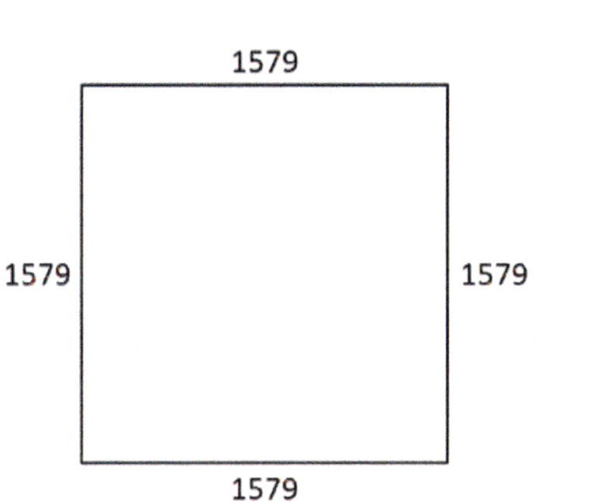

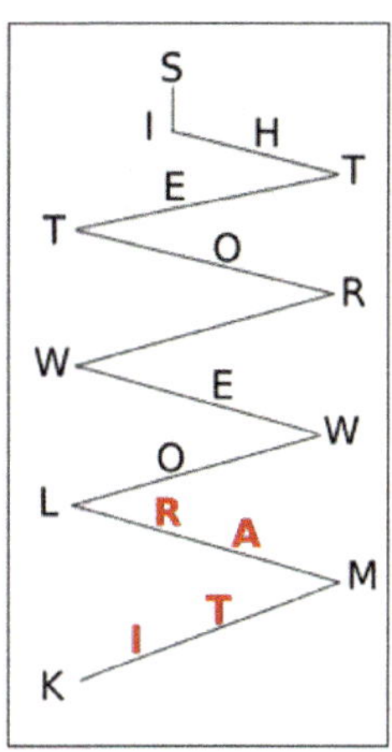

Part 2

Counting the letters on the left side of the zigzag - KIT MARLOWE WROTE THIS – yields a total of: 1835 + 1290 + 792 + 467 + 387 = 4771. In context of the square above, this is astonishingly propitious. 4771 measures the perimeter of that square which may be drawn inside a 1579-sided square and rotated such that its vertices divide the sides into sections of 493 and 1086. In other words, it splits the first square according to the values of 'Christopher' and 'Marlowe' exactly.

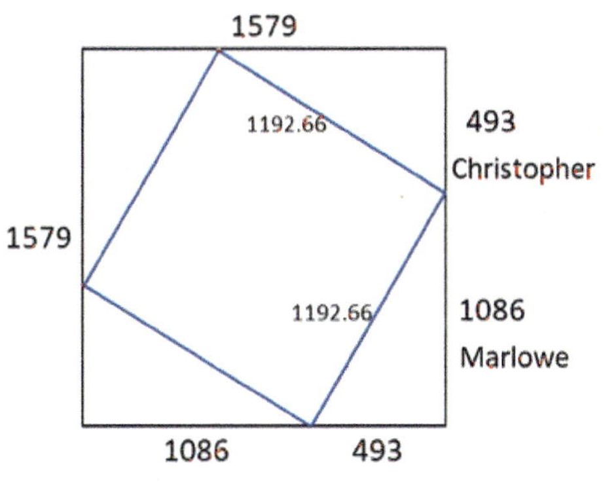

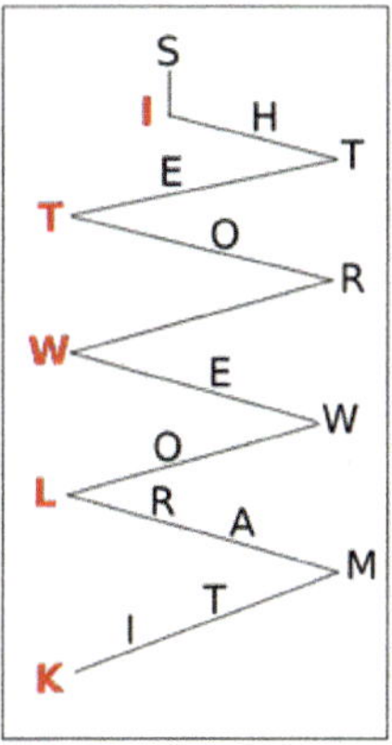

Perimeter of blue square: 1192.66 x 4 = 4770.65

How could two of the main structural features of a random zig-zag do this? Furthermore, how could they do this when the last word already sums to 1579, and when its centre and end letters divide 1579 perfectly according to its Golden Section proportions? The answer is that it is effectively impossible by chance. In fact, it would be remarkably challenging to design it.

Part 3

How might this impressive geometric signature be further developed? That is a question the constructor must have had in mind. It struck me, the most obvious way to do this would be to encircle the 1579-sided square. This would require a circle with a circumference of 7015: a diameter of 1579 x √2. I wondered if the letters down the right side of the zigzag would achieve this. If these and the terminal letter – KIT MARLOWE WROTE THIS – are counted, they yield a total of 1594 + 1160 + 615 + 417 + 373 = 4159. Unfortunately, this is well short. In fact, it is short by exactly 2856, but as this the value of his name written in Greek, Χριστοφερ Μαρλω, one may be entitled to think there is something worthy of investigation happening.

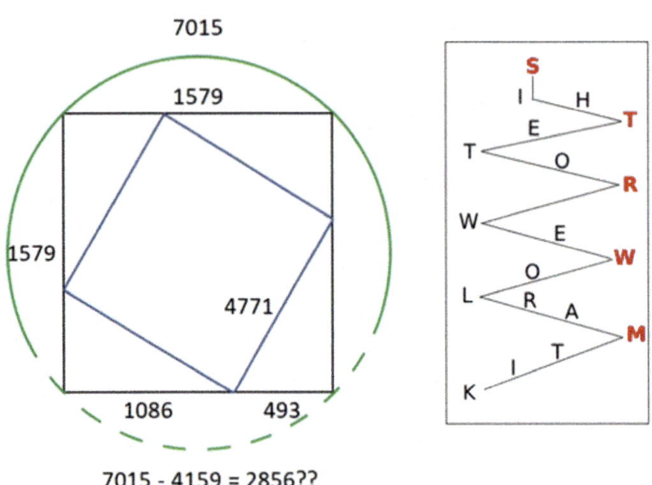

Perhaps the amount of shortfall is being drawn to our attention for some reason? Well, if 7015 is divided by 4159, it produces a decimal fraction of 1.6867. In this, there is an extremely precise measurement of the diagonal of the 4771-perimeter square, which sits in the 1579-sided square, and divides those sides in the proportions of 'Christopher' and 'Marlowe'. The actual measure is 1686.68.

This justifies completion of the circle and confirms the conceptualisation of 4771 as the perimeter of a square . . . which is very neat indeed. This goes beyond simple proof – it's the hallmark of genius.

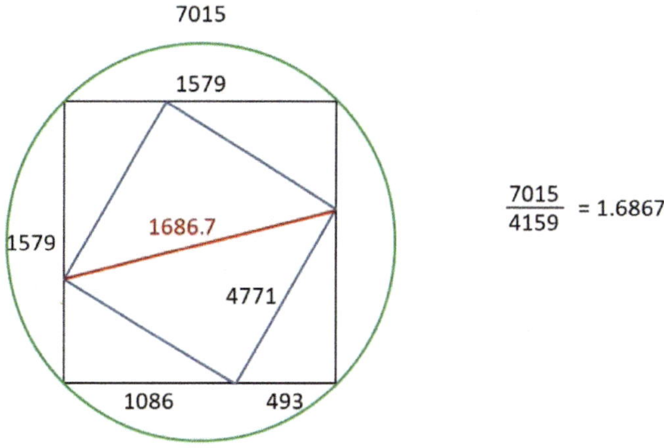

Part 4

The next stage requires nothing so complex, just all ten of the numbers forming the outside points of the zigzag:

1835 + 1290 + 792 + 467 + 387 + 1594 + 1160 + 615 + 417 + 373 = 8930

This measures the perimeter of the square which may be drawn around the 7015-circumference circle and whose sides measure 1579 x √2.[3]

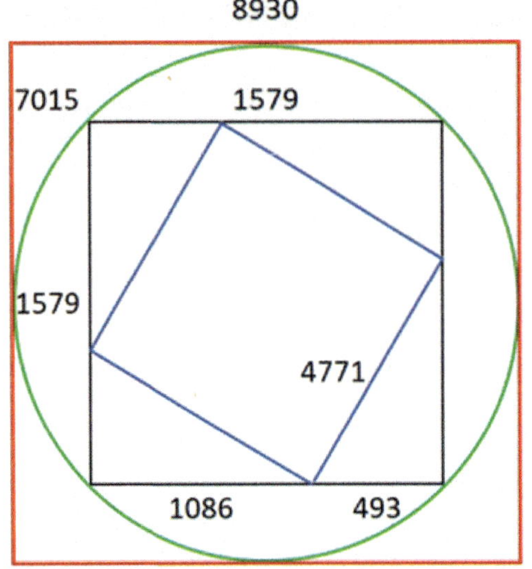

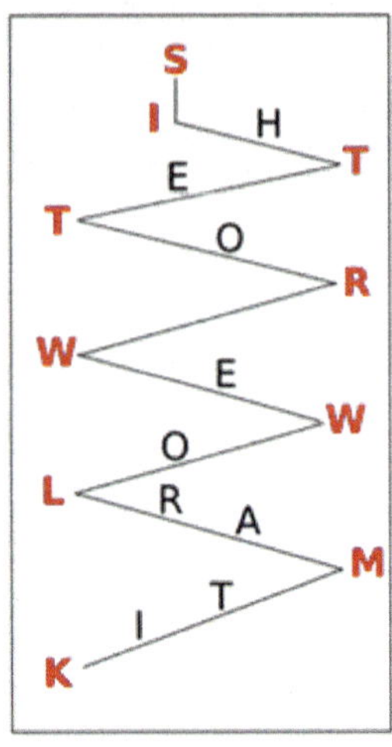

It can hardly be denied this is a highly impressive artefact to emerge from the main structural elements of an otherwise random path through an unsorted grid of letters. It is undeniably based on the number 1579, and further is broken down into components of 493 and 1086. Does it lend support the words of the acrostic message? What's the probability it just happens to be there by chance? How many monkeys with geometry kits and typewriters would be needed to produce a geometric signature for Christopher Marlowe of such perfection? Could anyone have done better?

Part 5

So far one component remains unaccounted for. This is the column of five remaining letters coming up the centre, all of which are located in the middle of three-letter lines. If the message were smoke, 'Brownian motion' would dictate that these should be devoid of the smallest nano-quark of significance; but not so if the message were engineered by one of the greatest minds of the Renaissance. The letters are KIT MARLOWE WROTE THIS and they have values of 1225 + 976 + 541 + 442 + 402 = 3586.

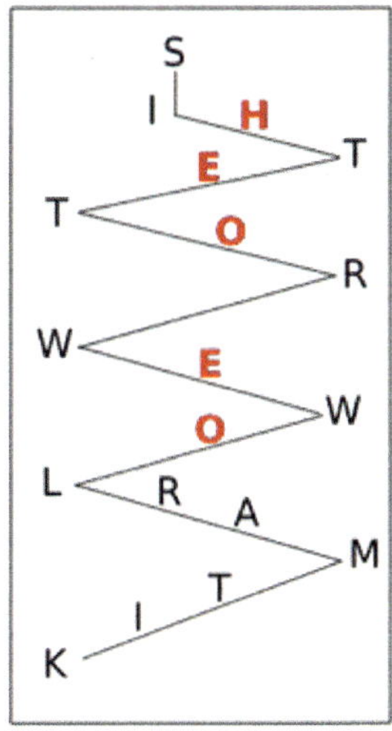

This number can be no accident because it measures the perimeter of a rectangle with sides of 214 and 1579. These are the values of 'Christopher Marlowe' counted by the two codes of English gematria, 'S' and 'L'. The poet's name is once more *squared*.

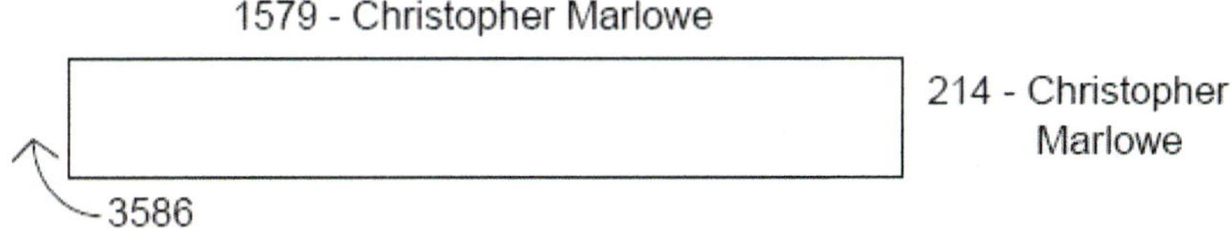

According to the S-code, his name is counted:

C	h	r	i	s	t	o	p	h	e	r	
3	8	17	9	18	19	14	15	8	5	17	133
				M	a	r	l	o	w	e	
				12	1	17	11	14	21	5	81
											214

A justification for using the subsidiary gematria code may lie in a surprisingly pertinent feature of the rectangle – namely, its diagonal.

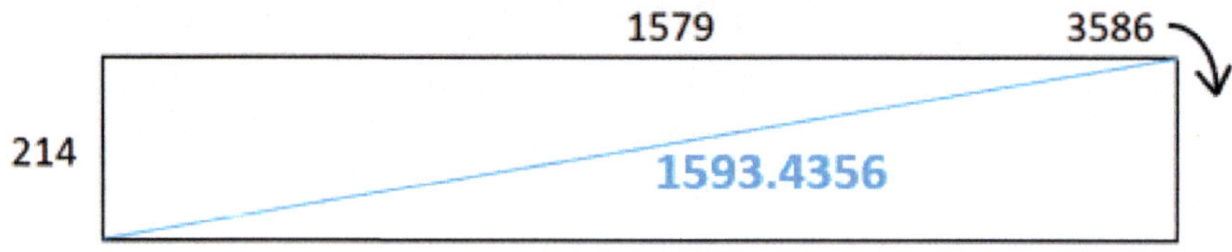

If the diagonal marks a year and a fraction thereof, it takes us to between 26th May and 8th June 1593 (in the Gregorian calendar) – according to how the fraction is rounded. Just between the two lies 30th May 1593, when the murder of England's pre-eminent playwright was reported in the port town of Deptford, and 1st June when a corpse with a mutilated face was buried in an unmarked grave in the parish churchyard.

Part 6

One way of looking at the message as a whole is to break it down into three discrete sections: the outside, the paired letters inside sections and the single letters inside sections. This yields three discreet 'squaring' figures for 1579: the square with sides of 1579, the square with sides of 1579 x √2 and the 1579 by 214 rectangle (6316, 8930 & 3586):

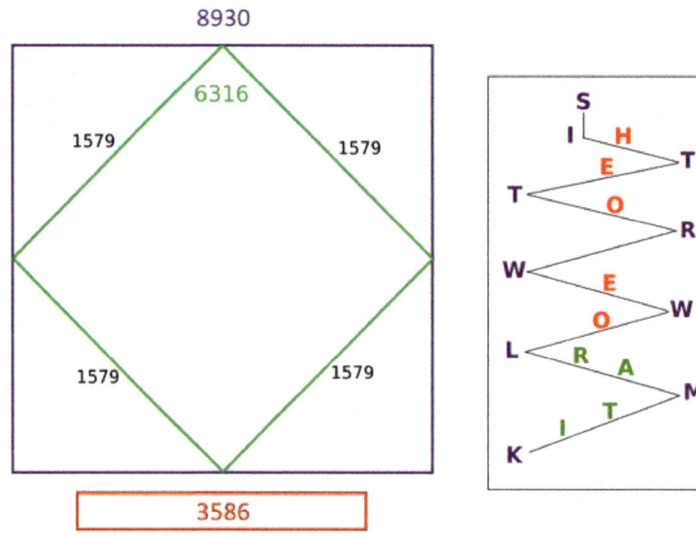

However, as two of the figures already interlock, it makes sense to integrate the 3586 rectangle, too. There is a visual hint for this: as the outside of the zigzag (the purple square) encloses the interior twinned points (the green square), it should also enclose the interior single points (the red rectangle). The obvious way of doing this is to place the red rectangle inside the 1579 square:

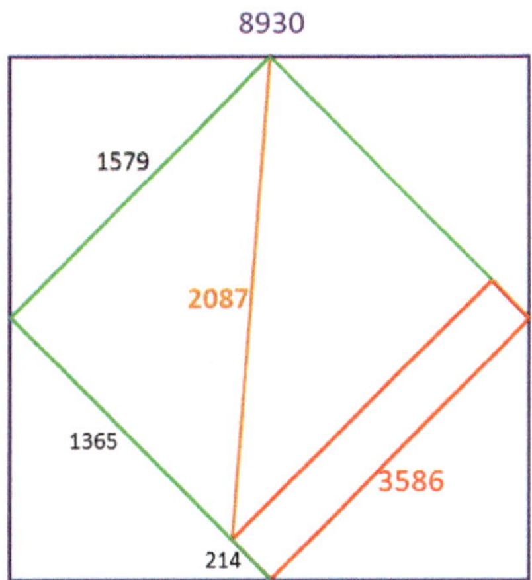

This placement leads to a new diagonal with a length of just over 2087. This number constitutes 1205 multiplied by the square root of three. As such, it can signify the diagonal of a cube with sides of 1205 – hence, a *cubing* symbol for 'Kit Marlowe'.

What is more, a new right-angle triangle is created. This has a perimeter of 1579 + 2087 + 1365 = 5031. If this number is extended through the addition of its divisors, it takes us to 8008:

1	5031
3	1677
9	559
13	387
39	129
43	117
8008	

8008 is relevant because it marks the difference between the 12 edges and the 4 diagonals of a cube whose sides measure 1579 – a *cubing* symbol of 'Christopher Marlowe':

$$(12 \times 1579) - (4 \times (1579 \times \sqrt{3})) = 8008.367$$

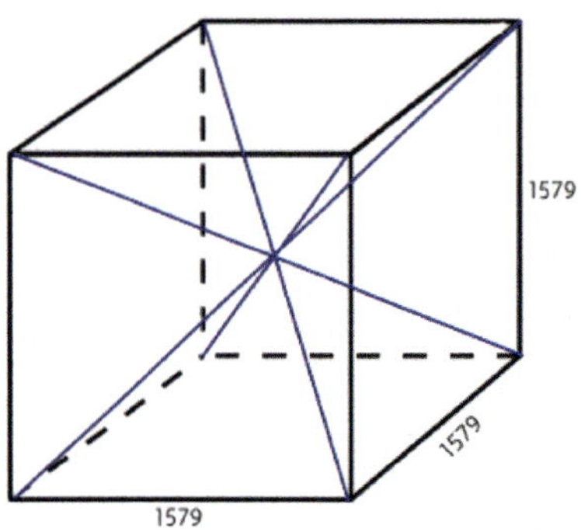

Part 7

The grand total of the letter locations for the whole message also tells of the constructor's skill rather than the cobbling and bodging that would be necessary to knock a random figure into service. The sum of these is 18832:

1835 + 1756 + 1675 + 1594 + 1493 + 1392 + 1290 + 1225 + 1160 + 976 + 792 + 615 + 541 + 467 + 442 + 417 + 402 + 387 + 373 = 18832

How, one might wonder, could 18832 have relevance to the name Christopher Marlowe? It couldn't be connected to the *squaring* of his name by means of Euclid's 47th Proposition, could it? Surely not.

By now, we are well aware the key to dividing a 1579-sided square into the proportions fitting 'Christopher' and 'Marlowe' lies in the right-angled triangle with perpendiculars of 493 and 1086, and hypotenuse of 1192.66. It so happens that if 18832 is divided by 1579, the result is 11.9265 – thus, coming within 0.99999 of the digits of the hypotenuse. No other five-digit number comes closer than 18832 to doing so.

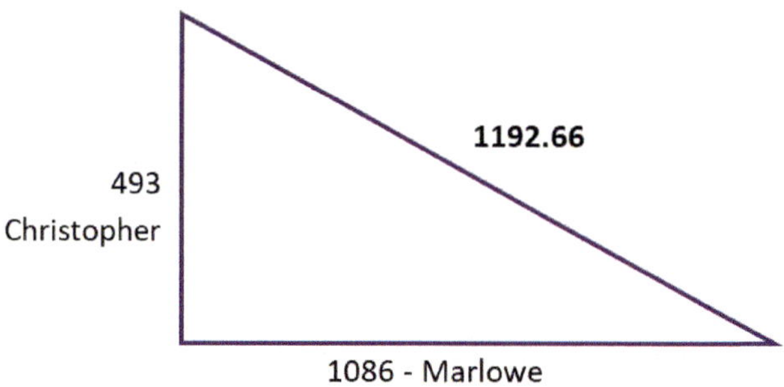

Part 8

There is more. Taking 1579 away from the total of 18832 can be justified as the trimming of the final word to leave just KIT MARLOWE WROTE. The residual value is 17253, and when this is divided by 1579, the experience is one of *déjà vu*. The result is 10.926 – which supplies the digits measuring the hypotenuse of a 119 by 1086 right-angled triangle, *squaring* the names 'Kit' and 'Marlowe'.

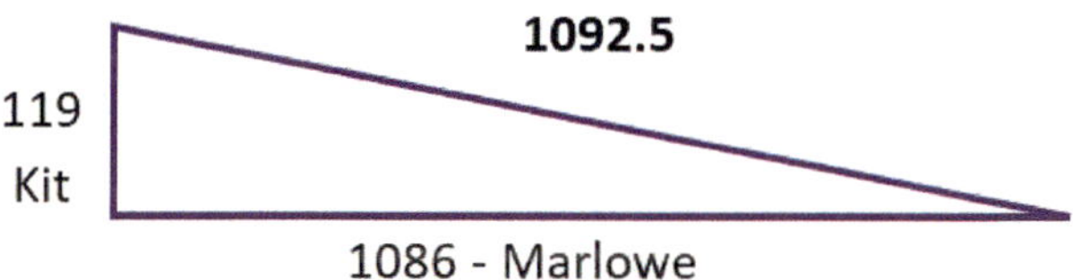

Part 9

Almost miraculously, there is a third relevant property of 18832 because it pulls the 1579-sided square up into three dimensions. It was seen how THIS is valued at 1579, and how the four letters at the centre of the first two lines are valued at 4 x 1579. If the latter denote the sides of a square, then the former can point in the direction of a third dimension – thereby indicating a cube. If we take these five lengths of 1579 away from 18832, the remainder is 10937. This figure supplies the (missing) four diagonals of the cube with sides of 1579. [4]

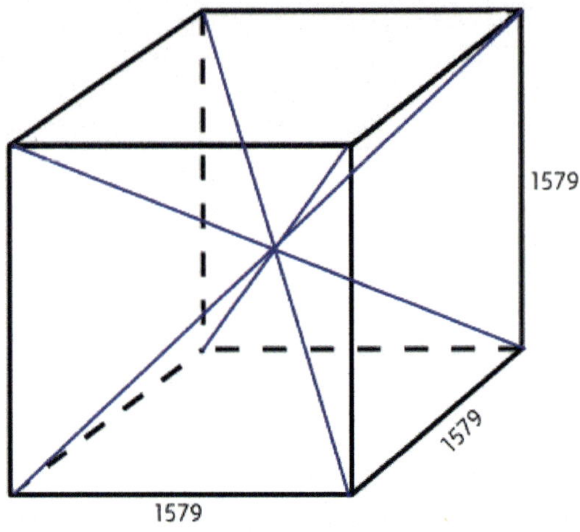

Part 10

An additional plank of support for this 1579-sided cube arrives courtesy of a feature noticed right at the beginning of the investigation. There are actually two regularly spaced 'KITM' letter sequences starting from line/square 1835. The one used for the primary message had a spacing of three across and six up while the other went two across and two up. This apparently redundant sequence has letter placement values of 1835 + 1809 + 1783 + 1759 = 7186. If this replaces the original 'KITM' value (of 1835 + 1756 + 1675 + 1594 = 6860), a new overall total for the message of 19158 is arrived at. [5]

One indication this could be significant comes because the new 'M' of 'MARLOWE' is located at 1759 – a *numerical anagram* of 1579. Then if 1579 is taken from 19158 (e.g. by once again cutting 'THIS'), the remainder is 17579, which can be regarded as another rearrangement of 1579. The process can then be continued until a total of twelve lengths of 1579 can be hewn – and just 210 remains. By this means, all twelve edges of a 1579-sided cube are supplied. The word 'cube' itself has a gematria value of 210.

C	U	B	E	
3	200	2	5	**210**

Part 11

The 7186 value of the new 'KITM' is even more significant when extended through the addition of its divisors:

1	7186
2	3593
	10782

10782 measures the combined perimeter and diagonals of a square with sides of 1579:

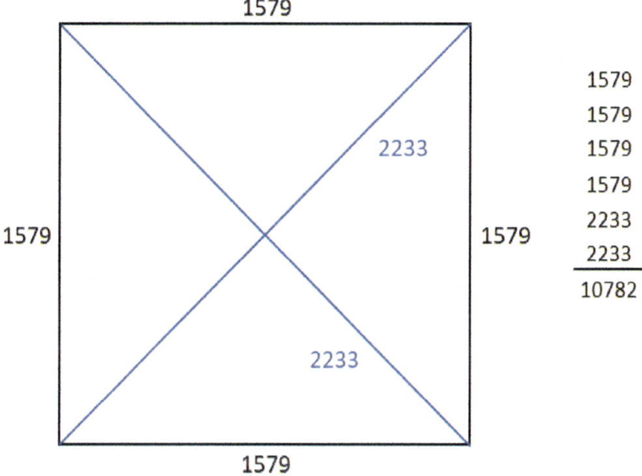

The skill with which this puzzle has been constructed is dizzying.

C. The Message Itself

So far, the gematria value of the message itself has not been addressed. Why did the author write '**Kit Marlowe wrote this**', rather than, for example, 'Chr. Marle penned these sugared lines'? Aside from being brief and to the point, the message must have been chosen because its gematria value is 2547. This measures the perimeter of *the other* right-angle triangle that *squares* his name. It has an upright of 493 and a hypotenuse of 1086:

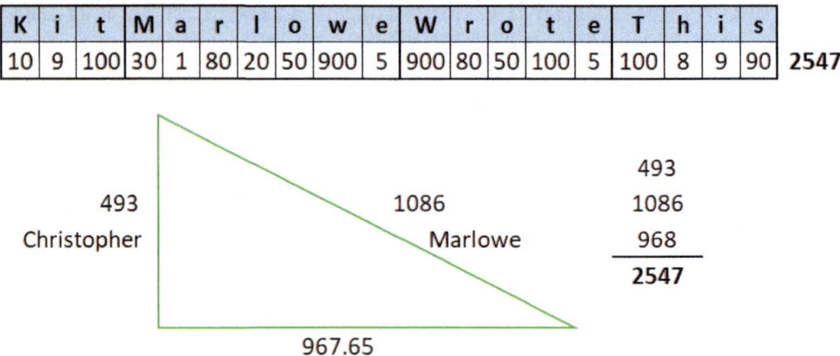

K	i	t	M	a	r	l	o	w	e	W	r	o	t	e	T	h	i	s	
10	9	100	30	1	80	20	50	900	5	900	80	50	100	5	100	8	9	90	**2547**

This triangle has an extraordinary benefit for the author in that it leads on to a rectangle with sides of 493 and 967.65. The rectangle has a perimeter of 2921. Here is the value of, **'Christopher Marlowe wrote this'**.

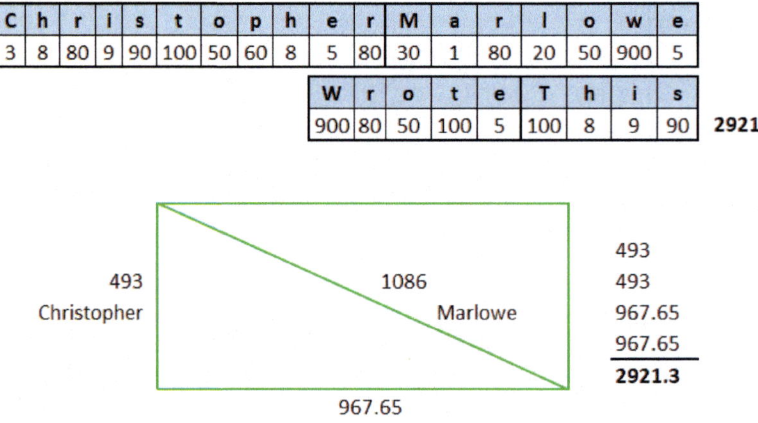

C	h	r	i	s	t	o	p	h	e	r	M	a	r	l	o	w	e
3	8	80	9	90	100	50	60	8	5	80	30	1	80	20	50	900	5

W	r	o	t	e	T	h	i	s	
900	80	50	100	5	100	8	9	90	**2921**

In geometric terms, the overall pattern fits neatly into a circle whose diameter is 1086 – 'Marlowe'. This circle simultaneously bounds the three corners of the 2547 triangle and the four corners of the 2921 rectangle:

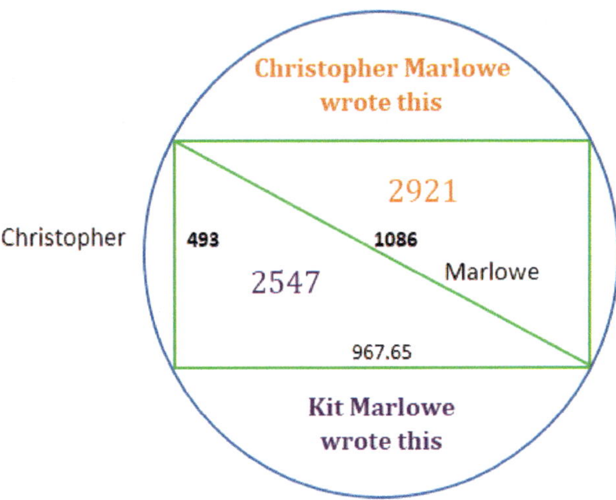

This figure unites the squaring of his name with the duplication of the message inside a 'Marlowe' circle. What is the probability of this fourfold 'coincidence'? How many atoms are there in the universe? More than are dreamt of in most cryptographers' philosophies.

Summary

The acrostic is 100% authentic. Kit Marlowe wrote it.

Chapter 9 Notes

---

[1] There are actually two sonnets with irregular line numbers. Sonnet 99 has 15 lines and sonnet 126 has 12 lines. These irregularities did not impact the basic form of thc grid.
[2] The third word - 'WROTE' - has a location total of 2857, which is within a single unit of the name Χριστοφερ Μαρλω – 'Christopher Marlowe' (2856).
[3] The exact figure is 8932.17. However, the 8930 perimeter square leads to an inner square with sides of 1578.62, which rounds to 1579.
[4] Each diagonal measures 1579 x rt3. Thus 2734.9 x 4 = 10939.6. However, if one works backwards from 10937, the diagonals lead to a cube with sides of 1578.62. Rounded to the nearest whole number, this gives 1579.
[5] This would require the message line to make a vertical rise of 19 squares from the new 'M' to the 'A' of 'MARLOWE'.

10

Kit's Cryptogram – Part 2

A critical validating feature of the acrostic has been the way every element of its design can be accounted for. There are no extraneous components and no loose ends. However, at the outset of the quest for a message, a great profusion of KITs was discovered. The only orderly thing about them seemed that they all sprouted from two points of origin: two 'K' nodes. What is going on here? Were these KITs thrown out like chaff to confuse radar-seeking missiles, or do they form part of some greater cryptogram?

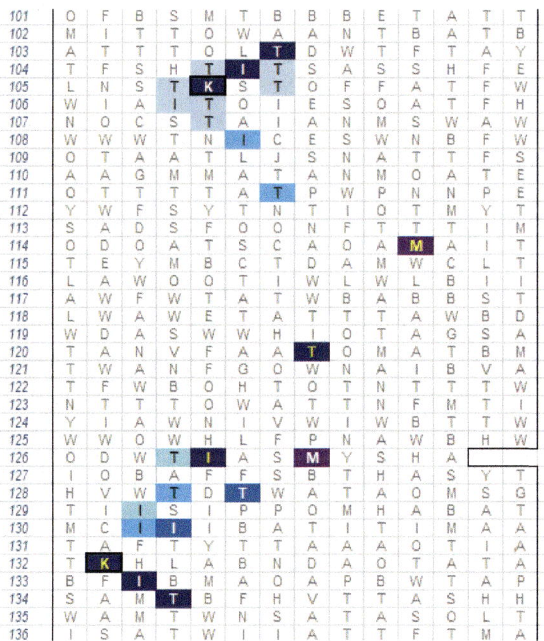

101	O	F	B	S	M	T	B	B	B	E	T	A	T	T
102	M	I	T	T	O	W	A	A	N	T	B	A	T	B
103	A	T	T	T	O	L	T	D	W	T	F	T	A	Y
104	T	F	S	H	T	I	T	S	A	S	S	H	F	E
105	L	N	S	T	K	S	T	O	F	F	A	T	F	W
106	W	I	A	I	T	O	I	E	S	O	A	T	F	H
107	N	O	C	S	T	A	I	A	N	M	S	W	A	W
108	W	W	W	T	N	I	C	E	S	W	N	B	F	W
109	O	T	A	A	T	L	J	S	N	A	T	T	F	S
110	A	A	G	M	M	A	T	A	N	M	O	A	T	E
111	O	T	T	T	T	A	T	P	W	P	N	N	P	E
112	Y	W	F	S	Y	T	N	T	I	O	T	M	Y	T
113	S	A	D	S	F	O	O	N	F	T	T	T	I	M
114	O	D	O	A	T	S	C	A	O	A	M	A	I	T
115	T	E	Y	M	B	C	T	D	A	M	W	C	L	T
116	L	A	W	O	O	T	I	W	L	W	L	B	I	I
117	A	W	F	W	T	A	T	W	B	A	B	B	S	T
118	L	W	A	W	E	T	A	T	T	T	A	W	B	D
119	W	D	A	S	W	W	H	I	O	T	A	G	S	A
120	T	A	N	V	F	A	A	T	O	M	A	T	B	M
121	T	W	A	N	F	G	O	W	N	A	I	B	V	A
122	T	F	W	B	O	H	T	O	T	N	T	T	T	W
123	N	T	T	T	O	W	A	T	T	N	F	M	T	I
124	Y	I	A	W	N	I	V	W	I	W	B	T	T	W
125	W	W	O	W	H	L	F	P	N	A	W	B	H	W
126	O	D	W	T	I	A	S	M	Y	S	H	A		
127	I	O	B	A	F	F	S	B	T	H	A	S	Y	T
128	H	V	W	T	D	T	W	A	T	A	O	M	S	G
129	T	I	I	S	I	P	P	O	M	H	A	B	A	T
130	M	C	I	I	I	B	A	T	I	T	I	M	A	A
131	T	A	F	T	Y	T	T	A	A	A	O	T	I	A
132	T	K	H	L	A	B	N	D	A	O	T	A	T	A
133	B	F	I	B	M	A	O	A	P	B	W	T	A	P
134	S	A	M	T	B	F	H	V	T	T	A	S	H	H
135	W	A	M	T	W	N	S	A	T	A	S	O	L	T
136	I	S	A	T	W	I	I	A	T	T	F	T	M	A

A. The 'KIT' Nodes

The first question that springs to mind is, what is the purpose of the second 'KIT node' at square 1462 (Sonnet 105, line 5)? Given the very precise planning we have seen already, it is unthinkable this other node would not be an integral part of the scheme. So, what function does it serve? How does it relate to the first 'KIT node', where the message begins?

To start with, I worked out the separation between the two 'K' letters. Moving from the origin of the message at 1835 (132/2) to the second node at 1462 (105/5) requires a shift of three squares to the right and 27 squares up. It then occurred to me that this step could be repeated. Making the same move of three right and 27 up from 1426 landed me at square 1086 (78/8). This is home territory: it is the square with the value of 'Marlowe'. So, of all the squares possible, the two 'KIT nodes' are perfectly aligned with the square carrying the number of 'Marlowe'. What are the odds: 'Kit' and 'Marlowe'? The chances are actually smaller than you might think because two squares in the grid picked at random will more often than not align with some location outside the grid. I am no statistician, but it seems clear there must be many thousands of possible locations. Would any other square among all those thousands be more suitable than 1086?

I was also gratified to find the requisite move of 3 x 27 defines a block of 81 squares, and 81 is the value of 'Marlowe' by the S-code. That should put a couple more zeros on the 'improbability quotient'. There is nothing random here.

Next, I found I was able to continue the line from the KITs, past 1086, and on to two more contact points before it went off the right edge. The five points lie at squares 1835, 1462, 1086, 711 & 336. What is striking about this group is that not only does 1086 lie at the centre of the line, but simple geometry dictates the sum of the numbers is 5430, which is 1086 times 5. Therefore, it gives the total length of a 1086-sided pentacle – the symbol of a man called 'Marlowe'. It is neat that it is entirely generated by the placement of the two 'KIT' nodes.

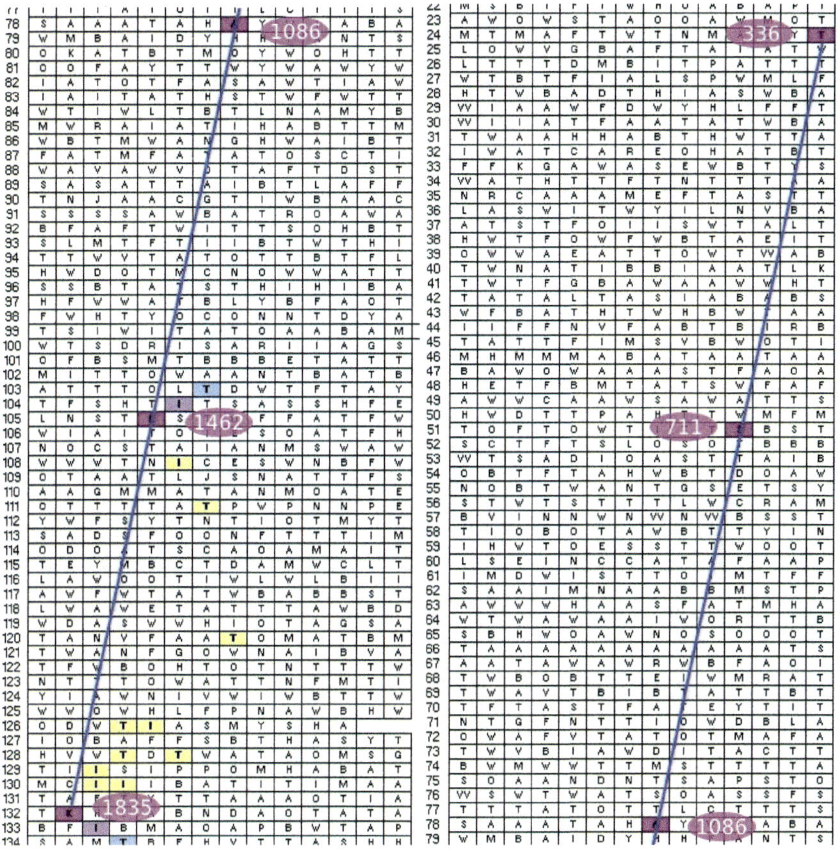

78	S	A	A	A	T	A	H	[illegible]	Y	[illegible]	[illegible]	A	B	A
79	W	M	B	A	I	D	Y	H	H	[illegible]	[illegible]	N	T	S
80	O	K	A	T	B	T	M	O	Y	W	O	H	T	T
81	O	O	F	A	Y	T	T	W	Y	W	A	W	Y	W
82	I	A	T	O	T	F	A	S	A	W	T	I	A	W
83	I	A	I	T	A	T	H	S	T	W	F	W	T	T
84	W	T	I	W	L	T	B	T	L	N	A	M	Y	B
85	M	W	R	A	I	A	T	I	H	A	B	T	T	M
86	W	B	T	M	W	A	N	G	H	W	A	I	B	T
87	F	A	T	M	F	A	I	A	T	O	S	C	T	I
88	W	A	V	A	W	V	O	T	A	F	T	D	S	T
89	S	A	S	A	T	T	A	I	B	T	L	A	F	F
90	T	N	J	A	A	C	G	T	I	W	B	A	A	C
91	S	S	S	S	A	W	B	A	T	R	O	A	W	A
92	B	F	A	F	T	W	I	T	T	S	O	H	B	T
93	S	L	M	T	F	T	I	I	B	T	W	T	H	I
94	T	T	W	V	T	A	T	O	T	T	B	T	F	L
95	H	W	D	O	T	M	C	N	O	W	W	A	T	T
96	S	S	B	T	A	T	S	T	H	I	H	I	B	A
97	H	F	W	W	A	T	B	L	Y	B	F	A	O	T
98	F	W	H	T	Y	O	C	O	N	N	T	D	Y	A
99	T	S	I	W	I	T	A	T	O	A	A	B	A	M
100	W	T	S	D	R	I	S	A	R	I	I	A	G	S
101	O	F	B	S	M	T	B	B	B	E	T	A	T	T
102	M	I	T	T	O	W	A	A	N	T	B	A	T	B
103	A	T	T	T	O	L	T	D	W	T	F	T	A	Y
104	T	F	S	H	T	I	T	S	A	S	S	H	F	E
105	L	N	S	T	[illegible]	S	[illegible]	[illegible]	F	F	A	T	F	W
106	W	I	A	I	T	O	[illegible]	E	S	O	A	T	F	H
107	N	O	C	S	T	A	I	A	N	M	S	W	A	W
108	W	W	W	T	N	I	C	E	S	W	N	B	F	W
109	O	T	A	A	T	L	J	S	N	A	T	T	F	S
110	A	A	G	M	M	A	T	A	N	M	O	A	T	E
111	O	T	T	T	T	A	T	P	W	P	N	N	P	E
112	Y	W	F	S	Y	T	N	T	I	O	T	M	Y	T
113	S	A	D	S	F	O	O	N	F	T	T	T	I	M
114	O	D	O	A	T	S	C	A	O	A	M	A	I	T
115	T	E	Y	M	B	C	T	D	A	M	W	C	L	T
116	L	A	W	O	O	T	I	W	L	W	L	B	I	I
117	A	W	F	W	T	A	T	W	B	A	B	B	S	T
118	L	W	A	W	E	T	A	T	T	T	A	W	B	D
119	W	D	A	S	W	W	H	I	O	T	A	G	S	A
120	T	A	N	V	F	A	A	T	O	M	A	T	B	M
121	T	W	A	N	F	G	O	W	N	A	I	B	V	A
122	T	F	W	B	O	H	T	O	T	N	T	T	T	W
123	N	T	T	T	O	W	A	T	T	N	F	M	T	I
124	Y	I	A	W	N	I	V	W	I	W	B	T	T	W
125	W	W	O	W	H	L	F	P	N	A	W	B	H	W
126	O	D	W	T	I	A	S	M	Y	S	H	A		
127	I	O	B	A	F	F	S	B	T	H	A	S	Y	T
128	H	V	W	T	D	T	W	A	T	A	O	M	S	G
129	T	I	I	S	I	P	P	O	M	H	A	B	A	T
130	M	C	I	I	I	B	A	T	I	T	I	M	A	A
131	T	A	F	T	Y	T	T	A	A	A	O	T	I	A
132	T	K	H	[illegible]	A	B	N	D	A	O	T	A	T	A
133	B	F	I	B	M	A	O	A	P	B	W	T	A	P
134	S	A	M	T	R	F	H	V	T	T	A	S	H	H

23	A	W	O	W	S	T	A	O	O	A	W	M	O	T
24	M	T	M	A	F	T	W	T	N	M	[illegible]	[illegible]	Y	T
25	L	O	W	V	G	B	A	F	T	A	I	A	T	V
26	L	T	T	T	D	M	B	I	T	P	A	T	T	T
27	W	T	B	T	F	I	A	L	S	P	W	M	L	F
28	H	T	W	B	A	D	T	H	I	A	S	W	B	A
29	VV	I	A	A	W	F	D	W	Y	H	L	F	F	T
30	VV	I	I	A	T	F	A	A	T	A	T	W	B	A
31	T	W	A	A	H	H	A	B	T	H	W	T	T	A
32	I	W	A	T	C	A	R	E	O	H	A	T	B	T
33	F	F	K	G	A	W	A	S	E	W	B	T	Y	S
34	VV	A	T	H	T	T	F	T	N	T	T	T	A	A
35	N	R	C	A	A	A	M	E	F	T	A	S	T	T
36	L	A	S	W	I	T	W	Y	I	L	N	V	B	A
37	A	T	S	T	F	O	I	I	S	W	T	A	L	T
38	H	W	T	F	O	W	F	W	B	T	A	E	I	T
39	O	W	W	A	E	A	T	T	O	W	T	VV	A	B
40	T	W	N	A	T	I	B	B	I	A	A	T	L	K
41	T	W	T	F	G	B	A	W	A	A	W	W	H	T
42	T	A	T	A	L	T	A	S	I	A	B	A	B	S
43	W	F	B	A	T	H	T	W	H	B	W	T	A	A
44	I	I	F	F	N	V	F	A	B	T	B	I	R	B
45	T	A	T	T	F	I	M	S	V	B	W	O	T	I
46	M	H	M	M	M	A	B	A	T	A	A	T	A	A
47	B	A	W	O	W	A	A	A	S	T	F	A	O	A
48	H	E	T	F	B	M	T	A	T	S	W	F	A	F
49	A	W	W	C	A	A	W	S	A	W	A	T	T	S
50	H	W	D	T	T	P	A	H	T	T	W	M	F	M
51	T	O	F	T	O	W	T	[illegible]	[illegible]	T	[illegible]	B	S	T
52	S	C	T	F	T	S	L	O	S	O	T	B	B	B
53	VV	T	S	A	D	I	O	A	S	T	T	A	I	B
54	O	B	T	F	T	A	H	W	B	T	D	O	A	W
55	N	O	B	T	W	A	N	T	G	S	E	T	S	Y
56	S	T	W	T	S	T	T	T	L	W	C	R	A	M
57	B	V	I	N	N	W	N	VV	N	VV	B	S	S	T
58	T	I	O	B	O	T	A	W	B	T	T	Y	I	N
59	I	H	W	T	O	E	S	S	T	T	W	O	O	T
60	L	S	E	I	N	C	C	A	T	A	F	A	A	P
61	I	M	D	W	I	S	T	T	O	I	M	T	F	F
62	S	A	A	I	M	N	A	A	B	B	M	S	T	P
63	A	W	W	W	H	A	A	S	F	A	T	M	H	A
64	W	T	W	A	W	A	A	I	W	O	R	T	T	B
65	S	B	H	W	O	A	W	N	O	S	O	O	O	T
66	T	A	A	A	A	A	A	A	A	A	A	A	T	S
67	A	A	T	A	W	A	W	R	W	B	F	A	O	I
68	T	W	B	O	B	T	T	E	I	W	M	R	A	T
69	T	W	A	V	T	B	I	B	T	A	T	T	B	T
70	T	F	T	A	S	T	F	A	T	E	Y	T	I	T
71	N	T	G	F	N	T	T	I	O	W	D	B	L	A
72	O	W	A	F	V	T	A	T	O	T	M	A	F	A
73	T	W	V	B	I	A	W	D	I	T	A	C	T	T
74	B	W	M	W	W	T	T	M	S	T	T	T	T	A
75	S	O	A	A	N	D	N	T	S	A	P	S	T	O
76	VV	S	W	T	W	A	T	S	O	A	S	S	F	S
77	T	T	T	A	T	O	T	T	L	C	T	T	T	S
78	S	A	A	A	T	A	H	[illegible]	Y	[illegible]	[illegible]	A	B	A
79	W	M	B	A	I	D	Y	H	H	[illegible]	[illegible]	N	T	S

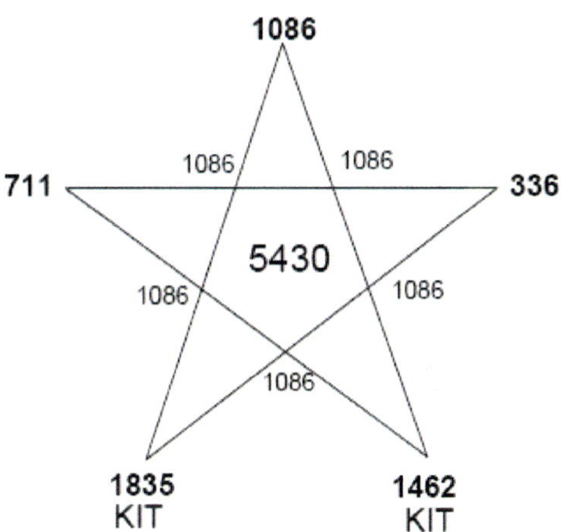

Since the 'K's of the two 'KIT' nodes line up meaningfully with other squares, I wondered if the 'I's and the 'T's might do, too. Plotting out from these letters yielded me two more squares for the 'I's and two more for the 'T's.

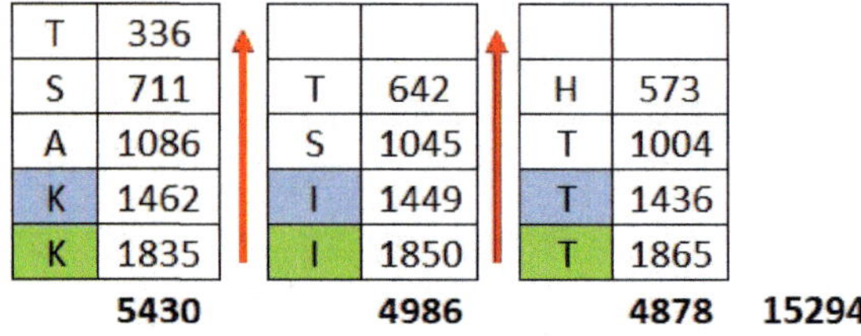

T	336					
S	711	T	642	H	573	
A	1086	S	1045	T	1004	
K	1462	I	1449	T	1436	
K	1835	I	1850	T	1865	
	5430		**4986**		**4878**	**15294**

The grand total of all the letter locations is 15294. This can be represented as the interlocking triangles of a hexagram with sides of 2549. As the sum of 1205 and 1344, this serves symbolically to bring together 'Kit Marlowe' and 'William Shakespeare'. Now, why would the author of the *Sonnets* want to suggest that?

W	i	l	l	i	a	m	S	h	a	k	e	s	p	e	a	r	e	
900	9	20	20	9	1	30	90	8	1	10	5	90	60	5	1	80	5	**1344**

B. The 'Kit' Lines

On the grid below, it can be seen that the 'KIT' node at 1462 is the origin of two iterations of that name plotted in straight lines, while the node at 1835 yields five of these (although one is superimposed on another). It looks like there may be another plan here. A logical inference is that these seven lines point to certain squares on the right edge of the grid.

The cryptographic purpose seems to be confirmed by the only square which is triangulated by lines coming from both nodes. This is square 1344, and, as seen above, 1344 is the gematria value of, 'William Shakespeare'.

95	H	W	D	D	I	M	C	N	D	W	W	A	I	I	
96	S	S	B	T	A	T	S	T	H	I	H	I	B	A	1344
97	H	F	W	W	A	T	B	L	Y	B	F	A	O	T	
98	F	W	H	T	Y	O	C	O	N	N	T	D	Y	A	
99	T	S	I	W	I	T	A	T	O	A	A	B	A	M	B
100	W	T	S	D	R	I	S	A	R	I	I	A	G	S	
101	O	F	B	S	M	T	B	B	B	E	T	A	T	T	
102	M	I	T	T	O	W	A	A	N	T	B	A	T	B	
103	A	T	T	T	O	L	T	D	W	T	F	T	A	Y	
104	T	F	S	H	T	I	T	S	A	S	S	H	F	E	1462
105	L	N	S	T	K	S	T	O	F	F	A	T	F	W	
106	W	I	A	I	T	O	I	E	S	O	A	T	F	H	
107	N	O	C	S	T	A	I	A	N	M	S	W	A	W	
108	W	W	W	T	N	I	C	E	S	W	N	B	F	W	1513
109	O	T	A	A	T	L	J	S	N	A	T	T	F	S	
110	A	A	G	M	M	A	T	A	N	M	O	A	T	E	
111	O	T	T	T	T	A	T	P	W	P	N	N	P	E	
112	Y	W	F	S	Y	T	N	T	I	O	T	M	Y	T	
113	S	A	D	S	F	O	O	N	F	T	T	T	I	M	
114	O	D	O	A	T	S	C	A	O	A	M	A	I	T	
115	T	E	Y	M	B	C	T	D	A	M	W	C	L	T	
116	L	A	W	O	O	T	I	W	L	W	L	B	I	I	
117	A	W	F	W	T	A	T	W	B	A	B	B	S	T	
118	L	W	A	W	E	T	A	T	T	T	A	W	B	D	
119	W	D	A	S	W	W	H	I	O	T	A	G	S	A	
120	T	A	N	V	F	A	A	T	O	M	A	T	B	M	1681
121	T	W	A	N	F	G	O	W	N	A	I	B	V	A	
122	T	F	W	B	O	H	T	O	T	N	T	T	T	W	
123	N	T	T	T	O	W	A	T	T	N	F	M	T	I	
124	Y	I	A	W	N	I	V	W	I	W	B	T	T	W	
125	W	W	O	W	H	L	F	P	N	A	W	B	H	W	
126	O	D	W	T	I	A	S	M	Y	S	H	A			
127	I	O	B	A	F	F	S	B	T	H	A	S	Y	T	
128	H	V	W	T	D	T	W	A	T	A	O	M	S	G	
129	T	I	I	S	I	P	P	O	M	H	A	B	A	T	
130	M	C	I	I	I	B	A	T	I	T	I	M	A	A	1835
131	T	A	F	T	Y	T	T	A	A	A	O	T	I	A	
132	T	K	H	L	A	B	N	D	A	O	T	A	T	A	1847
133	B	F	I	B	M	A	O	A	P	B	W	T	A	P	
134	S	A	M	T	B	F	H	V	T	T	A	S	H	H	
135	W	A	M	T	W	N	S	A	T	A	S	O	L	T	
136	I	S	A	T	W	I	I	A	T	T	F	T	M	A	
137	T	T	T	Y	I	B	W	W	W	W	O	T	I	A	
138	W	I	T	V	T	A	S	O	B	A	O	A	T	A	
139	O	T	W	V	T	D	W	I	L	H	A	T	Y	K	
140	B	M	L	T	I	T	A	N	F	A	N	M	T	B	
141	I	F	B	W	N	N	N	T	B	D	W	T	O	T	
142	L	H	O	A	O	T	A	R	B	W	R	T	I	B	
143	L	O	S	I	W	C	T	N	S	W	B	A	S	I	
144	T	W	T	T	T	T	A	W	A	S	B	I	Y	T	2015

19	D	A	F	N	H	F	Y	M
20	A	H	A		A	B	B	M
21	S	S	[illegible]	H	A	A	L	I
22	M	S	E	A	B	A	P	T
23	A	W	C	A	W	336		T
24	M	T	M	[illegible]	A	D	Y	T
25	L	O	V		I	A	T	W
26	L	T	T	[illegible]	A	T	T	T
27	W	T	E	P	W	M	L	F
28	H	T	V	A	S	W	B	A
29	VV	I	A	[illegible]	L	F	F	T
30	VV	I	I		T	W	B	A
31	T	W	A	H	W	T	T	A

The adjacent-letter 'KIT' at 1835 points down by the same means to square 2015. The significance of this number almost certainly lies in its the sum of its divisors, which is exactly twice 1344.

1	2015	
5	403	
13	155	
31	65	
	2688	1344 x 2

It may therefore be inferred the purpose for which these 'KIT' lines has been set out is to unite the true author with his pen-name.

The fact that we find the number 1344 indicated three times by the prime 'KIT'-lines – those made from adjacent squares – may have been planned because it points, via a geometric route to 2856, the value of Χριστοφερ Μαρλω – 'Christopher Marlowe'.

An equilateral triangle with three sides of 1344 may be contained in a circle with a circumference of 4875.5. This comes within 0.999999 of the combined sides and diagonals of a square with a perimeter of 2856.

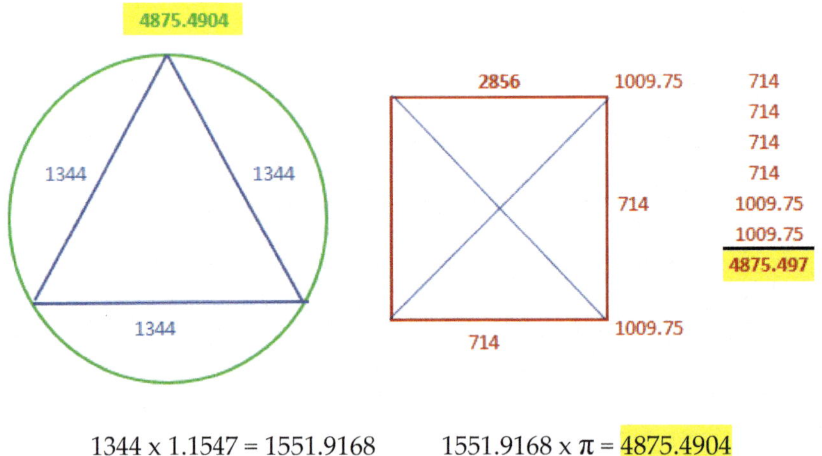

1344 x 1.1547 = 1551.9168 1551.9168 x π = 4875.4904

The same combination of names crops up when all seven 'KIT' lines are projected to the right edge. They point to five letter squares: 1344, 1513, 1681, 1847 and 2015. The sum of these figures is 8400. This gives the perimeter of a rectangle with two sides of 1344 – 'William Shakespeare', and two sides of 2856 – Χριστοφερ Μαρλω.

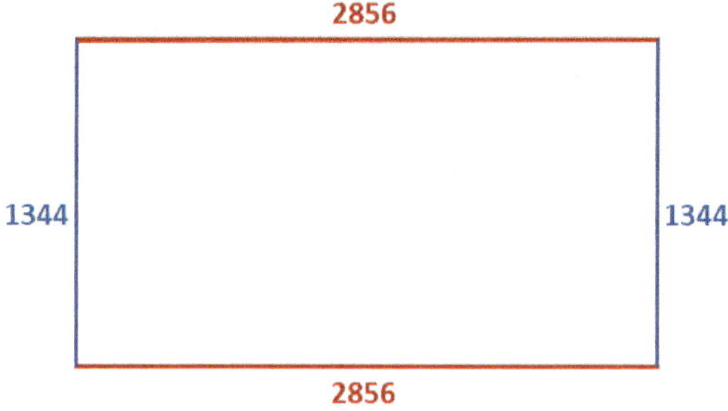

Another consideration is that 8400, as the sum of the five terminal points, can represent a pentagram with sides of 1680. This figure may be inscribed within a circle with a circumference of:

$$\pi\ (1680 \times 1.051462) = 5550$$

In the grid, 5550 appears as the location value of the letter squares giving the lower of the prime 'KIT'-lines: 1835 + 1850 + 1865 = 5550. The intentionality here is almost certainly because the addition of 1680 and 5550 makes 7230. As 1205 x 6, this presents 'Kit Marlowe' by hexagonal geometry.

The Many Mysteries of 8064

There is one more square picked out on the right edge of the grid. Square 336 is indicated by the line from the two nodal 'K's that runs through square 1086. No other squares are indicated on the edge by the 'KIT' lines or nodes. If 336 is taken from 8400, the remainder is 8064. As 1344 x 6, this presents 'William Shakespeare' by hexagonal geometry.

If this all feels unsettlingly familiar, it should do. Adding the sixfold Kit Marlowe figure of 7230 to the sixfold William Shakespeare number 8064 makes 15294. We just saw this above from the plotted projection of the two primary 'KIT's. 15294 was interpreted as a hexagram fusing Kit Marlowe together with William Shakespeare. This repetition of results helps to provide confirmation of their intentional nature.

The number 8064 can also be arrived at by a completely different route. It was mentioned above that just six lines in the *Sonnets* start with the letter 'K' and that two of these have been designated 'KIT nodes': 1462 and 1835. The other four are found at sonnet lines 33/3, 40/14, 80/2 and 139/14. These have combined locations of 451 + 560 + 1108 + 1945 = 4064. The number 4064 is directly linked to 1344 and 8064 because the factors of 1344 sum to 4064, and the factors of 4046 sum to 8064:

1	1344
2	672
3	448
4	336
6	224
7	192
8	168
12	112
14	96
16	84
21	64
24	56
28	48
32	42
4064	

1	4064
2	2032
4	1016
8	508
16	254
32	127
8064	

Thus all 6 'K' squares in the grid take us to both 1344 and 8064.

The peculiar prominence given 8064 suggests it may have further significance. If an 8064 hexagram, with sides of 1344, is drawn in a circle, a vesica can be drawn around it in the form of an eye – another 'eye of Horus'. In this case, each of the two circles forming the vesica will have a circumference of 9751.

> 1344 x 1.1547 = 1551.9168 (vesica width)
> 1551.9168 x 4.18879 = 6500.6536 (vesica perimeter)
> (6500.6536 x 3) ÷ 2 = 9750.98

9751 is the mirror of 1579 – 'Christopher Marlowe'. What is more, the circles in combination will have a total of 9751 x 2 = 19502. This provides an exact measure of a square and its two diagonals with sides of 2856 – Χριστοφερ Μαρλω. The accuracy comes within 0.9999997 of true.

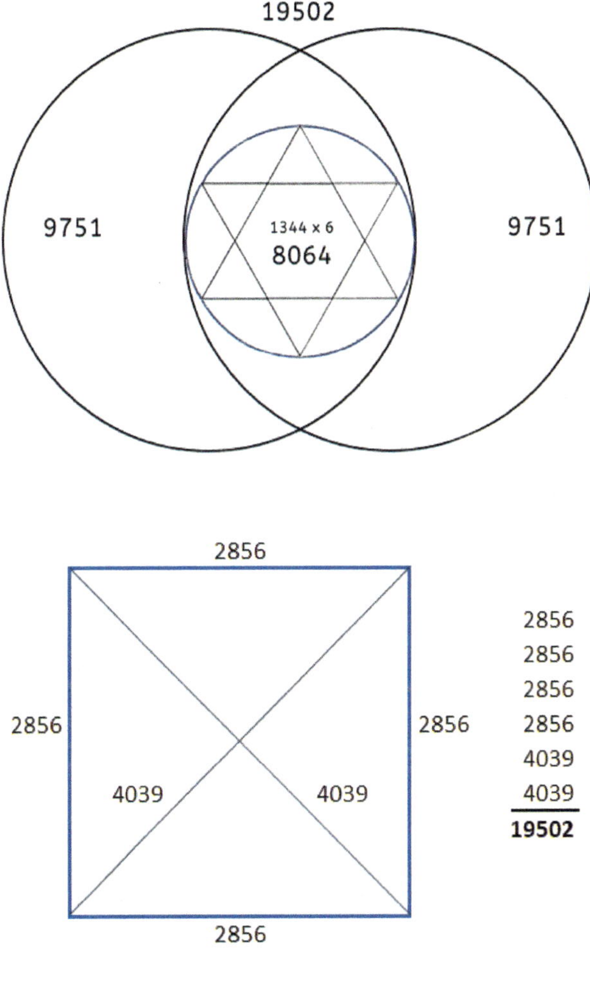

The two circles: 19501.9879
The 2856 square: 19501.9939

The 9751 circle also leads to 2856 by an entirely different route. A square can be drawn within the 9751 circle and inside that another circle drawn touching its sides. The inner circle will have a circumference of 6895. The difference between the two circles is 9751 – 6895 = 2856.

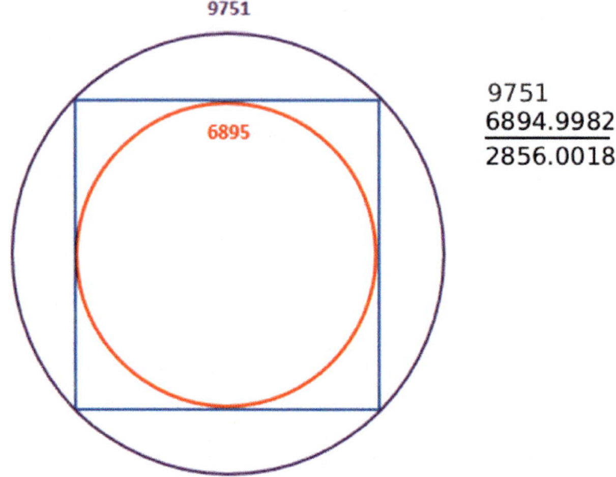

If an 8064 circumference circle is used in an identical configuration, the inner circle will measure 5702. The difference between the two is 2362 – Χρισ̲τ̲οφερ Μαρλω.

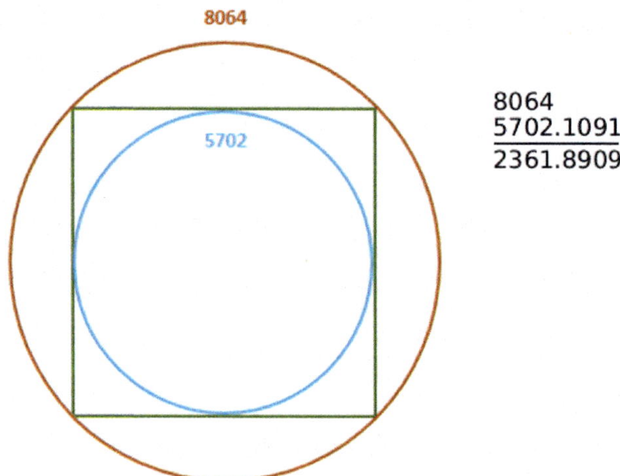

A non-circular route to the same relationship comes when we discover that 8064 measures the perimeter of right-angled triangle with two perpendiculars of a 2362. This is a 2362-sided square split by its diagonal: (2 x 2362) + (2362 x √2).

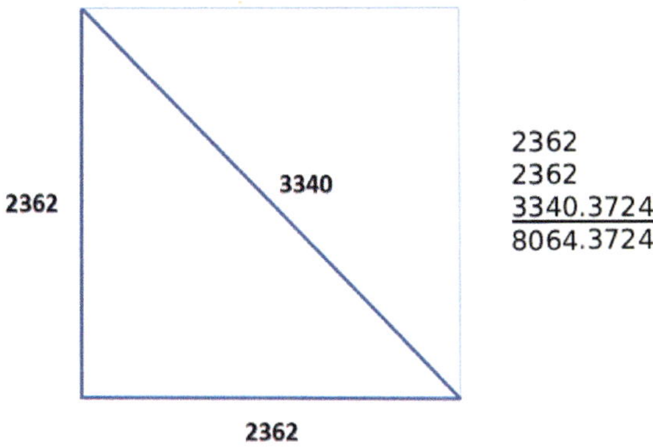

Therefore, it is not surprising the author with two names was keen to double-reference this number.

Doubling Up

The tidy-minded, those who fret about loose-ends, might be concerned that just as two 'KIT' lines point to square 1344, two (superimposed) lines point to 1513. These anxious folk need have no fear. The reason for this is rather clever. The effect of the doubling is to give the seven line termini a grand total of:

1344 + 1344 + 1513 + 1513 + 1681 + 1847 + 2015 = **11257**

This leads to a purely algebraic confirmation of the scheme's intentionality because 1513 ÷ 1344 = **1.1257**.

It may even be that the reverse is purposeful, too: 1344 ÷ 1513 = 0.8883. This leads to a slightly less accurate, but more personal result, because 8883 measures a 1301-sided square and its two diagonals (or more precisely 1300.885). It thereby squares, Κιτ Μαϱλω – 'Kit Marlowe'.

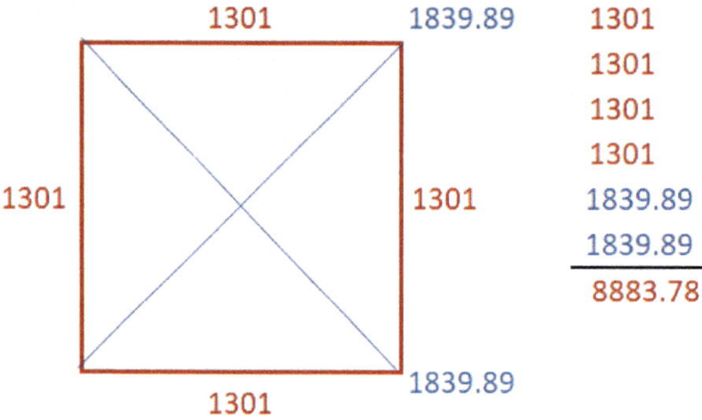

As if that weren't enough, the three line termini which are not doubled have independent significance. These sum as:

1681 + 1847 + 2015 = **5543**

This has another squaring function because it measures a 493 x 1086 – 'Christopher Marlowe' – rectangle and its diagonals:

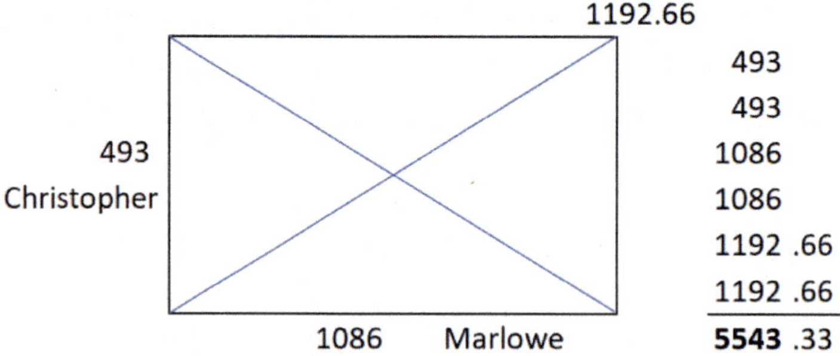

A final feature of the lines lies in a point of intersection. The line coming down from 1462 crosses the three lines rising from 1835, but only at one point does it precisely triangulate a square. This happens at 1591 – representing the eighth line of Sonnet 114. I like to think this is a strategic choice because 1591 nails the gematria value of, '*Marlowes Sonnets*'. Should future editions of *Shakespeares Sonnets* carry this new name?

C. The 'KIT' Letters

Some of the 'KIT' features have yet to be explained. The most obvious of these is the cluster of seven adjacent-square 'KIT's starting from the 'K' at 1462. The relevant letters occupy ten squares, with some overlaps (boxed):

102	M	I	T	T	O	W	A	A	N				
103	A	T	T	T	O	L	T	D	W				1436
104	T	F	S	H	T	I	T	S	A		1448	1449	1450
105	L	N	S	T	K	S	T	O	F	1461	1462		1464
106	W	I	A	I	T	O	I	E	S	1475	1476		
107	N	O	C	S	T	A	I	A	N		1490		
108	W	W	W	T	N	I	C	E	S			1505	
109	O	T	A	A	T	L	J	S	N				
110	A	A	G	M	M	A	T	A	N				
111	O	T	T	T	T	A	T	P	W				1548
112	Y	W	F	S	Y	T	N	T	I				

The sum of the ten square locations used is, 1436 + 1448 + 1449 + 1450 + 1461 + 1462 + 1464 + 1475 + 1476 + 1490 = 14611. If divided by the number of 'KIT's it represents, which is 7, the result is 2087. This is the value of 1205 – 'Kit Marlowe' – multiplied by the square root of three. In geometric terms it can measure the diagonal of a 1205-sided cube.

A different way to count the locations is to add the seven sets of three squares making the seven independent 'KIT's. These seven sum as 4347 + 4359 + 4361 + 4375 + 4398 + 4413 + 4427 = 30680. If divided by seven, it yields a value of 4383. This is very suitable because it comprises the sum of 1835, 1462 and 1086: in other words, the location value of the two 'KIT' nodes and the square they triangulate – which has the value of 'Marlowe'. What is even neater is that 4383 divided by three is 1461, and this is the gematria value of, 'Kit Wrote This' – in other words, the acrostic message without the 'Marlowe'.[1]

Kit would have been especially pleased with the total of 14611 (above) because it constitutes a numerical anagram of 14161. This is 119 squared – and we already know 119 is the gematria value of 'Kit'. Those who look down on anagrams will be relieved, or dismayed, to learn the exact number can be found at the lower 1835-node. Here it forms the sum of all the 'KIT' locations except the adjacent-square 'KIT' (valued at 5550):

1675 + 1755 + 1756 + 1781 + 1783 + 1794 + 1808 + 1809 = 14161

119	W	D	A	S	W	W	H	I	O							
120	T	A	N	V	F	A	A	T	O							1675
121	T	W	A	N	F	G	O	W	N							
122	T	F	W	B	O	H	T	O	T							
123	N	T	T	T	O	W	A	T	T							
124	Y	I	A	W	N	I	V	W	I							
125	W	W	O	W	H	L	F	P	N							
126	O	D	W	T	I	A	S	M	Y			1755	1756			
127	I	O	B	A	F	F	S	B	T							
128	H	V	W	T	D	T	W	A	T			1781		1783		
129	T	I	I	S	I	P	P	O	M		1794					
130	M	C	I	I	I	B	A	T	I		1808	1809				
131	T	A	F	T	Y	T	T	A	A							
132	T	K	H	L	A	B	N	D	A	1835						
133	B	F	I	B	M	A	O	A	P		1850					
134	S	A	M	T	B	F	H	V	T			1865				
135	W	A	M	T	W	N	S	A	T							

By the S-code, the name 'Kit' is valued at 38. This is indicated if the total of the 'straight adjacent-square 'KIT's' is divided by the total of the 'straight non-adjacent-square 'KIT's':

(4347 + 5550) ÷ (4515 + 5266 + 5348 + 5424 + 5427) = 0.38

It even appears when the 'straight adjacent-square 'KIT's' are divided by 'crooked adjacent-square 'KIT's' (albeit with a rounding of the decimal fraction):

(4347 + 5550) ÷ (4359 + 4361 + 4375 + 4398 + 4413 + 4427) = 0.3758

If 5550 is added to 14611, a grand total for all eight adjacent-square 'KIT's is found (i.e. 7 at the top node and 1 at the lower node): 5550 + 14611 = 20161. This, divided by 8 is 2520. It thereby provides another number uniting the value of the poet's name with his pen-name by means of a right-angled triangle:

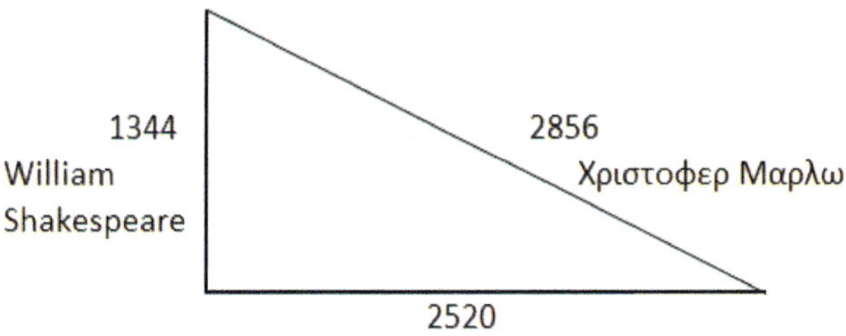

It will also be noticed, the perimeter of this triangle is 6720, which is 5 x 1344.

Finally, it can be seen that all thirteen 'KIT's in the grid are made up from 23 letters. The grand total of the letter locations can be calculated as 37375. When divided by 23, it yields a figure of exactly 1625. 1625 unites the names 'Marlowe' and 'Shakespeare' using both 'S' and 'L' codes:

1086 + 81 + 355 + 103 = 1625

G. The Cryptogram as a Whole

There are thirteen 'KIT's in the grid, but one of them is used in the message. Therefore, the whole plan combines **'Kit Marlowe wrote this'** with twelve other 'KIT's. Geometrically, the latter can represent the twelve edges of a 119-sided cube: hence, a *cubing* of the name '**Kit**'.

The cube requires 12 perfectly formed 'KIT's, however these twelve actually stem from just two 'K's, one of which is used in the message. The independent letters constitute 1 'K', 7 'I's and 12 'T's. These have a gematria total of 10 + (7 x 9) + (12 x 100) = 1273. There is also the 'M' from the alternative start to the message, and this is valued at 30. The message itself is valued at 2547. Therefore, the gematria total of all the 40 letters in the cryptogram is 2547 + 1273 + 30 = 3850.

This *squares the circle* for the cryptogram because a square of 3849.77 (3850) perimeter has an area equal to that of a circle of 1086 diameter. Aside from 1086 being the value of **'Marlowe'**, this is the circle that encloses both a right-angled triangle of perimeter 2547 –

'Kit Marlowe wrote this', and a rectangle of perimeter 2921 – **'Christopher Marlowe wrote this'**.

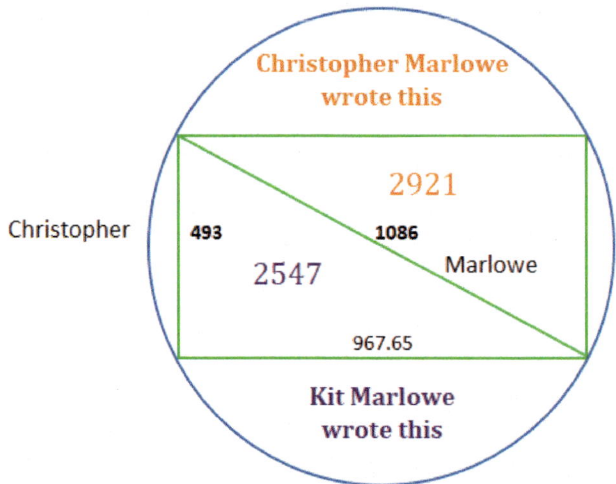

If extraordinary claims demand extraordinary evidence, we have now found it. The 40-letter cryptogram including the message **'Kit Marlowe Wrote This'** is completely valid; and, it can only have been constructed by the author of *Shake-speares Sonnets* – our ever-living poet, Christopher Marlowe.

Chapter 10 Notes

[1] It is also noticeable that 14611 divided by ten (its constituent parts) leads to 1461, too.

11
The Ouroboros

Some things just keep giving. The acrostic message is one of them; and I don't think it will stop any time soon. At some stage, while working on the cryptogram, I discovered that the beginning of the message is connected to the end by its numerical properties. It seemed like a neat feature and worthy of an aside or a footnote but not much more than that. Little did I realise, it points to something rather more substantial.

By now you will be aware that the first letter of the message, the 'K' of 'KIT', comes at line 1835. Despite appearances, this number doesn't have so much going for it. It certainly doesn't have a big list of divisors. You can divide it by 1, or you can divide it by 5 to get 367. It has no other whole number divisors. If you sum these, its 'aliquot parts', they come to 373.

1	1835
5	367
	373

373 may be small, but it's important, because square 373 is where the message ends – at the 'S' of 'THIS'. It means the beginning and the end of the message are tied together like a snake swallowing its tail.

The ouroboros is an ancient symbol of regeneration, cyclicity and eternity. In mythology, it is a creature that never dies. That is the message Kit wished to convey in his sonnets. Like his great hero Ovid, he didn't want to be forgotten: not ever. And, now that we understand his message, he never will be.

If Marlowe's circling snake depended simply on the aliquot parts of 1835, it would be a poor skinny thing. Three modest numbers hobbled together don't quite have the chutzpah we have come to expect from the maestro. If we want the message to really spin throughout aeons of time, we have to return to the source. That means the 19 lines whose first letters make up its body.

S-not	S-gem	*Line*		L-not	L-gem
93	423	*1835*	**K**nowing thy heart torment me with disdaine,	1152	3377
87	403	*1756*	**I**f Nature (soueraine misteres ouer wrack)	1119	3659
124	389	*1675*	**T**o waigh how once I suffered in your crime.	1569	3442
121	482	*1594*	**M**ine eie well knowes what with his gust is greeing,	2776	4925
65	341	*1493*	**A**nd peace proclaimes Oliues of endlesse age,	227	1669
71	436	*1392*	**R**eturne forgetfull Muse,and straight redeeme,	287	1903
59	272	*1290*	**L**ike a deceiued husband,so loues face,	149	2145
55	339	*1225*	**O**f faults conceald,wherein I am attainted:	970	2046
97	389	*1160*	**W**hen others would giue life,and bring a tombe.	1981	3592
58	379	*976*	**E**ither not assayld,or victor beeing charg'd,	801	2246
110	339	*792*	**VV**hen you haue bid your seruant once adieue.	1851	4400
73	367	*615*	**R**eceiuing naughts by elements so sloe,	307	2306
111	457	*541*	**O**h absence what a torment wouldst thou proue,	2112	4236
118	489	*467*	**T**is not enough that through the cloude thou breake,	550	2217
68	281	*442*	**E**xceeded by the hight of happier men.	203	1332
70/72	289	*417*	**T**he sad account of fore-bemoned mone,	277/279	1063
119	360	*402*	**H**aplye I thinke on thee, and then my state,	488	1807
115	392	*387*	**I** tell the Day to please him thou art bright,	484	1795
94	365	*373*	**S**aue that my soules imaginary sight	409	2681
1710	**7252**			**17714**	**50841**
1708				**17712**	

As ever, when first encountering these daunting-looking columns of numbers, John Dee's acerbic observation from *Monas Hieroglyphica* springs to mind, "Here the vulgar eye will see nothing but obscurity, and will despair considerably." I certainly did for the longest time.

When all else fails, one can do worse than add together the totals for each of the four codes:

1710 + 7252 + 17714 + 50841 = 77517

After a great deal of fruitless trial and error, I decided to see what would happen if I treated 77517 as the area of a circle. So, I divided by π, took the square root and multiplied by 2, to get the diameter:

77517 ÷ 3.1415926 = 24674.43
√24674.43 = 157.081
157.081 x 2 = 314.16

Amazing! The diameter of the circle is π itself, x 100. With two hops of the decimal place, it gives π to within 0.99999 accuracy. What this means is that the circumference must be π squared, because you multiply the diameter by π to find that length.

Thus, the whole message comes in the form of a great circle. It is a massive, archetypal circle on a scale of 100. It embodies the most important constant in geometry, and it does so twice – once on its own and once by means of its square. It is extremely significant.

It was shortly after that Eureka moment when I found myself assailed by a new thought. I had the uncanny feeling I might have missed something. Looking carefully through the nineteen lines (not unlike a princess looking under her mattresses), I discovered the discomforting presence of a hyphen. It was lurking in line 417, where the 'T' at the start of 'THIS' in the message comes from. For the notarikon count, I had taken the delightful expression 'fore-bemoned' to be two words rather than one. With the letter 'b' valued at 2 by both codes, the grand total for the 19 lines now went down by 4, to 77513. While this total was a tiny fraction less accurate at generating π, it actually helped because it gave an average area for the circle of 77515. This leads to a circle diameter of 100 x 3.1415786. In other words, it now comes to within 0.999996 of the figure a modern calculator will spit out. It's not bad for the days of quills, parchment and chamber-pots emptying at twelve o'clock.

In the afterglow of my discovery, I continued playing with the numbers. An obvious permutation was to put 77513 and 77517 together.

$$77513 + 77517 = 155030$$

It was while juggling around with this number, something very shocking happened. I made the momentous decision to divide it by five.

$$155030 \div 5 = 31006$$

When I looked that number up, I almost choked on that hyphen. It turns out that 31.006 is π cubed. So, the tiny punctuation mark buried in the message had just converted the double whammy of π and π squared to π cubed – accurate to five digits.

It was therefore by three permutations of the constant π that Kit Marlowe wrote his claim into eternity. His message is written in the form of a circle that will never end.

I was absolutely delighted with my discovery. However as my mind whirled around, I was now assailed by another niggle. It is apparent 155030 isn't exactly π^3. It is actually 5000 times greater. Obviously Kit and his mathematical buddies were aware of this, so I wondered if there was any context that might help account for the factor of 5000.

The place I suspected was where the extra quantity of 77513 originated: that mischievous little hyphen in line 417. When I looked up 417 in my numerical database, I found the answer right away. The number 5000 crops up prominently in the *New Testament*:

it is the number of people Jesus miraculously fed with bread and fishes. In *Matthew* 14, we read:

> *19* And he commanded the multitude to sit down on the grass, and took the five loaves, and the two fishes, and looking up to heaven, he blessed, and brake, and gave the loaves to his disciples, and the disciples to the multitude.
> 20 And they did all eat, and were filled: and they took up of the fragments that remained twelve baskets full.
> 21 And they that had eaten were about five thousand men, beside women and children.

If we take 5000 diners and divide their food according to 12 baskets, each basket will cater for 416.66 people. Since we can't have fractional people, we must round it up to 417. Thus the hyphen had to be placed in line 417, and nowhere else. So, by means of a famous miracle, 155030, boils down to 31.006. It is very very clever indeed.

I think it is additionally gratifying that line 417 supplies the first letter in the word 'This' – which has letter placement values summing to 1579 – 'Christopher Marlowe'. One also might be tempted to interpret the letter 'T' (its *raison d'etre* for inclusion in the message) by its gematria value of 100, and thereby allow for the factor by which π and π^2 were raised.

It next occurred to me to study the two gematria totals of the 19 lines: 7252 and 50841. It seems that the 'S' code total of 7252 may be relevant to the circular theme by means of its aliquot parts:

1	7252
2	3626
4	1813
7	1036
14	518
28	259
37	196
49	148
74	98

7910

7910 miles is a fair measure of the polar diameter of the earth – the axis about which it rotates each day. The modern figure is accepted to be 7900 miles. It thereby provides a cosmological measure of the line about which all measurements of earthly time are based.

The greater figure of 50841, the 'L' gematria total, is even more satisfactory when extended through the full addition of its divisors:

1	50841
3	16947
7	7263
9	5649
21	2421
27	1883
63	807
189	269

86400

The diameter of the sun has been reckoned, all the way from antiquity to the present day, as being 864,000 miles. Thus, the two gematria totals from the 19 message lines point to the axes of the Earth and the Sun. These are the poles around which these bodies perform their eternal whirling dance.

For critics who might bemoan the absence of a zero from the total, they would do well to concentrate their minds on the number of seconds in a day:

$$60 \times 60 \times 24 = 84{,}600$$

If a larger unit of time were demanded, we would need to recast our gaze on the message lines. Sharp eyes will notice the 'W' of line 792 is actually printed 'VV'. If counted with a double 'V', the gematria total of the message rises from 2547 to 3047. This number seems to make sense in combination with 2547 through the addition of their divisors:

		1	2547	
1	3047	3	849	
11	277	9	283	
3336		3692		**7028**

7028 supplies the value of the twelve months of the year, in the Latin calendar:

> Januarius, Februarius, Martius, Aprilis, Maius, Junius, Quinctilis, Sextilis, September, October, November, December
> 1221 + 673 + 510 + 269 + 330 + 1139 + 550 + 623 + 377 + 290 + 912 + 134 = 7028

Thus, the message lines give us both the diurnal rotation of the Earth about its axis and the annual rotation of the Earth around the Sun. And if we return where we started, in Sonnet 1, we also have the 12 signs of the Zodiac, which oversee the rise and fall of empires as they crawl imperceptibly around each great year of precession.

Conclusion

With his message concealed in *Shakespeares Sonnets* brought to light, Kit Marlowe is finally set free. From henceforth, his name will never be forgotten.

> Therefore when Flint and Iron weare away,
> Verse is immortall, and shal nere decay.
> To Verse let Kings giue place, and Kingly showes,
> And banks ore which gold-bearing Tagus flowes.
> Let base conceited witts admire vilde things,
> Faire Phoebus lead me to the Muses springs.
> About my head be quiuering mirtle wound,
> And in sad Louers heads let me be found.
> The Liuing, not the Dead can enuy bite,
> For after Death all men receiue their right.
> Then though Death rakes my bones in funeral fire,
> Ile liue, and as he puls me downe mount higher.

AFTERWORD

Words are powerful. God knows. Four short words hidden in a poem are all it takes to rewrite history. On their account, one of the foundational pillars of Western literature is torn down. Millions of hours of scholarship and the fond dreams of countless devotees are brought to nothing. The loss is incalculable. And yet it is necessary. There is always room for the truth, and the truth is inevitably greater than any legend built from wishful thinking and the all-too-human propensity for self-delusion. The faithful will feel bereft, and the experts will have egg on their faces. So be it.

The world will have to come to terms with Kit Marlowe and his afterlife as Shake-speare. Those who despise Marlowe, and there are many, will have to square his youthful Promethean spirit with the mature genius of Shakespeare. If they truly love Shakespeare, they could do worse than reflect on his words in *Sonnet* 121:

121

TIS better to be vile then vile esteemed,
When not to be, receiues reproach of being,
And the iust pleasure lost, which is so deemed,
Not by our feeling, but by others seeing.
For why should others false adulterat eyes
Giue salutation to my sportiue blood?
Or on my frailties why are frailer spies;
Which in their wils count bad what I think good?
Noe, I am that I am, and they that leuell
At my abuses, reckon vp their owne,
I may be straight though they them-selues be beuel
By their rancke thoughtes, my deedes must not be shown

Vnlesse this generall euill they maintaine,
All men are bad and in their badnesse raigne.

In coming to terms with this new reality, there is much to look forward to. While it may be overly optimistic to imagine that in this life the truth will set anyone completely free, it can be a liberating force. If we allow ourselves to celebrate the unbinding of Kit Marlowe from the shield behind which he was forced to hide, we can also start to free ourselves from the defensive illusions we hold about ourselves. We should not forget, it is great writers like Shakespeare who hold up the mirror wherein we see our own images reflected.

Appendix 1

The Gematria Codes

English

Short Code

a	b	c	d	e	f	g	h
1	2	3	4	5	6	7	8
i/j	k	l	m	n	o	p	q
9	10	11	12	13	14	15	16
r	s	t	u/v	w	x	y	z
17	18	19	20	21	22	23	24

Long Code (Agrippa)

a	b	c	d	e	f	g	h	i
1	2	3	4	5	6	7	8	9
k	l	m	n	o	p	q	r	s
10	20	30	40	50	60	70	80	90
t	u	x	y	z	j	v	*hi*	w
100	200	300	400	500	600	700	*800*	900

Greek

Greek Short Code

α	β	γ	δ	ε	ζ	η	θ
1	2	3	4	5	6	7	8
ι	κ	λ	μ	ν	ξ	ο	π
9	10	11	12	13	14	15	16
ρ	σ/ς	τ	υ	φ	χ	ψ	ω
17	18	19	20	21	22	23	24

Greek Long Code

α	β	γ	δ	ε	F/στ	ζ	η	θ
1	2	3	4	5	6	7	8	9
ι	κ	λ	μ	ν	ξ	ο	π	ϙ
10	20	30	40	50	60	70	80	90
ρ	σ/ς	τ	υ	φ	χ	ψ	ω	ϡ
100	200	300	400	500	600	700	800	900

Hebrew

Hebrew Short Code

א	ב	ג	ד	ה	ו	ז	ח
1	2	3	4	5	6	7	8
ט	י	כ	ל	מ	נ	ס	ע
9	10	11	12	13	14	15	16
פ	צ	ק	ר	ש	ת		
17	18	19	20	21	22		

Hebrew Long Code

א	ב	ג	ד	ה	ו	ז	ח	ט
1	2	3	4	5	6	7	8	9
י	כ	ל	מ	נ	ס	ע	פ	צ
10	20	30	40	50	60	70	80	90
ק	ר	ש	ת	ך	ם	ן	ף	ץ
100	200	300	400	500	600	700	800	900

Appendix 2

Geometric Ratios

Constants:

Pi/π = 3.1415926536 (approximately 22/7 or 355/113)
Phi/φ = 1.6180339887 'The Golden Section' $\varphi^3 = 4.236$
$\sqrt{2}$ = 1.4142135624
$\sqrt{3}$ = 1.7320580756

Right-angled triangle

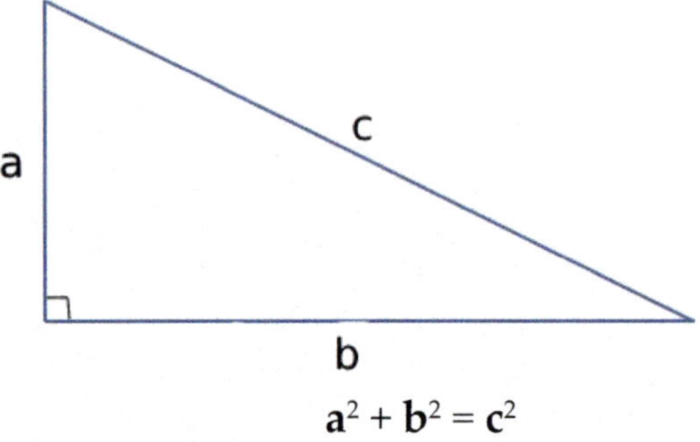

$$\mathbf{a}^2 + \mathbf{b}^2 = \mathbf{c}^2$$

A circle with a diameter of **c** (the hypotenuse) will intersect all 3 corners of a right-angled triangle.

Square

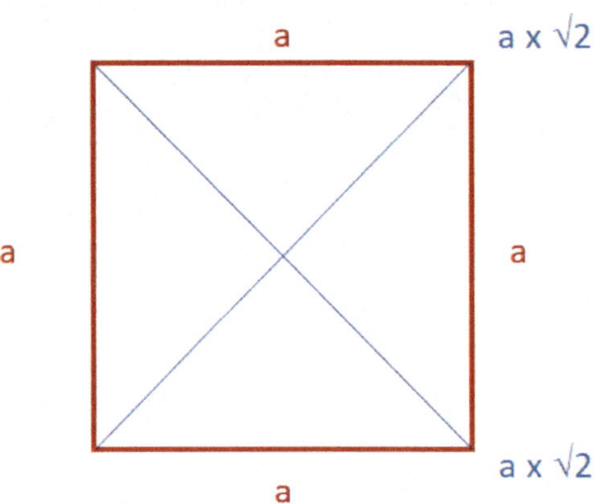

The diagonal is the side length multiplied by √2

Pentagram

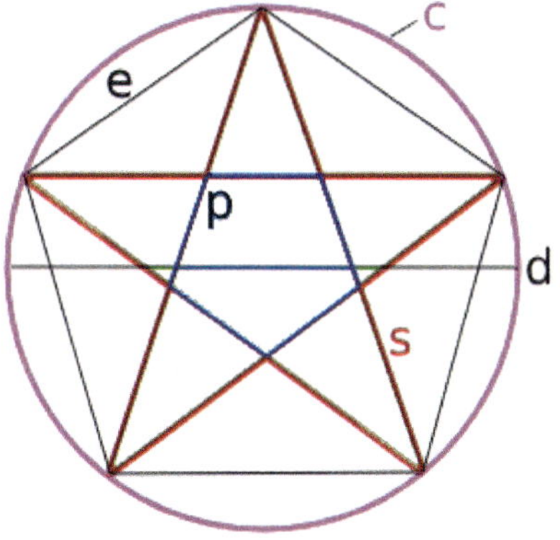

Pentagram length = **s** x 5
Internal pentagon perimeter **p** = (**s** x 5) ÷ 4.236 (φ^3)
External pentagon perimeter **e** = (**s** x 5) ÷ 1.618
Circle diameter **d** = **s** x 1.051462 1.051462 = 2 x √(2 ÷ (5 + √5))

Hexagram

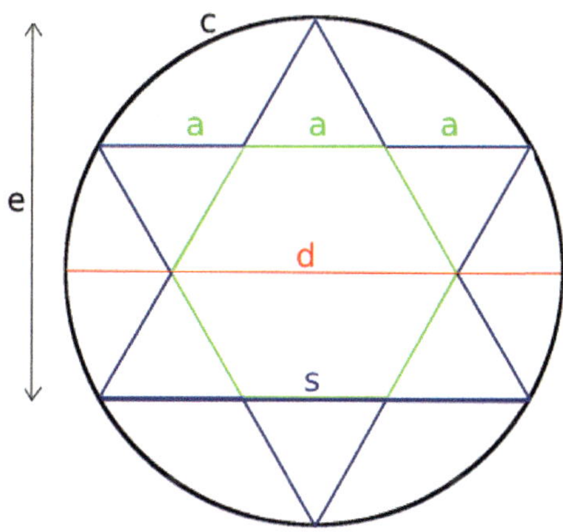

e (the height of an equilateral triangle) = **s** ÷ 1.1547
d (circle diameter) = **s** x 1.1547 $1.1547 = (2 \times \sqrt{3}) \div 3$
c (circle circumference) = **d** (diameter) x π
Circle area = $\pi \times r^2$ (r is radius, which is half the diameter)
3 x **a** = **s**

Vesica Piscis

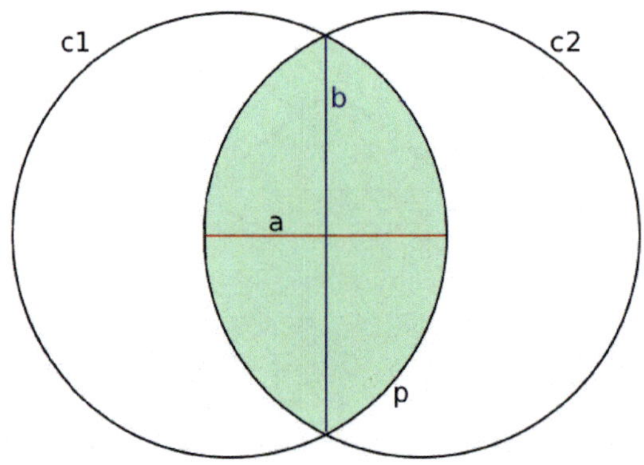

a x $\sqrt{3}$ = **b**
a x 4.18879 = **p** (perimeter of vesica piscis) $4/3\ \pi = 4.18879$
(**c**1 + **c**2) ÷ 3 = **p**
Area of vesica (green) is $((4\pi - 3\sqrt{3})\ a^2) \div 6$

Appendix 3
Gematria Counts in New Testament Greek

Luke 24, 2

And they found the stone rolled away from the sepulchre

ευρον	δε	τον	λιθον	αποκεκυλισμενον	απο	του	μνημειου	
625	9	420	169	1051	151	770	623	3818

John 21, 6

And he said unto them, Cast the net on the right side of the ship, and ye shall find. They cast therefore

ὁ	δὲ	εἶπεν	αὐτοῖς	Βάλετε	εἰς	τὰ	δεξιὰ	μέρη	τοῦ	πλοίου	τὸ	δίκτυον	καὶ	εὑρήσετε	ἔβαλον	οὖν	
70	9	150	981	343	215	301	80	153	770	660	370	854	31	1023	158	520	6688

John 21, 11 (Textus Receptus)

Simon Peter went up, and drew the net to land full of great fishes, an hundred

ανεβη	σιμων	πετρος	και	ειλκυσεν	το	δικτυον	επι	της	γης	μεστον	ιχθυων
66	1100	755	31	720	370	854	95	508	211	665	1869

and fifty and three: and for all there were so many, yet was not the net broken

μεγαλων	εκατον	πεντηκοντατριων	και	τοσουτων	οντων	ουκ	εσχισθη	το	δικτυον	
929	446	2144	31	2190	1270	490	1032	370	854	17000

John 21, 11 (Nestle-Aland)

Simon Peter went up, and drew the net to land full of great fishes, an hundred

ανεβη	ουν	Σιμων	Πετρος	και	ειλκυσεν	το	δικτυον	εις	την	γην	μεστον	ιχθυων
66	520	1100	755	31	720	370	854	215	358	61	665	1869

and fifty and three: and for all there were so many, yet was not the net broken

μεγαλων	εκατον	πεντηκοντατριων	και	τοσουτων	οντων	ουκ	εσχισθη	το	δικτυον	
929	446	2144	31	2190	1270	490	1032	370	854	17340

1 Corinthians 3, 13

The fire shall try every man's work of what sort it is

εκαστου	το	εργον	οποιον	εστιν	το	πυρ	δοκιμασει	
996	370	228	350	565	370	580	360	3819

1 Corinthians 15, 52

And the dead shall be raised incorruptible, and we shall all be changed

και	οι	νεκροι	εγερθησονται	αφθαρτοι	και	ημεις	αλλαγησομεθα	
31	80	255	761	991	31	263	398	2810

Revelation 21, 2

The holy city, new Jerusalem, coming down from God out of heaven

την	πολιν	την	αγιαν	ιερουσαλημ	καινην	καταβαινουσαν	απο	του	θεου	εκ	του	ουρανου	
358	240	358	65	864	139	1106	151	770	484	25	770	1091	6421

Revelation 22, 1

And he shewed me a pure river of water of life, clear as crystal,

και	εδειξεν	μοι	καθαρον	ποταμον	υδατος	ζωης	λαμπρον	ως	κρυσταλλον
31	139	120	251	611	975	1015	371	1000	1201

proceeding out of the throne of God and of the Lamb

εκπορευομενον	εκ	του	θρονου	του	θεου	και	του	αρνιου	
965	25	770	699	770	484	31	770	631	10859

BIBLIOGRAPHY

Acheson, Arthur. *Shakespeare and the Rival Poet*. New York: AMS Press, 1971 reprint of 1903 edn.

Agrippa, Henricus Cornelius. *Three Books of Occult Philosophy*. Antwerp: 1531. Modern edition translated by James Freake, edited & annotated by Donald Tyson. Saint Paul, MN: Llewellyn's Publications, 1993.

Akrigg, G.P.V. *Shakespeare & the Earl of Southampton*. London: Hamish Hamilton, 1968.

Arias Montanus, Benedictus. *Antiquitatum Judaicorum*, Leiden: Franciscus Raphelengius pour officine Plantin, 1593.

Auden, W.H. *'Introduction': Shakespeares Sonnets*, ed. William Burto. New York: New American Library (Signet Classic Shakespeare), 1964.

Bakeless, John. *The Tragicall History of Christopher Marlowe*. Connecticut: Harvard, 1942.

Barber, C.L. *'An Essay on the Sonnets'*, *The Laurel Shakespeare*, ed. Francis Ferguson: The Sonnets of Shakespeare. New York: Dell, 1960.

Barry, Kieren. *The Greek Qabalah - Alphabetic Mysticism and Numerology in the Ancient World*. York Beach, Maine: Samuel Weiser, 1999.

Beard, Thomas. *The Theatre of Gods Iudgements* . . . London: Adam Islip, 1597.

Boas, F.S. *Shakespeare and His Predecessors*. London: John Murray, 1896.

Bouriant, Urbain. *Description topographique et historique de l'Égypte, traduite en français par V. Bouriant*. Paris: Libraire de la Société Asiatique, 1895. There is an online version at https://gallica.bnf.fr/ark:/12148/bpt6k5828537q/f16.item
Broughton, James, 'Life and Writings of Christopher Marlowe'. *Gentleman's Magazine*, 1830.

Butler, Christopher. *Number Symbolism*. London: Routledge & Kegan Paul, 1970.

Camden, William. *Remaines of a greater worke, concerning Britaine, the inhabitants thereof, their languages, names, surnames, empreses, wise speeches, poësies, and epitaphes*. London: G.E., 1605.

Chambers, E.K. *Shakespearean Gleanings*. London: O.U.P., 1944.

Cheney, Patrick. *Shakespeare's Literary Authorship*. Cambridge: CUP, 2008.

Cordovero, Moses. *Pardes Rimmonim*. Cracow: 1591.

Cox, David Thomas and Cox, Jane. *Shakespeare in the Public Records*. London: HMSO, 1985.

Dee, John. *Mathematicall Praeface to The Elements of Geometrie by Euclid of Megara*. London: 1570. Facsimile edition by Kessinger publications, LLC, MT, USA (IBSN 0-7661-0766-3).

Dover Wilson, J. *The Essential Shakespeare*. Cambridge: CUP, 1932.

Dowden, Edward. *The Tragedies of William Shakespeare*. New York: International Collectors Library, 1912.

Drayton, Michael. *To My Most Dearely-loved Friend Henery Reynolds Esquire – Of Poets and Poesie*. London, 1627. Cited from: *The Minor Poems of Michael Drayton*. Cyril Brett, Ed. Oxford: Clarendon Press, 1907.

Durning-Lawrence, Edwin. *Bacon is Shake-speare*, New York: J. McBride, 1910.

Fludd, Robert. *Mosaicall Philosophy*. London: Humphrey Mosely, 1659.

Fowler, Alistair (ed.). *Silent Poetry, Essays in Numerological Analysis*, London: Routledge & Kegan Paul Ltd, 1970.

Fowler, Alistair. *Spenser and The Numbers of Time*. London: Routledge & Kegan Paul Ltd, 1964.

Fowler. Alistair. *Triumphal Forms - Structural Patterns in Elizabethan Poetry*. Cambridge: Cambridge University Press, 1970.

French, Peter. *John Dee – The World of an Elizabethan Magus*. London & New York: Ark Paperbacks, 1987 (first published 1972).

Friedman, William F. and Elizebeth S. *The Shakespearean Ciphers Examined*. London/New York: C.U.P., 1957.

Furnivall, F.J. *'Introduction', The Leopold Shakespeare*. London: Cassell Petter & Galpin, c.1877.

Greene, Robert. *Greenes Groats-worth of Witte, Bought with a Million of Repentance*. London: William Wright, 1592.

Greenwood, George Granville. *Is There a Shakespeare Problem?*, London: John Lane at the Bodley Head, 1916.

Hall, Joseph. *Virgidemiarum*. London: Robert Dexter, 1597.

Harriet, Joseph. *Shakespeare's Son-in-Law: John Hall, Man and Physician*. Hamden, Conn.: Archon Books, 1964.

Harrison, G.B. *'Introduction'. The Sonnets and A Lover's Complaint*. London: Penguin Books Ltd., 1938.

Hoffman, Calvin. *The Murder of the Man who was Shakespeare*. London: Max Parrish, 1955.

Horozco, Juan de. *Sacra Symbola*. Agriento: 1601.

Hotson, Leslie. *Mr W. H.* London: Rupert Hart-Davis, 1964.

Hotson, Leslie. *Shakespeare's Sonnets Dated*. New York: Oxford University Press, 1949.

Jonson, Ben. *Discoveries*, 1641, Conversations with William Drummond of Hawthorndon 1619, Bodley Head Quartos series, ed. G.B. Harrison, 1923.

Josephus, Flavius. Jewish Antiquities. trans. William Whiston. Ware: Wordsworth Editions, 2006.

Kuriyama, Constance Brown. *Christopher Marlowe: A Renaissance Life*. Ithaca and London: Cornell University Press, 2002.

Lee, Sidney. *A Life of William Shakespeare*. London: Smith, Elder & Co., 1899.

Lubbock, Percy, ed. *The Letters of Henry James*. New York: Charles Scribner's Sons, 1920.

MacLure, Millar, ed. *Marlowe: The Critical Heritage, 1588-1896*. London-Boston-Henley: Routledge & Kegan Paul, 1979.

Mackey, Albert. *An Encyclopedia of Freemasonry and its Kindred Sciences*. 2 Vols. New York: Masonic History Company, 1914.

Mackey, Albert. *The History of Freemasonry*. New York: Masonic History Company, 1898.

Marston, John. *The Metamorphosis of Pigmalions Image And Certaine Satyres*. London: Edmond Matts, 1598.

Meres, Francis. *Palladis Tamia*. Vol. 14. Scholars' facsimiles & reprints, 1938.

Michell, John. *City of Revelation*. London: Garnstone Press, 1972.

Michell, John. *The Dimensions of Paradise.* Kempton, Il.: Adventures Unlimited Press, 2001.

Moses de Leon. Sefer Zohar [Heb.]. Mantua: 1558.

Murphy, Donna. The Marlowe-Shakespeare Continuum: Christopher Marlowe, Thomas Nashe, and the Authorship of Early Shakespeare and Anonymous Plays. Newcastle Upon Tyne: Cambridge Scholars Publishing: 2013.

Nashe, Thomas. *Lenten Stuffe.* London: N.L. & C.B., 1599.

Nashe, Thomas. *The Unfortunate Traveller or the Life of Jack Wilton.* London: C. Burby, 1594.

Norman, Charles. *The Muses Darling.* New York: Macmillan, 1947.

Norton, Charles Eliot. *The Letters of William James.* Boston: The Atlantic Monthly Press, 1920.

Peele, George. *The Honour of the Garter,* London: John Busbie, 1593.

Petowe, Henry. *The Second Part of Hero and Leander Conteyning Their Further Fortunes.* London: Andrew Harris, 1598.

Pike, Albert. *Morals and Dogma of the Ancient and Accepted Rite of Freemasonry,* Charleston, 1871.

Pinksen, Daryl. *Marlowe's Ghost: The Blacklisting of the Man Who Was Shakespeare. New York: iUniverse, Inc, 2008.*

Price, Diana. *Shakespeare's Unorthodox Biography: New Evidence of an Authorship Problem.* Westport, CT: Greenwood, 2001.

Reynolds, Henry. *Mythomystes wherein a short suruay is taken of the nature and value of true poesy and depth of the ancients above our moderne poets.* London: Henry Seyle, 1632.

Robbins, R. *Secular Lyrics of the XIVth and XVth Centuries.* Oxford: Clarendon Press, 1952.

Schoenbaum, Samuel. *Shakespeare's Lives.* OUP, Oxford and New York, 1970.

Scholem, G. *Kabbalah,* Meridian/Penguin, New York, 1978.

Selenus, Gustavus. *Cryptomenytices et cryptographiae libri IX in quibus & planissima steganographiae à Johanne Trithemio...* Lüneburg: 1624.

Shakespeare, William. *Mr. William Shakespeares Comedies, Histories, & Tragedies.* London: Jaggard & Blount, 1623.

Shakespeare, William. *Shake-speares Sonnets.* London: Thomas Thorpe, 1609.

Schlegel, A.W. *A Course of Lectures on Dramatic Art and Literature*, trans. John Black, revised by AJW Morrison. London: Henry G. Bohn, 1846.

Spender, Stephen. *'The Alike and the Other', The Riddle of Shakespeares Sonnets.* ed. Edward Hubler, New York: Basic Books, 1962.

Stirling, William. *The Canon – An exposition of the pagan mystery perpetuated in the Cabala as the rule of all the arts.* London: Elkin Press, 1897. Modern ed. London: Garnstone Press, 1974.

Swinburne, A.C. *Letters on the Elizabethan Dramatists.* London: privately printed, 1910.

Thompson, E. Maunde. *Shakespeare's Handwriting: A Study.* Oxford: Clarendon Press, 1916.

Tompkins, Peter. *Secrets of the Great Pyramid*, New York: Galahad Books, 1971.

Trevor Roper, Hugh. *Réalités* (English Edition), November 1962.

Twain, Mark. *Is Shakespeare Dead?* New York: Harper and Row, 1909.

Vaughan, Thomas. *Lumen de Lumine.* London: H. Blunden, 1651.

Vaughan, William. *The Golden-groue Moralized in Three Bookes . . .*. London, Simon Stafford, 1600.

Vendler, Helen. *The Art of Shakespeare's Sonnets.* Cambridge, MA: The Belknap Press of Harvard University Press, 1997.

Wells, Stanley and Gary Taylor (et al), *William Shakespeare, a textual companion.* Oxford: Clarendon Press, 1987.

Wraight, A.D. & Stern, Virginia F. *In Search of Christopher Marlowe.* Chichester: Adam Hart Ltd., 1965.

Wraight, A.D. *Christopher Marlowe and Edward Alleyn.* Chichester: Adam Hart, Ltd., 1993.

Wraight, A.D. *The Story the Sonnets Tell.* Chichester: Adam Hart, Ltd., 1994.

Yates, Frances. *The Occult Philosophy in the Elizabethan Age.* London & New York:

Routledge Classics, 2001 (first published 1979).

Ziegler, Wilbur. *It Was Marlowe: A Story of the Secret of Three Centuries*. Chicago: Donohue, Hennebury & Co, 1895.

ABOUT THE AUTHOR

Peter Bull was born and brought up in England but spent 30 years working overseas as an English language instructor. He is now retired and lives in the UK. His research into gematria and the symbolic language of numbers stems from a deep conviction that this is the means to unlock the mystery of *Shakespeare's Sonnets* and similar works of esoteric literature. Peter's website has further information about his research: https://shake-scene.com